"The Bible alone, and the Bible in its entirety, is the
Word of God written and is therefore inerrant in the
autographs." - The Evangelical Theological Society

INERRANCY
OF SCRIPTURE

How Can We Believe Inerrancy of
Scripture In the Originals When We
Don't Have the Originals?

EDWARD D. ANDREWS

INERRANCY OF SCRIPTURE

How Can We Believe Inerrancy of Scripture in the Originals When We Don't Have the Originals?

Edward D. Andrews

Christian Publishing House

Cambridge, Ohio

CHRISTIAN PUBLISHING HOUSE

FOUNDED 2005

Unless otherwise stated, Scripture quotations are from Updated American Standard Version (UASV) Copyright © 2022 by Christian Publishing House

INERRANCY OF SCRIPTURE: How Can We Believe Inerrancy of Scripture In the Originals When We Don't Have the Originals? by Edward D. Andrews

- **ISBN-10:** 194958612X
- **ISBN-13:** 978-1949586121

Table of Contents

Book Description

"Inerrancy of Scripture: How Can We Believe Inerrancy of Scripture in the Originals When We Don't Have the Originals?" delves into the complexities surrounding the authenticity and inerrancy of the Bible. Author and conservative Bible scholar, provides a comprehensive exploration of how faith in the inerrancy of Scripture can be maintained even in the absence of original biblical texts.

Throughout the book, the author examines the formation of the Canon, scrutinizes the doctrine of biblical inerrancy and infallibility, and explores why we don't necessarily need the original manuscripts to believe in the inerrancy of Scripture. The discourse extends to why the Holy Spirit would allow for errors in copies after inspiring the original inerrant texts and probes how we can reconcile belief in inerrant originals when we don't possess them.

Diving into the book writing process of the New Testament, the author discusses the place of writing, the role of the scribe, and the influence of inspiration and inerrancy during the writing process. Further sections of the book tackle the issues of textual variants, the early Christian view of the integrity of the Greek New Testament books, and the legacy of the Hebrew Scriptures.

As skepticism grows in the modern age, the author brings attention to the dangers of skepticism, ambiguity, and uncertainty, and offers readers a faithful response to selective skepticism when it comes to God and the Bible. The book also explores the role of the Holy Spirit in the inspiration of the Bible's authors and presents explanations for common Bible difficulties.

"Inerrancy of Scripture" concludes with a thoughtful consideration of why God has allowed the proliferation of different religions, numerous Christian denominations, and a multitude of textual variants in the books He inspired.

This work serves as a detailed and nuanced study for those seeking to navigate the intersections of faith, historical criticism, and scriptural understanding in the pursuit of biblical inerrancy. Ideal for scholars, theologians, and anyone seeking a deeper understanding of the reliability of Scripture, this book is an invaluable addition to your theological library.

Preface

In the Preface of "Inerrancy of Scripture: How Can We Believe Inerrancy of Scripture in the Originals When We Don't Have the Originals?", I find it crucial to underscore the primary intent behind this work. It is not merely an intellectual pursuit to theorize and dissect, but rather an endeavor of faith—an effort to unite historical scholarship with sincere belief.

The questions we will explore in this book are not new. In fact, they have been posed for centuries by believers and skeptics alike. How can we trust in the inerrancy of Scripture when the original documents have not survived? Why would an omniscient God allow for errors in copies of His divinely inspired texts? These are not inquiries to take lightly, nor are they challenges to dismiss outright. Instead, they provide an opportunity to probe deeper into our understanding of God's Word and His purposes.

We will embark on this exploration together, with an open mind and a respectful approach towards differing perspectives. We will delve into the formation of the Canon, analyze the concepts of biblical inerrancy and infallibility, and investigate the original manuscripts' absence. As we examine textual variants and the preservation of the Greek New Testament, we will also consider the role of the Holy Spirit in the inspiration of Scripture.

Additionally, this book will reflect on the proliferation of various religions, numerous Christian denominations, and the myriad of textual variants in the books inspired by God. By engaging with these challenging topics, we aspire to bring clarity and reaffirm faith amidst an increasingly skeptical world.

While this journey is a scholarly pursuit, it remains, at its core, a personal one. It's about your relationship with God's Word, your understanding of it, and ultimately, your faith. As you turn the pages, may you find not just answers, but also an enriched relationship with the God who inspired these Scriptures.

I invite you to approach this book with an open heart and a ready mind, prepared to delve into these substantial questions. The path ahead may be challenging at times but remember: the pursuit of truth is rarely easy, but always rewarding.

Edward D. Andrews

Chief Translator of the Updated American Standard Version

Introduction

As we commence our journey through this book, "Inerrancy of Scripture: How Can We Believe Inerrancy of Scripture in the Originals When We Don't Have the Originals?", it is essential to acknowledge the crossroads at which we find ourselves. On one hand, we grapple with historical reality: the original biblical manuscripts have been lost to time, and in their stead, we have copies—many with minor variations. On the other hand, we grapple with a theological doctrine: the belief in the inerrancy of Scripture, which asserts that the Bible is completely free from error in its original form.

The tension between these two aspects presents an intriguing paradox—one that has sparked countless debates and given rise to numerous theories. Yet, we are not daunted. In fact, it is in the crucible of this tension that our exploration takes on even greater significance. For this is not merely an academic exercise; rather, it is an exploration of faith, a deepening of our understanding of God's Word, and an opportunity to clarify misconceptions that often arise in such discussions.

In the chapters that follow, we will examine the complex process of Canon formation, the doctrine of inerrancy and infallibility, and the implications of not having the original manuscripts. We will grapple with questions around the Holy Spirit's role in inspiring the Scriptures, the existence of textual variants, and the perspectives of the early Christians on the integrity of the Greek New Testament. As we delve into these subjects, we shall also engage with the skepticism and doubts that sometimes pervade discussions on religious texts, and the varied reactions these elicit.

This book is designed as a journey—a journey that invites you to engage with the material, to reflect on your understanding, and to consider the implications of the ideas presented. As such, it seeks not to impose answers, but to promote informed dialogue, careful reflection, and sincere seeking of the truth.

The belief in the inerrancy of Scripture is not a peripheral issue; it strikes at the heart of our faith and our understanding of God's revelation. How we approach and resolve this paradox impacts not only our theological perspectives but also our relationship with God and His Word. It is my sincere hope that this exploration will inspire us to navigate these complexities with wisdom, grace, and a deeper understanding of God's intentions in His revelation to humanity.

Let us, then, begin this journey—armed with curiosity, guided by respect for differing viewpoints, and above all, driven by a desire to deepen our understanding and love for God's Word.

CHAPTER 1 God's Word: Understanding the Canon and Its Formation

The Bible and Its Canon

The term "Bible," which is the name we use to refer to the collection of sacred texts of Christianity, has an interesting etymology. It is derived from the Greek word' bi·bli′a,' which translates to 'little books.' This term was originally rooted in 'bi′blos,' the word used to describe the inner part of the papyrus plant. In ancient civilizations, this plant was processed into a form of "paper" that was used for writing. This connection comes from the Phoenician port of Gebal, known as Byblos by the Greeks, which was a key hub for the import of papyrus from Egypt. As a result, the term' bi·bli′a' became associated with writings, scrolls, documents, books, or scriptures - even collections of books in a library.

Interestingly, the word "Bible" is not typically found within the texts of translations of the Holy Scriptures, regardless of the language of translation. However, by the second century B.C., the collection of inspired books of the Hebrew Scriptures was referred to as 'ta bi·bli′a' in Greek. Daniel 9:2 (A.S.V.) provides evidence of this, as the prophet Daniel says, "In the first year of his reign, I, Daniel, perceived in the books the number of years that, according to the word of Jehovah to Jeremiah the prophet, must pass before the end of the desolations of Jerusalem, namely, seventy years." The Septuagint, a Greek translation of the Hebrew Scriptures, uses the term 'bi′blois,' a form of 'bi′blos,' in this verse. Similarly, in 2 Timothy 4:13 (ESV), Paul asks Timothy to bring "the scrolls," or 'bi·bli′a' in Greek, when he comes to visit. These Greek words, in their various forms, appear over 40 times in the New Testament and are typically translated as "scroll(s)" or "book(s)."

'Bi·bli'a' was eventually used in Latin as a singular term, and it was from Latin that the term "Bible" was introduced into English.

Despite the fact that the Bible was composed by many different human authors and has been translated into many languages, it remains, in the most profound sense, the Word of God - a divine revelation to humanity. This perception is confirmed by the terminology used by the biblical authors themselves. They used phrases such as "expression of Jehovah's mouth" (Deuteronomy 8:3, ESV), "sayings of Jehovah" (Joshua 24:27, A.S.V.), "commandments of Jehovah" (Ezra 7:11, ESV), "law of Jehovah" (Psalm 19:7, A.S.V.), "word of Jehovah" (Isaiah 38:4, ESV), every word that comes from the mouth of God' (Matthew 4:4, ESV), and "we declare to you by a word from the Lord" (1 Thessalonians 4:15, ESV), indicating their understanding of the divine origin of these writings.

The Divine Library: Unveiling the Composition and Canon of the Bible

The Bible, as we know it today, is a compilation of ancient documents that were inspired by divine influence. Spanning over sixteen centuries, these texts were composed and assembled to form what has been fittingly termed in Latin by Jerome as the "Bibliotheca Divina," or the Divine Library. Similar to any other library, this Divine Library features a catalog—an official listing of authorized publications that align with the library's purpose and subject matter. This excludes any books that do not meet the set criteria. Jehovah God, acting as the Supreme Librarian, establishes the standard that dictates which writings are to be included. As a result, the Bible has a fixed catalog containing a total of 66 books, each guided and inspired by God's Holy Spirit.

The term' Bible canon' is often used to denote the collection, or list, of books acknowledged as genuine and divinely inspired Scripture. This term draws its roots from the original use of the reed (Hebrew, qa·neh') as a measuring rod in the absence of a piece of wood. The apostle Paul, in Galatians 6:16 and 2 Corinthians 10:13, extended the application of the Greek term 'ka·non" to indicate a "rule of conduct" as well as the "territory" measured out as his assignment. Thus, canonical books are those that are true and inspired, serving as a reliable benchmark in determining the correct faith, doctrine, and conduct. The usage of books that are not "straight" or truthful as a measuring guide can lead to misalignment in our "building" of faith, which will not withstand the scrutiny of the Master Surveyor, Jehovah God. As written in Proverbs 30:5-6 (A.S.V.), "Every word of God is tried: He is a shield unto them that take refuge in him. Add thou not unto his words, lest he reprove thee, and thou be found a liar." This further highlights the importance of sticking to the canon when seeking spiritual guidance.

Establishing Canonicity: Determining the Divinely Inspired Books of the Bible

How can we ascertain the canonicity—the divine authorization—of the 66 books that constitute the Bible? There are several divine indicators that help discern which documents have rightfully earned their place in this sacred anthology.

Primarily, these documents must focus on Jehovah's activities and purposes on earth. They should direct individuals towards His worship, instilling a profound reverence for His name and His divine intentions in the world. They must provide evidence of divine inspiration—indicative of their origin from the holy spirit. As stated in 2 Peter 1:21 (ESV), "For no prophecy was ever produced by the will of man, but men spoke from God as they were carried along by the Holy Spirit."

The texts must not promote superstition or creature worship; instead, they should encourage love and service to God. There must be an internal consistency within the texts; no single document should conflict with the overall harmony of the collection. Rather, each book should validate the single authorship—that of Jehovah God—through its unity with the others.

These documents are also expected to exhibit accuracy, even down to the smallest details. Beyond these fundamental criteria, other specific signs of inspiration—and thus canonicity—may depend on the unique content of each book. These have been discussed in the introduction of each individual book in the Bible.

There are also distinct circumstances associated with the Hebrew Scriptures and the Greek New Testament that aid in the establishment of the Bible canon. An example can be found in Isaiah 40:8 (A.S.V.), "The grass withereth, the flower fadeth; but the word of our God shall stand forever." This verse implies that the text is divinely inspired, as it claims to carry the enduring words of God, further supporting its canonicity.

Therefore, canonicity is not determined by mere human judgement, but by the divine characteristics inherent within the texts themselves, manifesting the Holy Spirit and timeless wisdom.

The Path to Canonicity: From Mosaic Law to the Hebrew Canon

It would be a misconception to assume that the recognition of inspired Scripture awaited the finalization of the Hebrew canon in the fifth century B.C.E. From the outset, the writings of Moses, guided by God's Holy Spirit, were accepted by the Israelites as divinely inspired. When finished, the Pentateuch — the first five books of the Old Testament — established the initial canon. Any subsequent revelations regarding Jehovah's purposes, shared through divinely inspired individuals, needed to align logically and harmoniously with the foundational principles of true worship found in the Pentateuch. This consistency is evident across the various books of the Bible, particularly those directly concerning the grand theme: the sanctification of Jehovah's name and the vindication of His sovereignty via the Kingdom under Christ, the Promised Seed.

Prophecy abounds in the Hebrew Scriptures. Through Moses, Jehovah provided a framework for validating the authenticity of a prophecy — determining whether it genuinely came from God, which in turn aided in determining the canonicity of a prophetic book. Deuteronomy 13:1-3 (A.S.V.) and 18:20-22 (A.S.V.) elaborate on this. Examining each of the prophetic books of the Hebrew Scriptures in conjunction with the Bible as a whole and secular history establishes that "the word" they spoke was indeed in Jehovah's name. This affirmation further underscores the prophecy's authenticity and inspiration.

Quotes from Jesus and the inspired authors of the Greek New Testament serve as a direct pathway to confirming the canonicity of many of the Hebrew Scriptures. However, this criterion may not be applicable to all books, such as Esther and Ecclesiastes. Another essential factor in considering canonicity is the logical presumption that Jehovah, who inspired men to record His divine messages, would also guide the collation of these inspired writings and the establishment of the Bible canon. By doing so, He ensures no ambiguity regarding what constitutes His Word of truth and the enduring measure of true worship. Only in this way could humanity continually receive 'a new birth through the word of God' and affirm that "the word of the Lord remains forever" (1 Peter 1:23, 25 ESV).

Constructing the Hebrew Canon

Jewish tradition attributes the initial compilation and cataloging of the Hebrew Scriptures canon to Ezra, with Nehemiah completing it. As an inspired Bible writer himself, as well as a priest, scholar, and official scribe of sacred writings (Ezra 7:1-11 A.S.V.), Ezra was uniquely qualified for this task. There is no substantial reason to dispute the traditional view that the Hebrew Scriptures' canon was finalized by the end of the fifth century B.C.E.

Today, we list 39 books in the Hebrew Scriptures; the traditional Jewish canon, while containing these same books, counts them as 24. By categorizing Ruth with Judges and Lamentations with Jeremiah, some authorities reduced the count to 22 books. This count matches the number of letters in the Hebrew alphabet, while still recognizing the same canonical writings. This exemplifies that while the form may change, the divine inspiration and canonicity of the Scriptures remain consistent. The following is the list of the 24 books according to the traditional Jewish canon:

The Law (The Pentateuch)

1. Genesis

2. Exodus

3. Leviticus

4. Numbers

5. Deuteronomy

The Prophets

6. Joshua

7. Judges

8. Samuel (First and Second together as one book)

9. Kings (First and Second together as one book)

10. Isaiah

11. Jeremiah

12. Ezekiel

13. The Twelve Prophets (Hosea, Joel, Amos, Obadiah, Jonah, Micah, Nahum, Habakkuk, Zephaniah, Haggai, Zechariah, and Malachi, as one book)

The Writings (Hagiographa)

14. Psalms

15. Proverbs

16. Job

17. The Song of Solomon

18. Ruth

19. Lamentations

20. Ecclesiastes

21. Esther

22. Daniel

23. Ezra (Nehemiah was included with Ezra)

24. Chronicles (First and Second together as one book)

Confirming the Hebrew Canon: The Influence of Christ and the Early Church

The canon that we recognize today as the Hebrew Scriptures was endorsed as inspired Scripture by both Christ Jesus and the early Christian congregation. Only from these texts did the inspired authors of the Greek New Testament draw their quotations, solidifying these works as God's Word by introducing such citations with phrases like "as it is written" (Romans 15:9 ESV). Jesus, when speaking of the comprehensive inspired Scriptures available during His ministry, alluded to the writings encapsulated in "the Law of Moses and the Prophets and Psalms" (Luke 24:44 ESV). Here, "Psalms," as the opening book of the Hagiographa, or the 'Writings,' represents this entire section.

The final historical book to be included in the Hebrew canon was Nehemiah. The guidance of God's Holy Spirit in this decision is evident as the book of Nehemiah singularly offers the initiating point for calculating Daniel's remarkable prophecy: from the issuance of the decree "to restore and build Jerusalem" until the arrival of the Messiah, there would span a period of 69 prophetic weeks (Daniel 9:25 A.S.V.; Nehemiah 2:1-8 A.S.V., 6:15 A.S.V.). Furthermore, the book of Nehemiah delivers the historical context for the last of the prophetic books, Malachi.

The inclusion of Malachi in the canon of inspired Scriptures is beyond doubt. Even Jesus, the Son of God, quoted from it on several occasions (Matthew 11:10, 14 ESV). While similar quotations are made from the majority of books in the Hebrew canon — all of which were written before Nehemiah and Malachi — the authors of the Greek New Testament do not quote from any purportedly inspired writings composed after the time of Nehemiah and Malachi and before the era of Christ. This affirms the traditional Jewish viewpoint, as well as the belief of the first-century C.E. Christian congregation, that the canon of the Hebrew Scriptures concluded with the writings of Nehemiah and Malachi.

The Apocryphal Books: A Study of Canon and Contention

The term "Apocrypha" refers to a set of books whose inclusion in certain versions of the Bible has sparked disagreement due to a lack of evidence suggesting divine inspiration. Originating from the Greek word a·po′kry·phos, meaning "carefully concealed" (Mark 4:22; Luke 8:17; Col. 2:3), this label denotes works of uncertain authorship or authority. Although these texts might offer value for personal reading, they lack indications of divine inspiration and were, therefore, not publicly read, hence the implication of "concealed."

The Council of Carthage, in 397 C.E., proposed the inclusion of seven Apocryphal books in the Hebrew Scriptures, in addition to appendices to the canonical books of Esther and Daniel. Yet, it was only in 1546, during the Council of Trent, that the Roman Catholic Church officially accepted these additions to its Bible catalog. These additions include Tobit, Judith, Additions to Esther, Wisdom, Ecclesiasticus, Baruch, three Additions to Daniel, First Maccabees, and Second Maccabees.

While First Maccabees, a book presenting the historical account of the Jewish fight for independence in the 2nd century B.C.E. under the Maccabean priestly family, offers historical interest, it isn't considered an inspired text. The remaining Apocryphal books, filled with myths, superstitions, and errors, were never referenced or quoted by Jesus or the authors of the Greek New Testament.

Flavius Josephus, a Jewish historian from the first century C.E., discusses all the books deemed sacred by the Hebrews in his work, "Against Apion" (I, 38-41 [8]). He asserts that the Hebrews possessed not a myriad of conflicting books, but only "two and twenty" (equivalent to our current 39), covering all recorded time. His account confirms that the canon of the Hebrew Scriptures had been established well before the first century C.E.

Biblical scholar Jerome, responsible for the Latin Vulgate translation of the Bible around 405 C.E., was clear about his stance on the Apocryphal books. Following the same count as Josephus, Jerome lists the 39 inspired books of the Hebrew Scriptures as 22 in his prologue to the books of Samuel and Kings in the Vulgate. He concludes, "Thus there are twenty-two books . . . This prologue of the Scriptures can serve as a fortified approach to all the books which we translate from the Hebrew into Latin; so that we may know that whatever is beyond these must be put in the apocrypha."

Canonical Controversy: An Examination of the Apocrypha

While the Apocryphal books may bear some historical merit, their claim to canonicity remains unsubstantiated. Evidence suggests that the Hebrew canon closed following the completion of the books of Ezra, Nehemiah, and Malachi in the fifth century B.C.E. The Apocrypha were never integrated into the Jewish canon of inspired Scriptures, and they remain excluded to this day.

Josephus, a first-century Jewish historian, highlighted the sacredness of a select few books of the Hebrew canon. He stated, "Our books, those which are justly accredited, are but two and twenty [the equivalent of the 39 books of the Hebrew Scriptures according to modern division], and contain the record of all time" (Against Apion, I, 38, 41 [8]). Josephus's comments suggest an awareness of the existence of Apocryphal books and their exclusion from the Hebrew canon due to "the failure of the exact succession of the prophets."

Some arguments advocating for the Apocrypha's canonicity stem from their presence in early versions of the Greek Septuagint translation of the Hebrew Scriptures, begun around 280 B.C.E. However, no original copies of the Septuagint exist to confirm the Apocryphal books' original inclusion. Most Apocryphal writings were, admittedly, composed after the initiation of the Septuagint's translation, excluding them from the original list of books chosen for translation. Thus, their incorporation into the Septuagint could only be considered an addition.

While Alexandrian Greek-speaking Jews incorporated the Apocrypha into the Septuagint and may have regarded them as part of an expanded canon, these texts were never included in the Jerusalem or Palestinian canon. At most, they were perceived as secondary writings without divine origin. The Jewish Council of Jamnia, around 90 C.E., definitively excluded these writings from the Hebrew canon. The apostle Paul in Romans 3:1, 2 asserts the necessity of acknowledging the Jewish stance in this matter.

Further evidence against the Apocrypha's canonicity lies in the fact that none of the Christian Bible authors quoted from these books. Although this is not definitive proof—some canonical books such as Esther, Ecclesiastes, and The Song of Solomon are also devoid of quotes—it is noteworthy that the Apocryphal books are never cited.

Another key consideration is the Apocrypha's inferior position among leading Bible scholars and "church fathers" of the early Common Era. Notable figures like Origen, Athanasius, Cyril of Jerusalem, Gregory of Nazianzus, and Amphilocius cataloged sacred writings in alignment with the Hebrew canon and either disregarded these additional texts or categorized them as secondary.

Jerome, recognized as "the best Hebrew scholar" of the early church and who completed the Latin Vulgate in 405 C.E., explicitly defined these writings as noncanonical, or "Apocrypha." In his prologue to the books of Samuel and Kings, he lists the inspired books of the Hebrew Scriptures in harmony with the Hebrew canon (grouping the 39 books as 22) and clarifies: "Thus there are twenty-two books . . . so that we may know that whatever is beyond these must be put in the apocrypha."

The Catholic Church began incorporating these additional texts into the canon largely due to Augustine (354-430 C.E.). However, even Augustine eventually conceded a distinction between the Hebrew canon's books and the "outside books." Despite this, the Catholic

Church, guided by Augustine's precedent, included these texts in the sacred books' canon confirmed by the Council of Carthage in 397 C.E. Yet it wasn't until 1546 C.E., at the Council of Trent, that the Roman Catholic Church definitively accepted these additions into its Bible catalog, a move that was necessary due to the church's divided opinions on these writings.

The internal evidence of the Apocryphal books, however, provides the most compelling case against their canonicity. These writings lack the prophetic component and often contradict the teachings of the canonical books. They're fraught with historical inaccuracies and geographical errors, and some authors even falsely present their works as those of earlier inspired authors. They bear the influence of pagan Greek culture and sometimes resort to extravagant language and literary style that is entirely uncharacteristic of the inspired Scriptures. Two of the authors imply their lack of divine inspiration (Prologue to Ecclesiasticus; 2 Maccabees 2:24-32; 15:38-40). Hence, the most substantial evidence against the Apocrypha's canonicity is the Apocrypha itself. A consideration of the individual books here follows:

A Deeper Examination of the Apocryphal Books

Tobit (Tobias)

The narrative describes Tobit, a devout Jew from the tribe of Naphtali, who lives in exile in Nineveh. After becoming blind due to a bizarre incident involving bird droppings, Tobit sends his son Tobias to Media to collect a debt. Guided by an angel disguised as a human, Tobias journeys to Ecbatana. During his journey, he acquires a fish's heart, liver, and gall. He marries a widow who had been plagued by a demon that killed her previous seven husbands on their wedding nights. Using the fish's heart and liver, Tobias drives the demon away and upon returning home, he cures his father's blindness using the fish's gall.

Given its origins in the third century B.C.E. and the numerous inaccuracies and superstitions woven into the narrative, Tobit cannot be considered divinely inspired. An example of the inaccuracies is the assertion that Tobit, in his youth, witnessed the revolt of the northern tribes in 997 B.C.E. after Solomon's death (Tobit 1:4,5), and that he was later deported to Nineveh in 740 B.C.E. (Tobias 1:11-13). This would necessitate a lifespan exceeding 257 years, contrary to Tobias 14:1-3, which states Tobit lived only 102 years.

Judith

This book recounts the story of Judith, a beautiful Jewish widow from "Bethulia". Nebuchadnezzar sends his officer Holofernes on a campaign to enforce universal worship of himself. Judith pretends to betray the Jews, gains access to Holofernes' camp, and eventually beheads the drunken Holofernes using his own sword, leading to a Jewish victory.

The Jerusalem Bible, in its introduction to the books of Tobit, Judith, and Esther, comments on the "bland indifference to history and geography" displayed in the book of Judith. One notable inconsistency is the claim that the events transpired during Nebuchadnezzar's reign in Nineveh, despite the historical record showing Nebuchadnezzar as the king of Babylonia who never reigned in Nineveh.

Additions to the Book of Esther

These additions form six supplementary passages, each contradicting the canonical record in one way or another. For instance, Mordecai is depicted as having been among the captives taken by Nebuchadnezzar in 617 B.C.E. and as an important man in the king's court over a century later. This contradicts the canonical Esther, as it implies Mordecai occupied a significant position very early in the king's reign.

Wisdom (of Solomon)

Despite attributing Solomon as its author in several verses (Wisdom 9:7,8,12), the text references passages from biblical books written centuries after Solomon's death and draws heavily from the Greek Septuagint, a translation that did not begin until 280 B.C.E. The writer also displays a significant influence of Greek philosophy, introducing ideas like the immortality of the human soul (Wisdom 2:23; 3:2,4) and the preexistence of human souls (8:19,20; 9:15), both of which are not consistent with canonical biblical teachings.

Ecclesiasticus

Also known as The Wisdom of Jesus, the Son of Sirach, this book contradicts canonical teachings such as Paul's assertion in Romans 5:12-19, which attributes the origin of sin to Adam. Ecclesiasticus, on the other hand, places the blame for sin's origin on women. In Ecclesiasticus 25:24, it states: "From a woman sin had its beginning, and because of her, we all die." This statement contradicts the canonical teaching in Genesis where Adam's disobedience is highlighted as the source of sin (Genesis 3:6,17), and in Romans where Paul attributes sin's origin to Adam (Romans 5:12-19). These inconsistencies raise questions about the book's divine inspiration.

Baruch and the Letter of Jeremiah

These two are sometimes combined into one book. The first is purportedly written by Baruch, Jeremiah's scribe, and contains admonitions and prophecies. The latter is supposedly a letter written by Jeremiah to the exiles in Babylon, warning them against idolatry.

Historical inaccuracies are present in these texts as well. For instance, the Book of Baruch claims to be written in Babylon after the destruction of Jerusalem in 607 B.C.E., yet it speaks of the people praying in the temple (Baruch 1:10). The Letter of Jeremiah, supposedly written before the exile, accurately describes the

Babylonian idols' adornment, an unlikely knowledge for someone not yet in Babylon.

The Song of the Three Young Men

This is an expansion of the events described in Daniel 3, placed between verses 23 and 24. It depicts Shadrach, Meshach, and Abednego in the fiery furnace, praising God in song.

This addition contradicts the book of Daniel, where it's recorded that Nebuchadnezzar saw four men, not three, walking in the furnace (Daniel 3:25). Moreover, the style and tone of this song differ markedly from the rest of the Book of Daniel.

Susanna

This narrative, appended to the book of Daniel as its 13th chapter in the Septuagint, tells the story of Susanna, a virtuous woman falsely accused of adultery by two wicked elders. Daniel's clever interrogation exposes the elders' lie, and Susanna is acquitted.

However, the plot seems more like a folktale than a historical account. The elders' lust, Susanna's unwavering virtue, and the dramatic courtroom scene where Daniel uncovers the truth are more characteristic of a morality tale rather than a divinely inspired biblical account.

Bel and the Dragon

This narrative is the 14th chapter of Daniel in the Septuagint. It contains two independent stories, one in which Daniel exposes the trickery of the priests of the god Bel, and the other where he kills a revered dragon-god by feeding it a mixture that causes it to burst.

Again, these stories resemble folktales more than historical accounts. The depictions of idol worship in Babylon are also inconsistent with the biblical account that the Babylonians were polytheistic but did not worship animals or serpents.

1 and 2 Maccabees

These books provide valuable historical information about the Jewish resistance against the Seleucid Empire, led by the Maccabee family. However, their historicity does not necessarily confer divine inspiration. These books contain teachings that contradict other parts of the Bible, such as the concept of intercession for the dead (2 Maccabees 12:42-45).

1 Maccabees

1 Maccabees presents an essential historical account of the Jewish fight for freedom during the second century B.C.E., starting from the reign of Antiochus Epiphanes in 175 B.C.E., up to the death of Simon Maccabaeus around 134 B.C.E. Despite being a vital source of historical information for this period, it didn't form part of the inspired Hebrew canon. It was likely written in Hebrew during the latter part of the second century B.C.E.

2 Maccabees

While it follows 1 Maccabees, 2 Maccabees overlaps with the same time period (circa 180 B.C.E. to 160 B.C.E.), but it wasn't written by the same author. Instead, the writer presents it as a summary of Jason of Cyrene's previous works.

Notably, the account introduces a claim that Jeremiah, at Jerusalem's destruction, moved the tabernacle and the Ark of the Covenant to a cave in the mountain where Moses viewed the land of Canaan (2 Maccabees 2:1-16). However, the temple had replaced the tabernacle some 420 years before this event.

Certain texts in this book are used to back Catholic doctrines such as punishment after death (2 Maccabees 6:26), intercession by the saints (15:12-16), and prayers for the dead (12:41-46). The book was likely written in Greek between 134 B.C.E. and Jerusalem's fall in 70 C.E.

Authenticating the Canon of the Greek New Testament

The Roman Catholic Church has asserted its authority over the canonization of the Bible, referencing the Council of Carthage in 397 C.E. as the occasion for formalizing the biblical catalog. This claim, however, contradicts the historical reality. The canon, which includes the Greek New Testament, was established before this Council, not by ecclesiastical decrees, but under the guidance of the Holy Spirit - the same Spirit that inspired the writing of these sacred texts. Later catalogers, while not divinely inspired, acknowledged the Bible canon as ordained by God's Spirit.

Many fourth-century catalogues of the Greek New Testament, predating the aforementioned Council, align precisely with our current canon, except for a few that omit the Book of Revelation. Universal acceptance of the four Gospels, the Acts of the Apostles, and 12 of Apostle Paul's letters was achieved by the end of the second century C.E. A few minor texts took longer to gain canonical recognition, possibly due to limited initial circulation.

One of the most intriguing early catalogs is the Muratorian Fragment, a Latin document from the latter part of the second century C.E. This Fragment, discovered by L. A. Muratori in the Ambrosian Library in Milan, Italy, provides an invaluable account of the early Christian view on canonical works.

This Fragment attests to the four Gospels, the Acts of the Apostles, Paul's epistles, the Apocalypse of John, Jude's epistle, and two of John's epistles. It hints at a broad consensus on the composition of the New Testament by the second century C.E. Some uncertainties, such as the apparent absence of mention of Peter's first epistle, are thought to be due to lost sections of the text.

By around 230 C.E., Origen accepted the canonical status of the books of Hebrews and James, both missing from the Muratorian Fragment. Despite some doubts, the recognition of these books further indicates that by this time, the majority of the Greek New

31

Testament was accepted as canonical. Later, influential figures like Athanasius, Jerome, and Augustine concurred with earlier lists and defined the same 27 books we now recognize as the canon.

Despite the lack of precise lists prior to the Muratorian Fragment, it is evident that the composition of the Greek New Testament was not arbitrary. It only became necessary to compile such lists in response to the proliferation of apocryphal literature and divergent interpretations of Scripture, like those propagated by Marcion in the second century C.E. The establishment of the canon, however, remains a work of divine inspiration rather than human intervention.

Distinguishing the Inspired Greek New Testament from Apocryphal Texts

A discernible distinction exists between the inspired Greek New Testament scriptures and the apocryphal writings. Evidence within the texts themselves substantiates this differentiation. The apocryphal texts, characterized by their inferior quality, often exhibit elements of whimsy and immaturity. Moreover, these writings are frequently flawed with inaccuracies, further attesting to their uninspired status.

From the second century C.E. onward, a large body of writings emerged, claiming divine inspiration and canonicity, often imitating the Gospels, Acts, letters, and revelations contained in the canonical books of the Greek New Testament. These writings attempt to fill gaps left by the inspired writings or support doctrines that contradict the Bible.

For instance, works like the Infancy Gospel of Thomas and the Protevangelium of James present fanciful accounts of Jesus's childhood miracles, which depict Jesus as a capricious and petulant child (in contrast with Luke 2:51-52). Additionally, "Acts," like the "Acts of Paul" and the "Acts of Peter," promote abstinence from sexual relations, even suggesting that apostles advised women to separate from their husbands, a clear contradiction of Paul's teachings in 1 Corinthians 7.

Despite these writings' significance in influencing sacred legends and ecclesiastical traditions, they were not accepted as inspired or canonical in the earliest collections of the Greek New Testament, similar to how the pre-Christian Hebrew Scriptures did not include the earlier Apocryphal writings.

Note the following statements by scholars on these noncanonical books:

"There is no question of any one's having excluded them from the New Testament: they have done that for themselves."—M. R. James, *The Apocryphal New Testament,* pages xi, xii.

"We have only to compare our New Testament books as a whole with other literature of the kind to realize how wide is the gulf which separates them from it. The uncanonical gospels, it is often said, are in reality the best evidence for the canonical."—G. Milligan, *The New Testament Documents,* page 228.

"It cannot be said of a single writing preserved to us from the early period of the Church outside the New Testament that it could properly be added to-day to the Canon."—K. Aland, *The Problem of the New Testament Canon,* page 24.

The Formation and Authenticity of the Greek New Testament

Intriguingly, all authors of the Greek New Testament had significant ties to the initial governing body of the Christian congregation, which comprised of apostles personally chosen by Jesus Christ. Matthew, John, and Peter belonged to the original 12 apostles, whereas Paul, though recognized as an apostle later, wasn't counted among the original 12. Matthew, John, and Peter, together with James, Jude, and likely Mark, were present during the special outpouring of the Holy Spirit at Pentecost. Moreover, Peter categorically included Paul's letters alongside "the rest of the Scriptures" (2 Pet. 3:15-16, ESV).

Mark and Luke were intimate associates and travel companions of Paul and Peter (Acts 12:25, 1 Pet. 5:13, Col. 4:14, 2 Tim. 4:11). All these writers were gifted with miraculous abilities through the Holy Spirit, either by the special outpouring at Pentecost, when Paul was converted (Acts 9:17-18), or likely in Luke's case, through the laying on of the apostles' hands (Acts 8:14-17). Consequently, all Greek New Testament were written during the period when the special gifts of the Holy Spirit were operational.

Our faith in the omnipotent God, the Inspirer and Protector of His Word, assures us that He guided the compilation of its different components. Thus, we confidently accept the 27 books of the Greek New Testament in addition to the 39 of the Hebrew Scriptures as the singular Bible, authored by Jehovah God. Comprising 66 books, His Word is our guide, and its overall harmony and balance attest to its completeness. We extend all praise to Jehovah God, the Creator of this unparalleled book! It possesses the power to thoroughly equip us and guide us on the path to life. Therefore, let us seize every opportunity to use it wisely.

CHAPTER 2 The Reliability of the Bible: Exploring Inerrancy and Infallibility

The Authority of Scripture: Understanding Inerrancy and Infallibility

The authority of Scripture, especially its reliability, is a foundational belief for Christians. The conviction that the Bible is both inerrant and infallible upholds its divine authority and solidifies the believer's trust in its teachings.

The Inerrancy of Scripture

Inerrancy denotes the belief that the Bible, in its original autographs, is free from error in all that it affirms, whether that relates to doctrine, ethical instruction, or matters of history and science. This belief is rooted in the understanding that the Scriptures are "breathed out by God" (2 Timothy 3:16, ESV), and since God is incapable of falsehood, it follows that his word must also be truthful.

For instance, when the Bible presents the creation account in Genesis, an inerrantist view upholds that this account is truthful in all that it affirms. This does not imply a literalistic reading of "day" as a 24-hour period, as the text's genre and context might suggest a figurative interpretation. It does affirm that God created the world and all life within it, contrary to atheistic evolution.

The doctrine of inerrancy affirms the historical reliability of the Bible, such as the exodus of the Israelites from Egypt (Exodus 14), David's reign as king (2 Samuel 5), and the life, death, and resurrection of Jesus Christ (Matthew, Mark, Luke, John). It underscores the fact that these aren't just mythological stories but are grounded in historical realities.

The Infallibility of Scripture

35

Closely tied to inerrancy is the concept of infallibility. While inerrancy speaks to the factual correctness of the text, infallibility emphasizes its unfailing truthfulness, especially concerning matters of faith and practice. The Bible is considered the ultimate and reliable authority for faith, doctrine, and conduct.

The infallibility of Scripture is seen, for instance, in passages like Romans 3:23-24 (ESV): "for all have sinned and fall short of the glory of God, and are justified by his grace as a gift, through the redemption that is in Christ Jesus." This passage makes clear the universal reality of sin and God's provision of salvation through Jesus, teachings that are infallibly true and essential to Christian faith and practice.

The Importance of Inerrancy and Infallibility

Both inerrancy and infallibility are necessary for maintaining the authority of Scripture. Inerrancy protects against the skepticism that arises when the Bible is considered erroneous in factual details, while infallibility safeguards the Bible's ultimate authority in teaching us what to believe and how to live.

However, understanding these terms requires discernment. They do not imply that the Bible should always be read literally, as its various genres (historical narratives, poetry, prophecy, etc.) often employ figurative language. They affirm that the Bible is truthful in all it intends to teach.

A critical caveat is that inerrancy applies to the original autographs of Scripture, not necessarily to all copies and translations. While scholars have worked diligently to ensure our Bible's accuracy, occasional scribal errors or translation issues do not undermine the original texts' inerrancy.

Inerrancy and infallibility do not mean that the Bible provides exhaustive information on every topic. It gives us all we need for knowledge of salvation and godly living, but it is not primarily a science or history textbook, though it affirms truth in those areas.

Belief in the inerrancy and infallibility of Scripture undergirds the Bible's authority, offering a foundation of trustworthiness that allows believers to embrace its teachings with confidence. As God's revealed

Word, the Bible is a reliable guide in matters of faith and practice, providing truth without error, as Psalm 12:6 (ESV) affirms: "The words of Jehovah are pure words, like silver refined in a furnace on the ground, purified seven times." The conviction that God's word is both inerrant and infallible assures believers that they can trust it to be the authoritative and definitive guide for all of life.

Examining the Doctrine of Biblical Inerrancy and Infallibility

The doctrines of biblical inerrancy and infallibility are cornerstones of Christian belief about the nature and reliability of the Holy Scriptures. These twin doctrines hold that the Bible is free from error and dependable in its truth claims, respectively.

Doctrine of Biblical Inerrancy

The doctrine of inerrancy is rooted in the belief that the original manuscripts of the Bible, known as the autographs, are without error. This includes all affirmations about history, doctrine, morality, and even matters of science. Inerrancy, therefore, asserts the truthfulness and complete reliability of Scripture.

Consider, for example, the resurrection of Jesus Christ from the dead, as recorded in the Gospel accounts (Matthew 28, Mark 16, Luke 24, and John 20). This event is presented as a historical reality, and the doctrine of inerrancy holds that this account is accurate and true.

However, the doctrine of inerrancy doesn't necessarily imply that the Bible should be interpreted literally at all times. Biblical writers often used figurative language, metaphor, and other literary devices to convey their message. When the Bible is interpreted with the historical-grammatical method, these instances of non-literal language do not compromise inerrancy. Rather, they're part of the intended meaning of the text.

For instance, when Jesus says in John 15:5 (ESV), "I am the vine; you are the branches," he is not implying a literal horticultural reality, but a spiritual truth about our relationship to him. Understanding this requires correctly identifying the metaphor and interpreting it as the author intended. This is perfectly consistent with the doctrine of inerrancy.

Doctrine of Biblical Infallibility

The doctrine of infallibility complements inerrancy by asserting that the Scriptures are incapable of failing in their purpose: to guide us to truth and salvation. Infallibility applies especially to spiritual, moral, and doctrinal matters, affirming that the Bible reliably leads us to truth in these areas.

Take for example 2 Timothy 3:16 (ESV): "All Scripture is breathed out by God and profitable for teaching, for reproof, for correction, and for training in righteousness." This verse asserts the infallible nature of Scripture; it reliably equips believers for every good work.

Implications and Challenges

While these doctrines provide a strong foundation for the authority and trustworthiness of the Bible, they come with certain challenges. Understanding inerrancy and infallibility requires careful and thoughtful interpretation. Inerrancy applies to the original autographs, not to every subsequent copy or translation. Moreover, recognizing the variety of literary genres in the Bible is crucial in interpreting it appropriately.

Additionally, we must acknowledge that while the Bible is inerrant and infallible, our interpretations are not. We are fallible beings who often bring our biases and limitations to the text. Therefore, humility and a willingness to correct our misunderstandings are key in handling the Scriptures.

These doctrines also affirm the sufficiency of Scripture for its intended purposes. While the Bible may not provide exhaustive knowledge in every field of inquiry, it is infallible and inerrant in all it seeks to communicate, especially regarding God's character and His plan for human salvation.

In conclusion, the doctrines of biblical inerrancy and infallibility are vital components of a high view of Scripture. They affirm that the Bible, interpreted rightly, is a completely trustworthy guide in all matters of faith and practice. In the words of Psalm 119:160 (ESV), "The sum of your word is truth, and every one of your righteous rules endures forever." Trusting in the inerrancy and infallibility of the Scriptures, believers can confidently rely on the Bible as the ultimate standard of truth.

The Reliability of the Bible: An Exploration of Scripture's Inerrancy and Infallibility

The reliability of the Bible is a core belief in Christianity, and this belief is embodied in the doctrines of inerrancy and infallibility. These doctrines essentially state that the Bible, as the Word of God, is free from error (inerrancy) and incapable of misleading us in matters of faith and conduct (infallibility). They form the foundation of our trust in the Scriptures as the definitive guide to understanding God's will and His plan for salvation.

The Doctrine of Inerrancy

Inerrancy refers to the belief that the Scriptures in their original manuscripts (known as "autographs") are without error in all their affirmations. The doctrine encompasses all aspects of truth: historical, scientific, moral, and spiritual.

For instance, when Genesis 1:1 (ESV) states, "In the beginning, God created the heavens and the earth," believers who affirm inerrancy uphold this as a true account of the origins of the universe. This doesn't mean that we interpret every passage literally; rather, the doctrine of inerrancy asserts that the intended message of a passage is completely true.

For instance, when Jesus describes Himself as "the door" in John 10:9 (ESV), we understand this as metaphorical language. Jesus is not literally a door; instead, He is the way by which we may enter into

39

salvation. Recognizing the figurative language does not negate inerrancy; instead, it affirms the truthful message conveyed through this metaphor.

The Doctrine of Infallibility

Infallibility, on the other hand, refers to the trustworthiness of Scripture. It states that the Scriptures, because they are the Word of God, are reliable and will not lead us astray. They are our dependable guide for faith and life.

This is affirmed by verses like 2 Timothy 3:16-17 (ESV), which says: "All Scripture is breathed out by God and profitable for teaching, for reproof, for correction, and for training in righteousness, that the man of God may be complete, equipped for every good work." This verse not only asserts the divine origin of the Scriptures but also their efficacy for spiritual instruction and moral guidance.

Exploring Scripture's Reliability

Affirming the inerrancy and infallibility of Scripture does not mean that we ignore the human element of its composition. The biblical writers were humans, inspired by the Holy Spirit, and they employed various literary styles and devices. These range from historical narrative and legal codes to poetry, prophecy, and apocalyptic visions.

A crucial aspect of interpreting Scripture, therefore, is to discern the genre and historical context of each book, chapter, and verse. This is where the historical-grammatical method comes in: it seeks to understand the original meaning of a passage by studying the language, culture, and circumstances of the time it was written.

This approach is essential for correctly interpreting the Bible. For instance, the apocalyptic language of the book of Revelation, full of symbolism and imagery, is understood differently from the historical narrative of the book of Acts.

Conclusion

The doctrines of inerrancy and infallibility reinforce the authority and trustworthiness of the Bible. They affirm that Scripture, properly interpreted, is a reliable guide for faith and practice.

This belief does not exempt us from the challenge of accurate interpretation. As finite and fallible humans, our interpretations may at times be mistaken. However, the solution to this problem is not to discard or dilute these doctrines but to seek continually to improve our understanding and application of God's Word.

In this endeavor, we are comforted by Psalm 119:105 (ESV): "Your word is a lamp to my feet and a light to my path." This verse encapsulates the heart of the doctrine of the Bible's reliability: that God's Word, inerrant and infallible, is our sure guide in a dark and uncertain world. In a world that so often confuses and misleads, the Bible stands as a beacon of truth, illuminating our path and leading us toward God's intended destination.

The Inspiration and Truth of Scripture: Perspectives on Inerrancy and Infallibility

The doctrines of the inspiration, inerrancy, and infallibility of Scripture are crucial pillars in the field of biblical hermeneutics. These doctrines posit that the Bible, as the Word of God, is divinely inspired, without error in its original form, and incapable of failing or leading one astray in matters of faith and practice. These principles lend credibility and authority to the Bible, situating it as the ultimate guide for understanding God's will, nature, and His plan for humanity.

The Inspiration of Scripture

The belief in the inspiration of Scripture holds that God, through the Holy Spirit, guided human authors to record exactly what He intended, albeit without overriding their personality, style, and cultural context. This divine-human synergy produced texts that bear the full weight of divine authority.

A critical verse in this regard is 2 Peter 1:21 (ESV), which states, "For no prophecy was ever produced by the will of man, but men spoke from God as they were carried along by the Holy Spirit." This passage makes clear the dual nature of the Bible's authorship: human writers were used as instruments, yet it was ultimately God who spoke through them, ensuring the messages conveyed were His own.

The Inerrancy of Scripture

Inerrancy is the belief that the Bible, in its original manuscripts, is without error in all its affirmations, whether they be historical, scientific, or spiritual. This doesn't mean that we must take each passage literally. Rather, we need to take into account the literary devices, genres, and cultural context of each passage, aiming to grasp what the author intended to communicate.

As an example, when God declares in Jeremiah 23:24 (ESV), "Can a man hide himself in secret places so that I cannot see him? Do I not fill heaven and earth?" We understand this as conveying the omnipresence of God. Despite the metaphorical language, the assertion here is true: God is present everywhere.

The Infallibility of Scripture

Infallibility refers to the Bible's complete trustworthiness as our guide for faith and life. The infallibility of Scripture derives from its divine origin; because it is God-breathed, it is utterly reliable and cannot lead us astray.

Hebrews 4:12 (ESV) speaks to this aspect, "For the word of God is living and active, sharper than any two-edged sword, piercing to the division of soul and of spirit, of joints and of marrow, and discerning the thoughts and intentions of the heart." The passage attests to the dynamic, penetrating power of God's Word, revealing its divine authority and efficacy.

Perspectives on Inerrancy and Infallibility

Over time, different perspectives have emerged within Christianity concerning inerrancy and infallibility. Some groups emphasize a stringent literal interpretation of Scripture, arguing that the Bible is inerrant in all respects, including scientific and historical details. Others adopt a more nuanced view, asserting the Bible's inerrancy in matters of faith and practice, while accommodating apparent discrepancies in historical or scientific details.

Notwithstanding these differences, what remains consistent across all perspectives is the belief in the essential reliability and authority of Scripture. This belief forms the bedrock of Christian faith and practice, shaping our understanding of God, His intentions, and His redemptive plan.

The application of the historical-grammatical method plays a critical role here. It serves to discern the original meaning of the texts by examining their language, cultural background, and historical context. This approach equips us to understand and appreciate the richness and complexity of Scripture, thereby leading us towards a more accurate interpretation.

In conclusion, the doctrines of inspiration, inerrancy, and infallibility uphold the Bible as the divine and authoritative Word of God, making it an indispensable guide for Christian faith and life. As we embrace these doctrines, we are better equipped to interpret Scripture faithfully, to discern its timeless truths, and to apply its teachings to our lives. While interpretations may differ among various perspectives, the commitment to Scripture's reliability and authority remains foundational in biblical hermeneutics.

Scripture as Reliable Revelation: A Discussion of Inerrancy and Infallibility

Christianity upholds the Bible as the infallible and inerrant Word of God, bearing within its text the reliable revelation of Jehovah and His will for mankind. These assertions carry profound implications for biblical hermeneutics, serving as foundational precepts in the interpretation of Scripture.

Inerrancy and Infallibility: The Twin Pillars of Reliability

The doctrines of inerrancy and infallibility form two essential aspects of the Bible's reliability. Inerrancy holds that the Bible is free from error in its original autographs, extending to all subjects it addresses, whether theological, historical, or scientific. Infallibility posits that the Bible is incapable of teaching falsehood or leading one astray when it comes to faith and life. Together, these twin doctrines assert that the Bible is a trustworthy and authoritative guide, providing an accurate and true revelation of Jehovah.

A scriptural example of inerrancy and infallibility is seen in Isaiah 55:11 (ESV): "so shall my word be that goes out from my mouth; it shall not return to me empty, but it shall accomplish that which I purpose, and shall succeed in the thing for which I sent it." Here, Jehovah speaks to the certainty and efficacy of His words, emphasizing their purposeful and unerring nature.

The Bible as Reliable Revelation

To discuss Scripture as a reliable revelation is to assert that it faithfully discloses the character, will, and redemptive plan of Jehovah. This perspective understands the Bible not as a human construct but as divinely inspired, where human authors were guided by the Holy Spirit to pen what Jehovah intended (2 Peter 1:21, ESV).

Consider the book of Romans. Throughout, Paul presents a comprehensive revelation of the gospel - the righteousness of God revealed through faith in Jesus Christ (Romans 1:16-17, ESV). Here, the reliability of Scripture is manifested in its clear and consistent revelation of God's redemptive plan for humanity.

The Role of Historical-Grammatical Hermeneutics

The historical-grammatical approach plays a crucial role in recognizing and affirming the reliability of the Bible. This method encourages interpreters to seek the original intended meaning of Scripture by considering its historical, cultural, and grammatical context. For instance, when Jesus says, "I am the true vine, and my Father is the vinedresser" (John 15:1, ESV), the historical-grammatical approach would lead one to explore the agricultural imagery familiar to the original audience to understand its metaphorical significance.

Moreover, it would dissuade an allegorical interpretation, instead of encouraging interpreters to grasp what Jesus meant by that metaphor, and then that is what is to be taken literally. By providing objective guidelines, this method ensures that our interpretation is anchored in the text itself and not in our own presuppositions, lending further credibility to the reliability of Scripture.

Conclusion

The doctrines of inerrancy and infallibility underline the Bible's role as a reliable revelation of Jehovah's character, will, and plan for humanity. By adhering to these doctrines and employing a historical-grammatical approach to interpretation, we respect the divine authorship of the Bible. Through the Scripture's revealed truths, we can know Jehovah, understand His will, and live faithfully in response. Our confidence in the reliability of Scripture emboldens us to explore its depths, knowing that it accurately reveals the very heart of God and His plans for us. It reinforces our faith, guides our lives, and shapes our worldview. In essence, these doctrines are fundamental in maintaining the integrity of our engagement with God's Word.

CHAPTER 3 Why Do We Not Need the Original Manuscripts to Believe In the Inerrancy of Scripture?

Between 3,500 years ago and 2,460 years ago, some 32+ authors penned 39 books in the Middle East, compiling a history of the world from its creation to the flood of Noah, the confusing of the languages at Babylon, Abraham entering Canaan, to the formation of the Israelite nation, to the rise and fall of the Egyptian, Assyrian, Babylonian, Medo-Persian Empires. These 39 books became the most important collection of literature that the world has ever known. They would soon be joined by another 27 books, the second most important collection that was written some 2,000 years ago, covering the birth of the Roman Empire and the birth of the Son of God, as well as the birth and foundation of Christianity.

There was something different about this library of sixty-six books that had been penned over a 1600-year period. The authors came from every walk of life, from lowly fishermen and shepherds to military general, a physician, tax collector, kings, and the like. These 40+ men were moved along by the Holy Spirit so that what they produced was not theirs alone but belonged to one author, the Creator of all things, God himself. This means these sixty-six books possessed perfect content (fully inerrant/infallible) with no errors, mistakes, or contradictions. We still have translations of these writings today that can be read by almost everyone on earth. However, a question arises because the Holy Spirit did not move along with the copyists who had been making copies for thousands of years. We do not have the original manuscripts. We know that the thousands upon thousands of original language manuscripts (Hebrew O.T./Greek NT) and the versions all read differently, as there are hundreds of thousands of scribal errors. How can we be sure that what we have in our Bible translations is really an accurate translation of what the authors originally wrote?

How Our Bible Manuscripts Survived the Elements

One may wonder why more Old and New Testament manuscripts have not survived. Really, the better question would be, how come so many of our Bible manuscripts survived in comparison to ancient secular manuscripts? In ancient times, the primary materials used to receive writing were perishable papyrus and parchment. It must be remembered that the Christians suffered intense persecution during intervals in the first 300 years from Pentecost 33 C.E. With this persecution from the Roman Empire came many orders to destroy Christian texts. In addition, these texts were not stored in such a way as to secure their preservation; the Christians actively used them in the congregation and were subject to wear and tear. Furthermore, moisture is the enemy of papyrus, and it causes them to disintegrate over time. As we will discover, this is why the papyrus manuscripts that have survived have come from the dry sands of Egypt. Moreover, it seems not to have entered the minds of the early Christians to preserve their documents because their solution to the loss of manuscripts was just to make more copies. Fortunately, the process of making copies transitioned to the more durable animal skins, which would last much longer. Those that have survived, especially from the fourth century C.E. and earlier, are the path to restoring the original Greek New Testament.[1]

Both papyrus and parchment jeopardized the survival of the Bible because they were perishable materials. Papyrus, the weakest of the two, can tear and discolor. Because of moist climates, a sheet of papyrus can decay to the point where it is nothing more than a handful of dust. We must remember papyrus is a plant; when the scroll has been stored, it can grow mold and rot from dampness. It can even be eaten by starving rodents or insects, especially white ants (i.e., termites) when buried. When some of the manuscripts were first discovered

---

[1] Cf. J. H. Greenlee, *Introduction to New Testament Textual Criticism* (Peabody: Hendrickson, 1995), 11.

early on, they were exposed to excessive light and humidity, which hastened their deterioration.

While parchment is far more durable than papyrus, it will also perish in time if mishandled or exposed to the elements (temperature, humidity, and light) over time.[2] Parchment is made from animal skin, so it is also an insect victim. Hence, when it comes to ancient records, Everyday Writing in the Graeco-Roman East states, "survival is the exception rather than the rule." (R. S. Bagnall 2009, 140) Think about it for a moment; the Bible and its special revelation could have died from decay in the elements.

The Mosaic Law commanded every future king, "And when he sits on the throne of his kingdom, he shall write for himself in a book a copy of this law, approved by the Levitical priests." (Deuteronomy 17:18) Moreover, the professional copyist of the Hebrew Old Testament made so many manuscripts, by the time of Jesus and the apostles, throughout all of Israel and even into distant Macedonia, there were many copies of the Scriptures in the synagogues (Luke 4:16, 17; Acts 17:11) How did our Hebrew Old Testament and Greek New Testament survive the elements to the point where there are far more of them than any other ancient document. For example, 5,898 New Testament manuscripts are in the original Greek alone.

New Testament scholar Philip W. Comfort writes, "Jews were known to put scrolls containing Scripture in pitchers or jars in order to preserve them. The Dead Sea scrolls found in jars in the Qumran caves are a celebrated example of this. The Beatty Papyri were very likely part of a Christian library, which was hidden in jars to be preserved from confiscation during the Diocletian persecution."[3] Christianity was initially made up of Jewish Christians only for the first seven years (29-36 C.E.), with Cornelius being the first Gentile baptized in 36 C.E. Much of early Christianity (33-350 C.E.) was made up of Jewish Christians, who evidently carried over the tradition of putting "scrolls containing Scripture in pitchers or jars in order to preserve them." For this reason,

---

[2] For example, the official signed copy of the U.S. Declaration of Independence was written on parchment. Now, less than 250 years later, it has faded to the point of being barely legible.

[3] Philip Wesley Comfort and David P. Barrett, *The Text of the Earliest New Testament Greek Manuscripts* (Wheaton, IL: Tyndale House, 2001), 158.

some of our earliest Bible manuscripts have been discovered in unusually dry regions, in clay jars, and even in dark closets and caves.

Manuscripts Saved from Egyptian Garbage Heaps

Beginning in 1778 and continuing to the end of the 19th century, many papyrus texts were accidentally discovered in Egypt that dated from 300 B.C.E. to 500 C.E., almost 500 thousand documents in all. About 130 years ago, there began a systematic search. At that time, a continuous flow of ancient texts was being found by the native fellahin, and the Egypt Exploration Society, a British non-profit organization founded in 1882, realized that they needed to send out an expedition team before it was too late. They sent two Oxford scholars, Bernard P. Grenfell and Arthur S. Hunt, who received permission to search the area south of the farming region in the Faiyūm district. Grenfell chose a site called Behnesa because of its ancient Greek name, Oxyrhynchus. A search of the graveyards and the ruined houses produced nothing. The only place left to search was the town's garbage dumps, which were some 30 feet [9 m] high. It seems to Grenfell and Hunt that all was lost but they decided to try.

In January of 1897, a trial trench (excavation or depression in the ground) was dug, and it only took a few hours before ancient papyrus materials were found. These included letters, contracts, and official documents. The sand had blown over them, covering them, and for nearly 2,000 years, the dry climate had protected them.

It took only a mere three months to pull out and recover almost two tons of papyri from Oxyrhynchus. They shipped twenty-five large cases back to England. Over the next ten years, these two courageous scholars returned each winter to grow their collections. They discovered ancient classical writing, along with royal ordinances and contracts mixed in with business accounts, private letters, shipping lists, as well as fragments of many New Testament manuscripts.

Of what benefit was all these documents? Foremost, the bulk of these documents were written by ordinary people in Koine (common) Greek of the day. Many of the words that would be used in the marketplace, not by the elites, appeared in the Greek New Testament Scriptures, which woke scholars up to the fact that Biblical Greek was not some special Greek, but instead, it was the ordinary language of the common people, the man on the street. Thus, by comparing how the words had been used in these papyri, a clearer understanding of Biblical Greek emerged. As of the time of this writing, less than ten percent of these papyri have been published and studied. Most of the papyri were found in the garbage heap's top 10 feet 93 m] because the other 20 feet [6 m] had been ruined by water from a nearby canal. If we look at it simply, this would mean that the 500 thousand documents found could have been two million in total. Then, we must ponder just how many documents must have come through Oxyrhynchus that were never discarded in the dumps. We have almost a half million papyrus documents (likely there were millions more that did not survive) in garbage dumps in the dry sands of Oxyrhynchus, Egypt.

The end result is that the New Testament has been preserved in over **5,898** complete or fragmented Greek manuscripts, as well as some **10,000** Latin manuscripts and **9,300 manuscripts** in various other ancient languages, which include Syriac, Slavic, Gothic, Ethiopic, Coptic and Armenian. Some of these are well over 2,000 years old.

The Hebrew Scriptures ended up in the hands of the Masoretes (Mas·o·retes \ 'ma-sə-ˌrētes) scribe-scholars ('preservers of tradition') who worked between the 6th and 10th centuries C.E., based primarily in early medieval Palestine in the cities of Tiberias and Jerusalem. The Masoretes have not been adequately appreciated for their accomplishments. These nameless scribes copied the Hebrew Old Testament Scriptures meticulously and lovingly. As for the early Christian copyists of the New Testament, either literate or semi-professional copyists did the vast majority of the early papyri, with some done by professionals.

It is true that the Jewish copyists and the later Christian copyists were not led along by the Holy Spirit, and therefore, their manuscripts were not inerrant, infallible. Errors (textual variants) crept into the manuscripts unintentionally and intentionally. However, most of the Hebrew Old Testament and Greek New Testament have not been infected with textual errors. For the portions impacted with textual errors, it is the many tens of thousands of copies that we have to help us to weed out the errors. How? Well, not every copyist made the same textual errors. Hence, by comparing the work of different copyists and different manuscripts, textual scholars, we can identify the textual variants (errors), and remove those, which leaves us with the original content.

Yes, it would be the greatest discovery of all time if we found the original five books penned by Moses himself, Genesis through Deuteronomy. However, first, there would be no way of establishing that they were the originals. Second, truth be told, we do not need the originals. We do not need those original documents. What is so important about the documents? Nothing, it is the content of the original documents that we are after. And truly miraculously, we have more copies than needed to do just that. We do not need miraculous preservation because we have miraculous restoration. We now know beyond a reasonable doubt that the Hebrew Old Testament and the Greek New Testament critical texts are a 99.99% reflection of the content that was in those ancient original manuscripts.

CHAPTER 4 Why Would the Holy Spirit Miraculously Inspire 66 Fully Inerrant Texts and Then Allow Variant Errors in the Copies?

Divine Inspiration and Preservation of the Bible: A Scholarly Perspective

Renowned agnostic scholar of New Testament texts and early Christianity, Dr. Bart D. Ehrman, poses an interesting argument. He suggests, "For the only reason (I came to think) for God to inspire the Bible would be so that his people would have his actual words; but if he really wanted people to have his actual words, surely he would have miraculously preserved those words, just as he had miraculously inspired them in the first place. Given the circumstance that he didn't preserve the words, the conclusion seemed inescapable to me that he hadn't gone to the trouble of inspiring them" (Misquoting Jesus: The Story Behind Who Changed the Bible and Why, HarperSanFrancisco, 2005).

In response to this, Dr. Dirk Jongkind, a New Testament textual scholar, provides a succinct counter: "God chose not to give us exhaustive knowledge of every detail of the text, though he could have done so. Still, he has given us abundant access to his words. In other words, to say that God inspired the words of the New Testament does not mean that God is therefore under an obligation to preserve for us each and every detail" (An Introduction to the Greek New Testament, Produced at Tyndale House, Cambridge, Crossway).

Why didn't God inspire the copyists? This question has perplexed many and served as a point of contention for critics of the Bible. You may be here seeking a definitive answer to alleviate your doubts or a potent response for critics of the Bible. Be reassured that there are myriad credible responses to such critiques that may prompt them to reconsider. Yet, some queries may not find their comprehensive answers until the Second Coming. The discussion below addresses this very question. While you might be tempted to skip ahead, I recommend reading through for a more comprehensive understanding.

Unfortunately, some individuals harbor inflexible hearts and minds, echoing the Pharisaical attitudes of old. No amount of biblical wisdom, reason, or logic can penetrate their hardened hearts. If my years of teaching have taught me one thing, it is to quickly identify these individuals to avoid wasting precious time offering rational responses, only to have them summarily dismissed. Keep in mind, though, an angry or doubting person is not necessarily Pharisaical. Doubt and anger can stem from valid reasons. Signs of Pharisaical attitudes include disdain, mockery, and condescension. The comprehensive answer to the posed question lies below within the broader context.

Christian Bible students need to familiarize themselves with Old and New Testament textual studies, as they are fundamental to understanding the Scriptures. If we fail to ascertain what was originally written with reasonable certainty, how can we translate or interpret the perceived Word of God? Fortunately, we possess more New Testament manuscripts than any other ancient text, offering scholars a vast amount of material to establish the original words of the text. Many Greek and Latin classics rely on a single existing manuscript, with a few having just a handful and even fewer possessing a few hundred. In contrast, there are over 5,898 cataloged Greek New Testament manuscripts (as of January 2016), 10,000 Latin manuscripts, and another 9,300 manuscripts in languages such as Syriac, Slavic, Gothic, Ethiopic, Coptic, and Armenian.

The other difference between the New Testament manuscripts and those of the classics is that the existing copies of the New Testament date much closer to the originals. In the case of the Greek classics, some of the manuscripts are dated about a thousand years after the author had penned the book. Some of the Latin classics are dated from three to seven hundred years after the time the author wrote the book. To be fair and forthright, there are some ancient authors that have manuscripts that are dated relatively close and there are many copies. Some of Thucydides (an Athenian historian and general) 96 manuscripts on history for example is only 200 years removed from the originals. Some of Sophocles (an Athenian historian and general) 193 manuscripts on plays for example is only 100-200 years removed from the originals.

The New Testament Compared to Classical Literature

Author	Work	Writing Completed	Earliest MSS	Years Removed	Number of MSS
Homer	*Iliad*	800 B.C.E.	3rd century B.C.E.[4]	500	1,757
Herodotus	*History*	480–425 B.C.E.	10th cent. C.E.	1,350	109
Sophocles	*Plays*	496–406 B.C.E.	3rd cent. B.C.E.[5]	100-200	193
Thucydides	*History*	460–400 B.C.E.	3rd cent. B.C.E.[6]	200	96
Plato	*Tetralogies*	400 B.C.E.	895 C.E.	1,300	210
Demosthenes	*Speeches*	300 B.C.E.	Fragments from 1st cent. B.C.E.	200	340
Caesar	*Gallic Wars*	51-46 B.C.E.	9th cent. C.E.	950	251
Livy	*History of Rome*	59 B.C.E.–17 C.E.	5th cent. C.E.	400	150
Tacitus	*Annals*	100 C.E.	9th-11th cent. C.E.	750–950	33
Pliny, the Elder	*Natural History*	49–79 C.E.	5th cent. C.E. fragment	400	200
Eight Greek NT Authors	27 Books	50 – 98 C.E.	110-125 C.E.	12-27	5,898

[4] There are a number of fragments that date to the second century B.C.E. and one to the third century B.C.E., with the rest dating to the ninth century C.E. or later.

[5] Most of the 193 MSS date to the tenth century C.E., with a few fragments dating to the third century B.C.E.

[6] Some papyri fragments date to the third century B.C.E.

When we look at the Greek copies of the New Testament books, some portions are within decades of the original author's book. Sixty-two Greek papyri, along with five majuscules[7] date from 110 C.E. to 300 C.E.

Distribution of Greek New Testament Manuscripts

- The **Papyrus** is a copy of a portion of the New Testament made on papyrus. At present, we have 140 cataloged New Testament papyri, many dating between 110-350 C.E., but some as late as the 6th century C.E.

- The **Majuscule** or **Uncial** is a script of large letters commonly used in Greek and Latin manuscripts written between the 3rd and 9th centuries C.E. that resembles a modern capital letter but is more rounded. At present, we have 323 cataloged New Testament Majuscule manuscripts.

- The **Minuscule** is a small cursive style of writing used in manuscripts from the 9th to the 16th centuries, now having 2,951 Minuscule manuscripts cataloged.

- The **Lectionary** is a schedule of readings from the Bible for Christian church services during the year, in both majuscules and minuscules, dating from the 4th to the 16th centuries C.E., now having 2,484 Lectionary manuscripts cataloged.

We should clarify that of the approximate 24,000 total manuscripts of the New Testament, not all are complete books. There are fragmented manuscripts that have just a few verses, but there are manuscripts that contain an entire book, others that include numerous books, and some that have the whole New Testament, or nearly so. This is to be expected since the oldest manuscripts we have were copied in an era when copying the whole New Testament was not the norm, but rather a single book or a group of books (i.e., the Gospels

---

[7] Large lettering, often called "capital" or uncial, in which all the letters are usually the same height.

or Paul's letters). This still does not negate the vast riches of manuscripts that we possess.

What can we conclude from this short introduction to one aspect of NT textual studies? There is some irony here, in that secular scholars have no problem accepting the wording of classic authors, with their minuscule amount of evidence. However, they discount the treasure trove of evidence that is available to the New Testament textual scholar. Still, this should not surprise us as the New Testament has always been under-appreciated and attacked in some way, shape, or form over the past 2,000 years.

On the contrary, in comparison to classical works, we are overwhelmed by the quantity and quality of existing New Testament manuscripts. We should also keep in mind that seventy-five percent[8] of the New Testament does not even require the help of textual studies because that much of the text is unanimous, and thus, we know what it says. Of the other twenty-five percent, about twenty percent make up trivial scribal mistakes that are easily corrected. Therefore, textual studies focus mainly on a small portion of the New Testament text. The facts are clear: the Christian, who reads the New Testament, is fortunate to have so many manuscripts, with so many dating so close to the originals, with c. 300 hundred years (1730-2020) of hundreds of textual scholars who have established the text with a level of certainty unimaginable for ancient secular works.

After discussing the amount of New Testament manuscripts available, Atheist commentator Bob Seidensticker, writes, "The first problem is that more manuscripts at best increase our confidence that we have the original version. That does not mean the original copy was history …."[9] That is, Seidensticker is forced to acknowledge the reliability of the New Testament text as we have it today and can only try to deny what it says. He also tells us of the New Testament, "Compare that with 2000 copies of the Iliad, the second-best

---

[8] The numbers in this paragraph are rounded for simplicity purposes.

[9] 25,000 New Testament Manuscripts? Big Deal. – Patheos,

http://www.patheos.com/blogs/crossexamined/2013/11/25000-new-testament-manuscrip (Retrieved Monday, August 10, 2020).

represented manuscript."[10] Of those 1,757 copies of the Iliad, how far removed are they from the alleged originals? The Iliad is dated to about 800 B.C.E. B.C.E. There are a number of fragments of the Iliad that date to the second century B.C.E. and one to the third century B.C.E., with the rest dating to the ninth century C.E. or later. That would make these handful of fragmented manuscripts 500 years removed and the rest about 1,7000 years removed from their original.

The Range of Textual Criticism

The Importance and scope of New Testament textual criticism could be summed up in the few words used by J. Harold Greenlee; it is "the basic biblical study, a prerequisite to all other biblical and theological work. Interpretation, systemization, and application of the teachings of the NT cannot be done until textual criticism has done at least some of its work. It is, therefore, deserving of the acquaintance and attention of every serious student of the Bible."[11]

It is only reasonable to assume that the original 39 books of the Old Testament and the 27 books written first-hand by the New Testament authors have not survived. Instead, we only have what we must consider being imperfect copies. **Why the Holy Spirit would miraculously inspire 66 fully inerrant texts, and then allow human imperfection into the copies**, is not explained for us in Scripture. We do know that imperfect humans have tended to worship relics that traditions hold to have been touched by the miraculous powers of God or to have been in direct contact with one of his special servants of old. Ultimately, though, all we know is that God had his reasons for allowing the Old and New Testament autographs to be worn out by repeated use. From time to time, we hear of the discovery of a fragment possibly dated to the first century, but even if such a fragment is eventually verified, the dating alone can never serve as proof of an autograph; it will still be a copy in all likelihood.

---

[10] Ibid

[11] J. Harold Greenlee, Introduction to New Testament Textual Criticism (Grand Rapids, MI: Baker Academic, 1995), 8-9.

The Role of Divine Inspiration in Scripture Transmission: An Examination

When considering why God didn't inspire the copyists, we should also ask, "Why didn't He inspire translators, Bible scholars, and others involved in the propagation of His Word?" If His intent was to provide an entirely inerrant, authoritative, authentic, and accurate Word, then why not protect the Scriptures in all facets of transmission, including copying, translating, and interpreting? If people were guided by the Holy Spirit, it would become evident that they could not err, make a mistake, or deliberately alter the text while copying.

However, where would this inspiration stop? Would it extend to anyone attempting to copy the Scriptures, attempting to test if they could also be inspired? Over time, this could serve as empirical evidence for God's existence, negating the need for humanity to learn the object lesson inherent in the existence of sin and imperfection: that man cannot exist independently from his Creator. God created perfect humans, but through the abuse of free will, they rejected His sovereignty. He did not continue creating perfect humans, as though He had made a mistake. Instead, He gave us His perfect Word and allowed us to continue in our human imperfection, learning our object lesson.

As we find in Matthew 24:14 and Acts 1:8, God has intervened in human affairs countless times throughout the Bible and perhaps tens of thousands of times unbeknownst to us over the past 6,000+ years, to achieve His will and purposes. But none of His interventions have been continuous until the return of the Son. Perhaps God gave us a perfect copy of the sixty-six books and then, as with everything else, placed the responsibility of copying, translating, and interpreting on us, along with the Great Commission to proclaim and explain His Word to make disciples.

Some critics argue that if the original Scriptures were divinely inspired and fully inerrant, their subsequent copies must also remain inerrant for the inerrancy of the originals to hold value. They question, "If only the originals were inspired, and we do not have the originals, how can we be certain of any passage in Scripture?" In other words, they believe God would not permit His inspired, inerrant Word to suffer copying errors.

This line of thinking raises several other questions: Why didn't God produce the books Himself and miraculously deliver them to the people, as He gave the commandments to Moses? Why didn't He use angelic messengers or produce the message miraculously instead of using humans? We don't know why God didn't guide copyists with the Holy Spirit to produce perfect copies; this remains a mystery.

Yet, if we can restore the text to its original wording through the art and science of textual criticism, we essentially have the originals. Regarding errors in the copies, we can confidently say that the majority of the Greek text is unaffected by errors. Errors typically occur as variant readings, where different manuscripts disagree. These variants are mostly minor and easily identifiable. They don't impact significant doctrines, and rarely alter the meaning of a verse.[12] However, establishing the original text wherever there are variant readings remains vitally important. Every word matters!

The Intricacies of Divine Inspiration and Preservation in Biblical Texts

Undoubtedly, Jewish and Christian copyists of ancient times weren't moved by the Holy Spirit in the same way the original authors were, which resulted in their copies not being infallible or inerrant. Consequently, unintentional and intentional errors, or textual variants, managed to find their way into the manuscripts. Nevertheless, the vast majority of the Hebrew Old Testament and Greek New Testament remains free from such textual inaccuracies. It's the plethora of copies we possess that enable us to identify and rectify these errors. By cross-examining the work of various copyists and their respective

---

[12] Leading textual scholar Daniel Wallace tells us, after looking at all of the evidence, that the percentage of instances where the reading is uncertain and a well-attested alternative reading could change the meaning of the verse is a quarter of one percent, i.e., 0.0025%

manuscripts, textual scholars can discern these textual variants and eliminate them, restoring the content to its original form.

Unearthing the original five books penned by Moses, Genesis through Deuteronomy, or the original Gospels of Matthew, Mark, Luke, and John would indeed be an extraordinary find. However, two issues arise with this scenario. First, verifying their authenticity as the original documents would be an insurmountable task. Second, and more importantly, the physical originals aren't necessary. It's not the documents themselves that hold intrinsic value, but the content they bear.

Through a miracle of restoration rather than preservation, we have an abundance of copies that permit us to reconstruct the original content. It's this enormous body of textual evidence that confirms, beyond a reasonable doubt, that our Hebrew Old Testament and Greek New Testament critical texts reflect the original manuscripts' content with 99.99% accuracy. In essence, we don't need the original documents because we have, through the wealth of copies available to us, a near-perfect reflection of their content.

CHAPTER 5 How Can We Believe Inerrancy of Scripture In the Originals When We Don't Have the Originals?

For the conservative Evangelical Christian, one of their foundational doctrines is "The Bible alone, and the Bible in its entirety, is the Word of God written and is therefore inerrant in the autographs."[13]

How is this even possible for Christians to hold such an absolute view as absolute inerrancy when we do not have the original documents? Really, how could any reasonable, rational, logical person have such a view as Inerrancy of Scripture because we do not have the originals and so how could you ever prove that your statement is true? Moreover, only the original autographs published by the Bible authors themselves are absolutely inerrant. No copy or any translation is inerrant. The following statements below are common ways the Agnostic, atheist, Bible critic, and skeptic make just this argument.

First, the original manuscripts are not accessible today. If the scriptures derive their authority from their inspiration and inerrancy, then only the original manuscripts carry any authority, for the copies we have now are neither inspired nor inerrant. This forces the conclusion that every Bible believing Christian places his faith in an authority that doesn't exist.[14]

It has been frequently pointed out that if God thought errorless Scripture important enough to inspire its composition, he would surely also have further inspired its

---

[13] The Evangelical Theological Society Constitution (Retrieved Monday, August 10, 2020) https://www.etsjets.org/about/constitution

[14] Darin M. Weil, Inerrancy and It's Implications for Authority: Textual Critical Considerations in Formulating an Evangelical Doctrine of Scripture, Quodlibet Journal 4.4 (November 2002.

copying, so that it might remain error free. Surely a God who can inspire error-free composition could also inspire error-free copying. Since he did not, it would appear he did not think our possession of error-free Scripture very important. But if it is not important for us, why was it important originally?[15]

Presumably if we could ever recover the original manuscript of a NT book it would be very close to what its author intended. Even here, however, the text might not be completely correct. If the author wrote it himself, he could have made mistakes; if he dictated it to a scribe, the latter could have made mistakes.[16]

What does all this mean? The Agnostic, atheist, and Bible critics and skeptics in general believe that this kind of argument is their advantage over the Christians belief in absolute inerrancy of Scripture.

There are, unfortunately, fierce critics who reject any claims of veracity for these early manuscripts. Former evangelical Christian, now Agnostic New Testament Bible scholar, Dr. Bart Ehrman writes,

Not only do we not have the originals, we don't have the first copies of the originals. **We don't even have copies of the copies of the originals, or copies of the copies of the copies of the originals.** What we have are copies **made later—much later**. In most instances, they are copies made many *centuries* later. And these **copies all differ from one another, in many thousands of places**. As we will see later in this book, these copies **differ from one another in so many places that we don't even know how many differences** there are. Possibly it is easiest to put it in comparative terms: **there are more differences among our**

---

[15] Paul J. Achtemeier, The Inspiration of Scripture: Problems and Proposals (Philadelphia: Westminster John Knox, 1998), 71–72.

[16] Jack Finegan, *Encountering New Testament Manuscripts: A Working Introduction to Textual Criticism.* (Grand Rapids, MI: Eerdmans, 1974), 54.

manuscripts than there are words in the New Testament.[17] (Bold mine)

As we read these remarks, it is easy to get a sense of hopelessness because "all feels lost, for there is certainly no way to get back to the originals." Correct? Ehrman has had a long history of creating hopelessness for his readers, as he carries on his alleged truth quest. He asserts that even in the very few numbers of places that we might be sure about the *wording*, we cannot be certain about the *meaning*.

Blinded by Misguided Perceptions

Ehrman clearly has been immensely impacted by the fact that we do not have the originals or immediate copies. Here we have a world-renowned textual scholar and historian of early Christianity who is emphasizing that we do not have the originals nor the direct copies, and since there are so many copyist errors, it is virtually impossible to get back to the Word of God at all. Even if by some stroke of fortune, we could, we cannot know the meaning with assurance. Ehrman is saying to the lay reader: we can no longer trust the text of the Greek New Testament as the Word of God. If so, we would have to conclude that all translations are untrustworthy as well.

Ehrman has exaggerated the negative to his readers to the detriment of the positive in New Testament textual criticism. Mark Minnick assesses the latter nicely: "Doesn't the existence of these variants undermine our confidence that we have the very words of God inspired? No! The fact is that because we know of them and are careful to preserve the readings of every one of them, *not one word of God's word has been lost to us.*"[18] The wealth of manuscripts that we have for establishing the original Greek New Testament is overwhelming, in comparison to other ancient literature. We can only wonder what Ehrman does with an ancient piece of literature that has only one copy,

---

[17] Bart D. Ehrman, *MISQUOTING JESUS: The Story Behind Who Changed the Bible and Why* (New York, NY: Harper One, 2005), 10.

[18] Mark Minnick, "Let's Meet the Manuscripts," in *From the Mind of God to the Mind of Man: A Layman's Guide to How We Got Our Bible*, eds. James B. Williams and Randolph Shaylor (Greenvill, SC: Ambassador-Emerald International, 1999), p. 96.

and that copy is hundreds or even over a thousand years removed from the time of the original.

Consider a few examples. Before beginning, it should be noted that some of the classical authors are centuries, some are many centuries before the first century New Testament era, which is a somewhat unfair comparison. See the chart below which we had shown you in the previous chapter. It is placed here for your convenience of not having to flip back and look at it.[19]

The New Testament Compared to Classical Literature

Author	Work	Writing Completed	Earliest MSS	Years Removed	Number of MSS
Homer	*Iliad*	800 B.C.E.	3rd century B.C.E.[20]	500	1,757
Herodotus	*History*	480–425 B.C.E.	10th cent. C.E.	1,350	109
Sophocles	*Plays*	496–406 B.C.E.	3rd cent. B.C.E.[21]	100-200	193
Thucydides	*History*	460–400 B.C.E.	3rd cent. B.C.E.[22]	200	96
Plato	*Tetralogies*	400 B.C.E.	895 C.E.	1,300	210
Demosthenes	*Speeches*	300 B.C.E.	Fragments from 1st cent. B.C.E.	200	340
Caesar	*Gallic Wars*	51-46 B.C.E.	9th cent. C.E.	950	251
Livy	*History of Rome*	59 B.C.E.–17 C.E.	5th cent. C.E.	400	150
Tacitus	*Annals*	100 C.E.	9th-11th cent. C.E.	750–950	33

---

[19] The concept of this chart is taken from *The Bibliographical Test Updated - Christian Research* ... http://www.equip.org/article/the-bibliographical-test-updated/ May 04, 2017. However, some adjustments have been made as well as footnotes added.

[20] There are a number of fragments that date to the second century B.C.E. and one to the third century B.C.E., with the rest dating to the ninth century C.E. or later.

[21] Most of the 193 MSS date to the tenth century C.E., with a few fragments dating to the third century B.C.E.

[22] Some papyri fragments date to the third century B.C.E.

Pliny, the Elder	*Natural History*	49–79 C.E.	5th cent. C.E. fragment	400	200
Eight Greek NT Authors	27 Books	50 – 98 C.E.	110-125 C.E.	12-27	5,898

The Greek New Testament evidence, as we've mentioned previously, is over 5,898 Greek NT manuscripts (140 papyri, 323 majuscules, 2,951 minuscules, and 2,484 lectionaries)[23] that have been cataloged,[24] over 9,284 versions, and over 10,000 Latin manuscripts, not to mention an innumerable amount of church fathers' quotations. This places the Greek New Testament in a class by itself, because no other ancient document is close to this. However, there is even more. There are 60 Greek papyri, along with five majuscules manuscripts that date to the second and third centuries C.E. Moreover, these early papyri manuscripts are from a region in Egypt that appreciated books as literature, and were copied by semi-professional and professional scribes, or at least highly skilled copyists. This region produced what are known as the most accurate and trusted manuscripts.

---

[23] Of the 5,898 Greek NT manuscripts cataloged, 83 percent of them date after 1000 C.E., with 17% (889 manuscripts) dating from the second to the tenth century. Between the second to the tenth century we find in whole or in part 365 Gospels, 112 Acts and Catholic Epistles, 158 Epistles of Paul, 33 Revelation, and 313 lectionaries. The Gospel of Mark is the least attested **prior to the fourth century**, with chapters 2, 3, 10, and 13-16 having no representation at all. The Gospel of Mark is only represented in (P[45]), but about 78% of the Gospel is missing, and the fragment P[137], a codex, written on both sides with text from the first chapter of the Gospel of Mark; verses 7-9 on the recto side and 16-18 on the verso side. The Gospel of John on the other hand, prior to the fourth century it is very well attested, with only 14 verses not being covered between chapters 16 and 20. The Gospel of John is found in some of the earliest and most significant manuscripts (P[45] P[66] P[75]).

[24] While at present here in 2020, there are 5,898 manuscripts. There are **140 listed Papyrus** manuscripts, 323 Majuscule manuscripts, 2,951 Minuscule manuscripts, and 2,484 Lectionary manuscripts, bringing the total cataloged manuscripts to 5,898 manuscripts. However, you cannot simply total the number of cataloged manuscripts because, for example, P[11/14] are the same manuscript but with different catalog numbers. The same is true of P[33/5], P[4/64/67], P[49/65] and P[77/103]. Now this alone would bring our 140 listed papyrus manuscripts down to 134. 'Then, we turn to one example from our majuscule manuscripts where clear 0110, 0124, 0178, 0179, 0180, 0190, 0191, 0193, 0194, and 0202 are said to be part of 070. A minuscule manuscript was listed with five separate catalog numbers for 2306, which then have the letters a through e. Thus, we have the following GA numbers: 2306 for 2306a, and 2831- 2834 for 2306b-2306e.' – Invalid source specified. The problem is much worse when we consider that there are 323 Majuscule manuscripts and then far worse still with a listed 2,951 Minuscule and 2,484 Lectionaries. Nevertheless, those who estimate a total of 5,300 (Jacob W. Peterson, Myths and Mistakes, p. 63) 5,500 manuscripts (Dr. Ed Gravely / ehrmanproject.com/), 5,800 manuscripts **Invalid source specified.**, it is still a truckload of evidence far and above the dismal number of ancient secular author books.

Were the Scribes in the Early Centuries Amateurs?

We could **go on nearly forever** talking about specific places in which the texts of the New Testament came to be changed, either accidentally or intentionally. As I have indicated, the examples are **not just in the hundreds but in the thousands**. The examples given are enough to convey the general point, however: there are lots of differences among our manuscripts, differences created by scribes who were reproducing their sacred texts. **In the early Christian centuries, scribes were amateurs** and as such were more inclined to alter the texts they copied—or more prone to alter them accidentally—than were scribes in the later periods who, starting in the fourth century, began to be professionals.[25] [Bold mine]

Let us take just a moment to discuss Ehrman's statement, **"in the early Christian centuries, scribes were amateurs...."** In this book, we established just the opposite. Literate or semi-professional copyists did most of our early papyri, with some being done by professionals. As it happened, the few poorly copied manuscripts became known first, establishing a precedent that was difficult for some to discard when the truckload of evidence came forth that showed just the opposite. (Comfort P. , 2005, pp. 18-19)

Ehrman is misrepresenting the situation to his readers when he states, "We don't even have copies of the copies of the originals or copies of the copies of the copies of the originals." The way this is worded, he is saying that we do not have copies that are three or four generations removed from the originals. Ehrman cannot know this because we have 50 copies of the Greek NT that are 20 to 150 years removed from the death of the apostle John in 100 C.E. There is the possibility that any of these could be only third or fourth generation removed copies. Furthermore, they could have been copied from a

---

[25] Bart D. Ehrman, *MISQUOTING JESUS: The Story Behind Who Changed the Bible and Why* (New York, NY: Harper One, 2005), 98.

second or third generation. Therefore, Ehrman is misstating the evidence.

Let us do another short review of two very important manuscripts: P[75] and Vaticanus 1209 (B). P[75] is also known as Bodmer 14, 15. As has already been stated, papyrus is writing material used by the ancient Egyptians, Greeks, and Romans that was made from the pith of the stem of a water plant. These are the earliest witnesses to the Greek New Testament. P[75] contains most of Luke and John, dating from 175 C.E. to 225 C.E Codex Vaticanus is designated internationally by the symbol "B" (and 03) and is known as an uncial manuscript written on parchment. It is dated to the beginning of the fourth-century C.E. [c. 300-325] and originally contained the entire Bible in Greek. At present, Vaticanus' New Testament is missing parts of Hebrews (Hebrews 9:14 to 13:25), all of First and Second Timothy, Titus, Philemon, and Revelation. Initially, this codex probably had approximately 820 leaves, of which 759 remain.

What kind of weight or evidence do these two manuscripts carry in the eyes of textual scholars? Vaticanus 1209 is a key source for our modern translations. When determining an original reading, this manuscript can stand against other external evidence that would seem to the non-professional to be much more significant. P[75] also is one of the weightiest manuscripts that we have and is virtually identical to Vaticanus 1209, which dates 175 to 125 years later than P[75]. When textual scholars B. F. Westcott and F. J. A. Hort released their critical text in 1881, Hort said that Vaticanus preserved "not only a very ancient text but a very pure line of a very ancient text." (Westcott & Hort, 1882, p. 251) Later, scholars argued that Vaticanus was a scholarly recension: a critical revision or edited text. However, P[75] has vindicated Westcott and Hort because of its virtual identity with Vaticanus; it establishes that Vaticanus is essentially a copy of a second-century text, and likely, a copy of the original text, except for a few minor points.

Kurt Aland[26] wrote, "P[75] shows such a close affinity with the Codex Vaticanus that the supposition of a recension of the text at Alexandria, in the fourth century, can no longer be held."[27] David C. Parker[28] says of P[75] that "it is extremely important for two reasons: "like Vaticanus, it is carefully copied; it is also very early and is generally dated to a period between 175 and 225. Thus, it pre-dates Vaticanus by at least a century. A careful comparison between P[75] and Vaticanus in Luke by C.M. Martini demonstrated that P[75] was an earlier copy of the same careful Alexandrian text. It is sometimes called proto-Alexandrian. It is our earliest example of a controlled text, one which was not intentionally or extensively changed in successive copying. Its discovery and study have provided proof that the Alexandrian text had already come into existence in the third century." (Parker, 1997, p. 61) Let us look at the remarks of a few more textual scholars: J. Ed Komoszewski, M. James Sawyer, and Daniel Wallace.

> Even some of the early manuscripts show compelling evidence of being copies of a much earlier source. Consider again Codex Vaticanus, whose text is very much like that of P[75] (B and P75 are much closer to each other than B is to [Codex Sinaiticus]). Yet the papyrus is at least a century older than Vaticanus. When P[75] was discovered in the 1950s, some entertained the possibility that Vaticanus could have been a copy of P[75], but this view is no longer acceptable since the wording of Vaticanus is certainly more primitive than that of P75 in several places.' They both must go back to a still earlier common ancestor, probably one that is from the early second century.[29]

---

[26] (1915 – 1994) was Professor of New Testament Research and Church History. He founded the Institute for New Testament Textual Research in Münster and served as its first director for many years (1959–83). He was one of the principal editors of The Greek New Testament for the United Bible Societies.

[27] K. Aland, "The Significance of the Papyri for New Testament Research," 336.

[28] Professor of Theology and the Director of the Institute for Textual Scholarship and Electronic Editing at the Department of Theology and Religion, University of Birmingham. Scholar of New Testament textual criticism and Greek and Latin paleography.

[29] J. ED Komoszewski; M. James Sawyer; Daniel B Wallace, *Reinventing Jesus* (Grand Rapids, MI, 2006), 78.

Comfort comments on how we can know that Vaticanus is not a copy of P[75]: "As was previously noted, Calvin Porter clearly established the fact that P[75] displays the kind of text that was used in making codex Vaticanus. However, it is unlikely that the scribe of B used P[75] as his exemplar because the scribe of B copied from a manuscript whose line length was 12–14 letters per line. We know this because when the scribe of Codex Vaticanus made large omissions, they were typically 12–14 letters long.[30] The average line length for P[75] is about 29–32 letters per line. Therefore, the scribe of B must have used a manuscript like P[75], but not P[75] itself."[31]

Ehrman suggests that the early Christians were not concerned about the integrity of the text, its preservation of accuracy. Let us consult the second-century evidence by way of Tertullian (155-240 C.E.).[32]

> Come now, you who would indulge a better curiosity, if you would apply it to the business of your salvation, run over the apostolic churches, in which the very thrones[33] of the apostles are still pre-eminent in their places,[34] in which their own **authentic writings** are read, uttering the voice and representing the face of each of them severally.[35] (Bold mine)

What did Tertullian mean by "authentic writings"? If he was referring to the Greek originals, and it seems that he was, according to the Latin–it is an indication that some of the original New Testament books were still in existence at the time of his penning this work. However, let us say that it is simply referring to well-preserved copies. In any case, this shows that the Christians valued the preservation of accuracy.

---

[30] Brooke F. Westcott and Fenton J. A. Hort, *Introduction to the New Testament in the Original Greek* (New York: Harper & Bros., 1882; reprint, Peabody, Mass.: Hendrickson, 1988), 233–34.

[31] (Comfort & Barret, The Text of the Earliest New Testament Greek Manuscripts, 2001)

[32] Tertullian (160 – 220 C.E.), was a prolific early Christian author from Carthage in the Roman province of Africa.

[33] Cathedrae

[34] Suis locis praesident.

[35] Alexander Roberts, James Donaldson and A. Cleveland Coxe, The Ante-Nicene Fathers Vol. III: Translations of the Writings of the Fathers Down to A.D. 325 (Oak Harbor: Logos Research Systems, 1997), 260.

We need to visit an earlier book by Ehrman for a moment, *Lost Christianities*, in which he writes, "In this process of recopying the document by hand, what happened to the original of 1 Thessalonians? For some unknown reason, it was eventually thrown away, burned, or otherwise destroyed. Possibly, it was read so much that it simply wore out. The early Christians saw no need to preserve it as the `original' text. They had copies of the letter. Why keep the original?" (Ehrman B. D., 2003, p. 217)

Here Ehrman is arguing from silence. We cannot read the minds of people today, let alone read the minds of persons 2,000 years in the past. It is a known fact that congregations valued Paul's letters, and Paul exhorted them to share the letters with differing congregations. Paul wrote to the Colossians, and in what we know as 4:16, he said, "And when this letter has been read among you, have it **also read in the church of the Laodiceans**; and see that you also read the letter from Laodicea." The best way to facilitate this would be to send someone to a congregation, have them copy the letter and bring it back to their home congregation. On the other hand, someone could make copies of the letter in the congregation that received it and deliver it to interested congregations. In 1 Thessalonians, the congregation that Ehrman is talking about here, at chapter five, verse 27, Paul says, "I put you under oath before the Lord to **have this letter read to all the brothers**." What did Paul mean by "all the brothers"? It could be that he meant it to be used like a circuit letter, circulated to other congregations, giving everyone a chance to hear the counsel. It may merely be that, with literacy being so low, Paul wanted a guarantee that all were going to get to hear the letter's contents, and he simply meant for every brother and sister locally to have a chance to hear it in the congregation. Regardless, even if we accept the latter, the stress that was put on the reading of this letter shows the weight that these people were placed under concerning Paul's letters.[36] In addition, Comfort comments on how Paul and others would view apostolic letters:

---

[36] The exhortation ἐνορκίζω ὑμᾶς τὸν κύριον ἀναγνωσθῆναι τὴν ἐπιστολὴν πᾶσιν τοῖς ἀδελφοῖς ("I adjure you by the Lord that this letter be read aloud to all the brothers [and sisters]"), is stated quite strongly. ἐνορκίζω takes a double accusative and has a causal sense denoting that the speaker or writer wishes to extract an oath from the addressee(s). The second accusative, in this case τὸν κύριον ("the Lord"), indicates the thing or person by whom the addressees were to swear. The forcefulness of

Paul knew the importance of authorized apostolic letters, for he saw the authority behind the letter that came from the first Jerusalem church council. The first epistle from the church leaders who had assembled at Jerusalem was the prototype for subsequent epistles (see Acts 15). It was authoritative because it was apostolic, and it was received as God's word. If an epistle came from an apostle (or apostles), it was to be received as having the imprimatur [**approval**/authority] of the Lord. This is why Paul wanted the churches to receive his word as being the word of the Lord. This is made explicit in 1 Thessalonians (2:13), an epistle he insisted had to be read to all the believers in the church (5:27). In the Second Epistle to the Thessalonians, Paul indicated that his epistles carry the same authority as his preaching (see 2:15). Paul also told his audience that if they would read what he had written, they would be able to understand the mystery of Christ, which had been revealed to him (see Eph. 3:1–6). Because Paul explained the mystery in his writings (in this case, the encyclical epistle known as "Ephesians"), he urged other churches to read this encyclical (see Col. 4:16). In so doing, Paul himself encouraged the circulation of his writings. Peter and John also had publishing plans. Peter's first epistle, written to a wide audience (the Christian diaspora in Pontus, Galatia, Cappadocia, Asia, Bithynia—see 1 Pet. 1:1), was a published work, which must have been produced in several copies from the onset, to reach his larger, intended audience. John's first epistle was also published and circulated—probably to all the churches in the Roman province of Asia Minor. First John is not any kind of occasional epistle; it is more like a treatise akin to Romans and Ephesians in that it contains John's full explanation of the Christian life and doctrine as a model for all orthodox believers to emulate. The book of Revelation, which begins with seven epistles to seven churches in this same province,

---

this statement is highly unusual, and in fact it is the only instance in Paul's letters where such a charge is laid on the recipients of one of his letters.—Charles A. Wanamaker, The Epistles to the Thessalonians: A Commentary on the Greek Text (Grand Rapids, Mich.: W.B. Eerdmans, 1990), 208-09.

must have also been inititally published in seven copies, as the book circulated from one locality to the next, by the seven "messengers" (Greek *anggeloi*—not "angels" in this context). By contrast, the personal letters (Philemon, 1 and 2 Timothy, Titus, 2 John, 3 John) were not originally "published"; therefore, their circulation was small. Second Peter also had minimal circulation in the early days of the church. Because of its popularity, the book of Hebrews seemed to have enjoyed wide circulation—this was promoted by the fact that most Christians in the East thought it was the work of Paul and therefore was included in Pauline collections (see discussion below). The book of Acts was originally published by Luke as a sequel to his Gospel (see Acts 1:1–2). Unfortunately, in due course, this book got detached from Luke when the Gospel of Luke was placed in one-volume codices along with the other Gospels.[37]

Peter, as we have seen, also had this to say about Paul's letters: "there are some things in them [Paul's letters] that are hard to understand, which the ignorant and unstable twist to their own destruction, **as they do the other Scriptures**." (2 Pet 3:16) Peter viewed Paul's letters as being on the same level as the Old Testament, which was referred to as Scripture. In the second century (about 135 C.E.), Papias, an elder of the early congregation in Hierapolis, made the following comment.

> I will not hesitate to set down for you, along with my interpretations, everything I carefully learned then from the elders and carefully remembered, guaranteeing their truth. For unlike most people I did not enjoy those who have a great deal to say, but those who teach the truth. Nor did I enjoy those who recall someone else's commandments, but those who remember the commandments given by the Lord to the faith and proceeding from the truth itself. In addition, if by chance someone who had been a follower of the elders should come my way, I inquired about the words of the

---

[37] Philip Comfort, *Encountering the Manuscripts: An Introduction to New Testament Paleography & Textual Criticism* (Nashville, TN: Broadman & Holman, 2005), 17.

elders--what Andrew or Peter said, or Philip, or Thomas or James, or John or Matthew or any other of the Lord's disciples, and whatever Aristion and the elder John, the Lord's disciples, were saying. For I did not think that information from books would profit me as much as information from a living and abiding voice.[38]

As an elder in the congregation at Hierapolis, in Asia Minor, Papias was an unrelenting researcher, as well as a thorough compiler of information; he exhibited great indebtedness for the Scriptures. Papias determined properly that any doctrinal statement of Jesus Christ or his apostles would be far more appreciated and respected to explain than the unreliable statements found in the written works of his day. We can compare Jude 1:17, where Jude urges his readers to preserve the words of the apostles.

Therefore, the notion that the "early Christians saw no need to preserve it as the 'original' text" is far too difficult to accept when we consider the above. Moreover, imagine a church in middle America being visited by Billy Graham. Now imagine that he wrote them a warm letter, but one also filled with some stern counsel. Would there be little interest in the preservation of those words? Would they not want to share it with others? Would other churches not be interested in it? The same would have been even truer of early Christianity receiving a letter from an apostle like Peter, John, or Paul. There is no doubt that the "original" wore out eventually. However, they lived in a society that valued the preservation of the apostle's words, and it is far more likely that it was copied with care, to share with others, and to preserve. Moreover, let us acknowledge that their imperfections took over as well. Paul would have become a famous apostle who wrote a few churches, and there were thousands of churches toward the end of the first century. Would they have not exhibited some pride in the fact that they received a letter from the famous apostle Paul, who was martyred for the truth? Ehrman's suggestions are reaching and contrary to human nature.

---

[38] Michael W. Holmes, *The Apostolic Fathers: Greek Texts and English Translations,* 3rd Edition (Grand Rapids, MI: Baker Academic. 2007), 565.

However, Ehrman may not have entirely dismissed the idea of getting back to the original if he agreed with Metzger in their coauthored fourth edition of *The Text of the New Testament*. Metzger's original comments from previous editions are repeated there as follows.

> Besides textual evidence derived from New Testament Greek manuscripts and from early versions, the textual critic compares numerous scriptural quotations used in commentaries, sermons, and other treatises written by early church fathers. Indeed, so extensive are these citations that if all other sources for our knowledge of the text of the New Testament were destroyed, they would be sufficient alone for the reconstruction of practically the entire New Testament.[39]

How are we to view the patristic citations? Let us look at another book for which Ehrman was coeditor and a contributor with other textual scholars: *The Text of the New Testament in Contemporary Research* (1995). The following is from Chapter 12, written by Gordon Fee (*The Use of the Greek Fathers for New Testament Textual Criticism*).

> In NT textual criticism, patristic citations are ordinarily viewed as the third line of evidence, indirect and supplementary to the Greek MSS, and are often therefore treated as of tertiary importance. When properly evaluated, however, patristic evidence is of primary importance, for both of the major tasks of NT textual criticism: in contrast to the early Greek MSS, the Fathers have the potential of offering datable and geographically certain evidence. (Ehrman B. D., 1995, p. 191)

To conclude, we have established that Ehrman has painted a picture that is not quite the truth of the matter for the average churchgoer while saying something entirely different for textual scholars. Moreover, he does not help the reader to appreciate just how close the New Testament manuscript evidence is to the time of the original writings, in comparison to manuscripts of other ancient works,

---

[39] Bruce M. Metzger; Bart D. Ehrman, THE TEXT OF THE NEW TESTAMENT: *Its Transmission, Corruption, and Restoration,* 4th ed. (New York, NY: Oxford University Press, 2005), 126.

many of which are few in number and hundreds, if not a thousand years removed.

In addition, Ehrman has exaggerated the variants in the Greek New Testament manuscripts by **not** qualifying the level of variants. In other words, he has not explained how he counts them to obtain such high numbers. Moreover, Ehrman's unqualified statement, "in the early Christian centuries, scribes were amateurs," has been discredited as well. Either literate or semi-professional copyists did **most of** the early papyri, with some being done by professionals.

Textual scholar Philip W. Comfort[40] and others believe that the incredibly early Alexandrian manuscripts that we now possess are a reflection of what would have been found throughout the whole of the Greco-Roman Empire about 125–300 C.E. If we were to discover other early manuscripts from Antioch, Constantinople, Carthage, or Rome, they would be very similar to the early Alexandrian manuscripts. This means that these early manuscripts are a primary means of establishing the original text, and we are in a far better position today than were Westcott and Hort in 1881. Even still, there is a 99.5% agreement between the Westcott and Hort critical text and the 2012 Nestle-Aland 28th edition critical text. This certainly emphasizes what a tremendous job that Westcott and Hort had done when we consider all the early second and third century New Testament papyri that was discovered in the 20th century, and yet so few changes.

How do we know that the critical text NA28 and the UBS5 are reliable? In 1989, Eldon J. Epp noted that the papyri have added virtually no new substantial variants to the variants already known from our later manuscripts.[41] Even with the discovery of many other papyri over the last 25 years, the situation has remained the same. It can be said that after 135 years of early manuscript discoveries since Westcott and Hort of 1881, the above critical editions of the Greek New Testament have gone virtually unchanged. (Hill and Kruger 2012,

---

[40] Philip W. Comfort, *The Quest for the Original Text of the New Testament* (Eugene, Oregon: Wipf and Stock Publishers, 1992).

[41] E. J. Epp, 'The Significance of the Papyri for Determining the Nature of the New Testament Text in the Second Century: A Dynamic View of Textual Transmission', in W. L. Petersen, ed., *The Gospel Traditions in the Second Century* (Notre Dame: University of Notre Dame Press, 1989), 101

5) Hill and Kruger go on to say, "It also means that the fourth-century 'best texts,' the 'Alexandrian' codices Vaticanus and Sinaiticus, have roots extending throughout the entire third century and even into the second." (p. 6)

The most reliable of the earliest texts are P^1, $P^{4, 64, 67}$, P^{23}, P^{27}, P^{30}, P^{32}, P^{35}, $P^{39, P49, 65}$, P^{70}, P^{75}, P^{86}, P^{87}, P^{90}, P^{91}, P^{100}, P^{101}, P^{106}, P^{108}, P^{111}, P^{114}, and P^{115}. The copyists of these manuscripts allowed very few variants in their copies of the exemplars.[42] They had the ability to make accurate judgments as they went about their copying, resulting in superior texts. Whether their skills in copying were a result of their belief that they were copying a sacred text, or from their training, cannot be known. It could have been a combination of both. These papyri are of great importance when considering textual problems and are considered by many textual scholars to be a good representation of the original wording of the text that was first published by the biblical author. Still, "many of these manuscripts contain singular readings and some 'Alexandrian' polishing, which needs to be sifted out." (P. Comfort 2005, 269) Nevertheless, again, they are the best texts and the most faithful in preserving the original. While it is true that some of the papyri are mere fragments, some contain substantial portions of text. We should note too that text types really did not exist per se in the second century, and it is a mere convention to refer to the papyri as Alexandrian, since the best Alexandrian manuscript, Vaticanus, did exist in the second century by way of P^{75}.[43] It is not that the Alexandrian text existed, but rather P^{75}/Vaticanus evidence that some very strict copying with great care was taking place.[44]

---

[42] In 1988, the Alands, in the second edition of *The Text of the New Testament* (93-95), categorized thirty of the forty-four earliest manuscripts (40 papyri and 4 parchment) as "at least normal," "normal," and "strict," with the other fourteen being categorized as "free" or "like Codex Bezae (D)." At that time, the Alands did not rate P^{90} [2nd], P^{92}, [3rd/4th] and P^{95} [3rd], likely because they had only recently been discovered. However, we now have the Aland classification of "strict."

[43] The Coherence Based Genealogical Method, which was developed by Gerd Mink and assists scholars in developing genealogical trees of manuscripts, will be discussed in the forthcoming release, *An Essential Investigation of the Coherence-Based Geneological Method*, in 2020 by Dr. Don. Wilkins; but we should note here that it has no relation to the traditional text-type model. It is for this reason that scholars such as Holger Strutwolf have suggested that we abandon any references to the manuscripts by the tradition text-types.

[44] "What we do know, from the manuscript evidence, is that several of the earliest Christian scribes were well-trained scribes who applied their training to making reliable texts, both of the Old Testament

The Trustworthiness of Early Copyists

E. C. Colwell in his Methods in Establishing the Nature of Text-Types, 55, notes: "the overwhelming majority of readings were created before the year 200. But very few, if any, text-types were established by that time." G. D. Kilpatrick in his The Bodmer and Mississippi Collection, 42 says, "Apart from errors which can occur anywhere as long as books are copied by hand, almost all variants can be presumed to have been created by A.D. 200." And Kurt and Barbara Aland, The Text of the New Testament, 295 says, "practically all the substantive variants in the text of the New Testament are from the second century …"

Lee McDonald states,

> "Many mistakes in the manuscripts were made and subsequently transmitted in the churches. This suggests that these documents were not generally recognized as Scripture until the end of the second century C.E. Scribal attempts at improvements in the text occurred regularly, and apparently no attempts were made to stop this activity until the fourth century, when more stability in the text of the NT began to take place."[45]

Throughout much of the twentieth century, it was common to form three conclusions about the earliest copyists and their work:

(1) The first three centuries saw copyists who were semiliterate and unskilled in the work of making copies.

---

and the New Testament. We know that they were conscientious to make a reliable text in the process of transcription (as can been seen in manuscripts like P[4+64+67] and P[75]), and we know that others worked to rid the manuscript of textual corruption. This is nowhere better manifested than in P[66], where the scribe himself and the *diorthotes* (official corrector) made over 450 corrections to the text of John. As is explained in the next chapter, the *diorthotes* of P[66] probably consulted other exemplars (one whose text was much like that of P[75]) in making his corrections. This shows a standard Alexandrian scriptoral practice at work in the reproduction of a New Testament manuscript." (P. Comfort, Encountering the Manuscripts: An Introduction to New Testament Paleography and Textual Criticism 2005, 264)

[45] L. M. McDonald, The Biblical Canon (Peabody, Mass.: Hendrickson, 2007), 359. A similar argument is made by G. M. Hahneman, The Muratorian Fragment and the Development of the Canon (Oxford: Clarendon, 1992), 96; D. W. Riddle, 'Textual Criticism as a Historical Discipline', ATR 18 (1936): 227; and Parker, The Living Text, 202–5.

(2) Copyists in these early centuries felt as though the end was nigh, so they took liberties with the text in an attempt to strengthen orthodoxy.

(3) In the early centuries, manuscripts could be described as "free," "wild," "in a state of flux," "chaotic," "a turbid textual morass," i.e., a "free text" (so the Alands).

The first in the above would undoubtedly lead to many unintentional changes while the second would escalate intentional changes. J. Harold Greenlee had this to say:

> In the very early period, the NT writings were more nearly "private" writings than the classics . . . the classics were commonly, although not always, copied by professional scribes, the NT books were probably usually copied in the early period by **Christians who were not professionally trained** for the task, and **no corrector** was employed to check the copyist's work against his exemplar (the MS from which the copy was made) .... It appears that a copyist sometimes even took liberty to add or change minor details in the narrative books on the basis of personal knowledge, alternative tradition, or a parallel account in another book of the Bible .... **At the same time, the importance of these factors in affecting the purity of the NT text <u>must not be exaggerated</u>**. The NT books doubtless came to be considered as "literature" soon after they began to be circulated, with attention to the precise wording required when copies were made.[46] (Bold and underline mine)

Greenlee had not changed his position 14 years later when he wrote the following:

> The New Testament, on the other hand, was probably copied during the earliest period mostly by ordinary Christians **who were not professional scribes** but who

---

[46] J. Harold Greenlee, Introduction to New Testament Textual Criticism (Revised Edition, 1995), 51–52.

wanted a copy of the New Testament book or books for themselves or for other Christians.[47] (Bold mine)

The Alands in their *Text of the New Testament* saw the New Testament books as not being canonical, i.e., not viewed as Scripture in the first few centuries, so the books were subject to changes. They wrote, "not only every church but each individual Christian felt 'a direct relationship to God.' Well into the second century Christians still regarded themselves as possessing inspiration equal to that of the New Testament writings which they read in their worship service." Earlier they wrote, "That was all the more true of the early period when the text had not attained canonical status, especially in the early period when Christians considered themselves filled with the Spirit." They claimed that "until the beginning of the fourth century the text of the New Testament developed freely."[48]

Generally, once an established concept is set within the world of textual scholars, it is not easily displaced. During the start of the 20th century (1900–1940), there was a handful of papyri discovered that obviously represented the work of a copyist who had no training. It is during this time that Sir Frederic Kenyon, director and principal librarian of the British Museum for many years, said,

> The early Christians, a poor, scattered, often **illiterate** body, looking for the return of the Lord at no distant date, **were not likely to care** sedulously for minute accuracy of transcription or to preserve their books religiously for the benefit of posterity.[49]

The first papyri discovered (P[45], P[46], P[66]) showed this possibly could be the case. P[46] and P[66] were copied by professional scribes. P[45] contains much of Gospels and Acts and it varies with each biblical book. On P[45] Comfort writes that "professionals—at least, they display the reformed documentary hand." (Comfort & Barret, The Text of the

---

[47] J. Harold Greenlee, The Text of the New Testament: From Manuscript to Modern Edition (2008), 37.

[48] Kurt and Barbara Aland, THE TEXT OF THE NEW TESTAMENT: An Introduction to the Critical Editions and to the Theory and Practice of Modern Textual Criticism (Grand Rapids, MI: Wm. B. Eerdmans Publishing Co., 1995), 295, 69.

[49] F. Kenyon, Our Bible and the Ancient Manuscripts (1895), 157.

Earliest New Testament Greek Manuscripts, 2001, p. 159) However, Barbara Aland says that "P⁴⁵ has a great number of singular readings."[50] On the origin of these singular readings, E. C. Colwell comments:

> As an editor the scribe of P⁴⁵ wielded a sharp axe. The most striking aspect of his style is its conciseness. The dispensable word is dispensed with. He omits adverbs, adjectives, nouns, participles, verbs, personal pronouns— without any compensating habit of addition. He frequently omits phrases and clauses. He prefers the simple to the compound word. In short, he favors brevity. He shortens the text in at least fifty places in singular readings alone. But he does not drop syllables or letters. His shortened text is readable.[51]

So, it would seem that P⁴⁵, which came to light when it was purchased from some dealer in **1930-31**, was the predominant factor for the negative view of the copyist in early Christianity. However, as more papyri became known, especially after the discovery of P⁷⁵ in the **1950s** in Pabau, Egypt, it proved to be just the opposite. P⁷⁵ is generally described as "the most significant"[52] papyrus of the Greek New Testament to be discovered. These new discoveries prompted Sir Frederic Kenyon to write,

> We must be content to know that the general authenticity of the New Testament text has been remarkably supported by the modern discoveries which have so greatly reduced the interval between the original autographs and our earliest extant manuscripts, and that the differences of reading, interesting as they are, do not affect the fundamental doctrines of the Christian faith.[53]

Even though many textual scholars were crediting the Alands' *The Text of the New Testament* with their description of the text as "free," that

---

[50] Barbara Aland, *The Significance of the Chester Beatty in Early Church History, in:* The Earliest Gospels ed. *Charles Horton, London 2004, p. 110.*

[51] Ernest Cadman Colwell, "Scribal Habits in the Early Papyri: A Study in the Corruption of the Text," in: "The Bible in Modern Scholarship" ed. J. P. Hyatt, New York: Abingdon Press 1965, p.383.

[52] Aland and Aland, *The Text of the New Testament* (1989), p. 244

[53] F. Kenyon, Our Bible and the Ancient Manuscripts (1962), 249.

was not the entire position of the Alands. True, they spoke of the different text styles such as the "normal," "free" "strict" and the "paraphrastic." However, like Kenyon, they saw a need based on the evidence, which suggested a rethinking of how the evidence should be described:

> Our research on the early papyri has yielded unexpected results that require a change in the traditional views of the early text. We have inherited from the past generation the view that the early text was a "free" text, and the discovery of the Chester Beatty papyri seemed to confirm this view. When P[45] and P[46] were joined by P[66] sharing the same characteristics, this position seemed to be definitely established. P[75] appeared in contrast to be a loner with its "strict" text anticipating Codex Vaticanus. Meanwhile the other witnesses of the early period had been ignored. It is their collations which have changed the picture so completely.[54]

While we have said this previously, it bears repeating once again that *some* of the earliest manuscripts we now have indicate that a professional scribe copied them.[55] *Many* of the other papyri confirm that a semi-professional hand copied them, while *most* of these early papyri give evidence of being produced by a copyist who was literate and experienced. Therefore, either literate or semi-professional copyist did the vast majority of our early papyri, with some being done by professionals. As it happened, the few poorly copied manuscripts

---

[54] Kurt and Barbara Aland, *THE TEXT OF THE NEW TESTAMENT: An Introduction to the Critical Editions and to the Theory and Practice of Modern Textual Criticism* (Grand Rapids, MI: Wm. B. Eerdmans Publishing Co., 1995), 93-95.

[55] Some may argue that we can only be confident that we have good manuscripts of an "early" form of the text but not necessarily of the originally published text. This hypothesis cannot be disproven. However, I think it is highly doubtful for four reasons: (1) The intervening time between the publication date of various New Testament books (from AD 60–90) and the date of several of our extant manuscripts (from AD 100–200) is narrow, thereby giving us manuscripts that are probably only three to five "manuscript generations" removed from the originally published texts. (2) We have no knowledge that any of these manuscripts go back to an early "form" that postdates the original publications. (3) We are certain that there was no major Alexandrian recension in the second century. (4) Text critics have been able to detect any other second-century textual aberrations, such as the D-text, which was probably created near the end of the second century, not the beginning. Thus, it stands to reason that these "reliable" manuscripts are excellent copies of the authorized published texts." (Comfort P. , Encountering the Manuscripts: An Introduction to New Testament Paleography and Textual Criticism, 2005, p. 269)

became known first, establishing a precedent that was difficult for some to discard when the enormous amount of evidence came forth that showed just the opposite.

Distribution of Papyri by Century and Type				
DATE	ALEX	WEST	CAES	BYZ
100-150/175 C.E.	7Q4? 7Q5? $P^{4/64/67}$ P^{32} P^{46} P^{52} P^{66} P^{75} $^{P77/103}$ P^{87} P^{90} P^{98} (bad shape, differences) P^{109} (too small) P^{118} (too small) P^{137} 0189 P. Oxyrhynchus 405 P. Egerton 2	P^{104}	0	0
175-250 C.E.	P^1 P^5 P^{13} P^{20} P^{23} P^{27} P^{30} P^{35} P^{39} P^{40} P^{45} P^{47} $P^{49/65}$ P^{71} P^{72} P^{82} P^{85} P^{95} P^{100} P^{101} P^{106} P^{108} P^{111} P^{113} P^{115} P^{121} (too small) P^{125} P^{126} (too small) P^{133} P^{136} 0220 0232 P. Oxyrhynchus 406 P. Egerton 3	P^{29} (Metzger Western & Aland Free; too small to be certain) P^{38} P^{48} P^{69} 0171 0212 (mixed) P^{107} P^{110} (Independent)	0	0
250-300 C.E.	P^8 P^9 P^{12} P^{15} P^{16} P^{17} P^{18} P^{19} P^{24} P^{28} P^{50} P^{51} P^{53} P^{70} P^{78} P^{80} P^{86} P^{88} P^{89} (too small) P^{91} P^{92} P^{114} P^{119} P^{120} P^{129} (too small) P^{131} P^{132} too small) P^{134} 0162 0207 0231 P. Antinoopolis 54	P^{37} (Free, mostly Western)	0	0
290-390 C.E.	P^3 P^6 P^7 P^{10} P^{21} P^{54} P^{62} P^{81} P^{93} P^{94} P^{102} (too small) P^{117} (too	P^{21} (mixed) P^{25} (independent)	0	0

	small) P^{122} (too small) P^{123} P^{127} P^{130} (too small) P^{139} (too small) 057 058 059 / 0215 071 0160 0163 0165 0169 0172 0173 0175 0176 0181 0182 0185 0188 0206 0214 0217 0218 0219 0221 0226 0227 0228 0230 0242 0264 0308 0312 P. Oxyrhynchus 4010 P. Oxyrhynchus 5073	P^{112} (independent) P^{127} (independent; like no other)	
4th / 5th Century C.E.	P^{11} P^{14} $P^{33/P58}$ P^{56} P^{57} P^{63} P^{105} (too small) P^{124} 0254		069 P. Oxyrhynchus 1077?

Also, as we noted earlier, textual scholars such as Comfort[56] and others believe that the very early Alexandrian manuscripts that we now possess are a reflection of what would have been found throughout the whole of the Greco-Roman Empire from about 85–275 C.E. So these early papyri can play a major role in our establishing the original readings. While this is true, it might not be in the way that one might think. Have the early papyri made a difference in the critical text of the New Testament? Maurice A. Robinson has estimated that the current Nestle-Aland 28th edition of 2012 is 99.5 percent the same as the 1881 Westcott and Hort's edition of the Greek New Testament. From the Westcott and Hort Greek text of 1881 to the 25th edition of the Nestle-Aland Greek New Testament Text of 1963 was essentially based on the accumulated evidence from the days of Desiderius Erasmus in 1516, 1522 up unto the 19th/early 20th century, that is, the codices manuscripts, with Codex Vaticanus (c. 300–325 C.E.) and Codex

---

[56] Philip W. Comfort, The Quest for the Original Text of the New Testament (Eugene, Oregon: Wipf and Stock Publishers, 1992).

Sinaiticus (c. 330–360) leading the way. Again, there were no major changes from 1881 to the 2012 28th edition of the Nestle-Aland Text. However, that is, in fact, what makes the early papyri majorly important, extremely significant, very consequential, considerable evidence for establishing the original Greek New Testament. It simply gives validity to those who had placed much trust in the great majuscules.

However, Epp asks, "If Westcott-Hort did not utilize papyri in constructing their NT text, and if our own modern critical texts, in fact, are not significantly different from that of Westcott-Hort, then why are the papyri important after all?"[57] From there, Epp goes on to strongly advise that the papyri should play an essential role in three areas: (1) "to isolate the earliest discernable text-types, (2) assisting "to trace out the very early history of the NT text," and, (3) "Finally, the papyri can aid in refining the canons of criticism—the principles by which we judge variant readings—for they open to us a window for viewing the earliest stages of textual transmission, providing instances of how scribes worked in their copying of manuscripts."[58] We should add that the early papyri have changed decisions of textual scholars and committees so that they have not retained the readings of Westcott and Hort at times. So, even though there has been little change between the Westcott and Hort Greek New Testament of 1881 and the 2012 28th edition of the Nestle-Aland Greek New Testament, (1) the early papyri have reinforced what we already knew to be original and (2) helped us to improve the critical text ever slightly.

To offer just one example, both Metzger and Comfort inform us that it was the external evidence of the papyri that resulted in the change in the NU text, adopting the reading that was also in the Textus Receptus, as opposed to what was in the Westcott and Hort text.

Matthew 26:20 (WH)	Matthew 26:20 (TRNU)
20 μετα των δωδεκα μαθητων	20 μετα των δωδεκα

---

[57] The New Testament Papyrus Manuscripts in Historical Perspective, in To Touch the Text: Biblical and Related Studies in Honour of Joseph A. Fitzmyer, S. J. (ed. Maurya P. Horgan and Paul J. Kobelski; New York: Crossroad, 1989), 285 (there italicized) repr. in Epp, Perspectives, 338.

[58] Ibid., 288

With the twelve disciples	With the twelve

Metzger writes, "As is the case in 20:17,[59] the reading μαθηται after οἱ δώδεκα is doubtful. In the present verse [26:20] the weight of the external evidence seems to favor the shorter reading." (Metzger, 1994, p. 53) Comfort in his *New Testament Text and Translation* writes, "Even though both P[37] and P[45] are listed as 'vid,' it is certain that both did not include the word μαθητων because line spacing would not accommodate it. P[37] has the typical abbreviation for 'twelve,' as ῑβ; and P[45] has it written out as [δω]δεκα. P[64+67] is less certain, but line lengths of the manuscript suggest that it reads ῑβ (see *Texts of Earliest MSS*, 69)." Comfort more explicitly explains what Metzger hinted at; "The testimony of the papyri (with B and D) created a change in the NU text. Prior to NA26, the NU text included the word μαθητων ("disciples"). But the early evidence shows that this must have been a later addition." Comfort continues, "Such an addition is not necessary in light of the fact that Jesus' closest followers were often designated by the gospel writers as simply "the twelve." (Comfort P. W., 2008, p. 77)

Again, many textual scholars before 1961 believed that the early copyists of the New Testament papyri were among the untrained in making documents (P[45], P[46], P[47]; P[66] and P[72] in 2 Peter and Jude) and that the papyri were texts in flux.[60] It was not until the discovery of P[75] and other papyri that textual scholars began to think differently. Nevertheless, the attitude of the 1930s through the 1950s is explained well by Kurt and Barbara Aland:

---

[59] 20:17 τοὺς δώδεκα [μαθητάς] {C}

Although copyists often add the word μαθηταίto the more primitive expression οἱ δώδεκα (see Tischendorf's note *in loc.* and 26.20 below), a majority of the Committee judged that the present passage was assimilated to the text of Mark (10:32) or Luke (18:31). In order to represent both possibilities it was decided to employ square brackets. (Metzger, 1994, p. 42)

On 20:17, Comfort writes, "Either reading could be original because they both have good support and because the gospel writers alternated between the nomenclature 'the twelve disciples' and 'the twelve.'" (Comfort P. W., 2008, p. 60)

[60] Kurt and Barbara Aland write, "By the 1930s the number of known papyri had grown to more than forty without any of them arousing any special attention, despite the fact that many of them were of a quite early date. (Aland & Aland, 1995, p. 84)

Of special importance are the early papyri, i.e., of the period of the third/fourth century. As we have said, these have an inherent significance for the New Testament textual studies because they witness to a situation before the text was channeled into major text types in the fourth century. Our research on the early papyri has yielded unexpected results that require a change in the traditional views of the early text. We have inherited from the past generation the view that the early text was a "free" text,[61] and the discovery of the Chester Beatty papyri seemed to confirm this view. When P[45] and P[46] were joined by P[66] sharing the same characteristics, this position seemed to be definitely established. (Aland & Aland, 1995, p. 93)

Before P[75] and other early papyri, scholars were under the impression that scribes must have used manuscripts of untrained copyists to make a recension (critical revision, i.e., revised text); and this, according to scholars prior to 1961, was how Codex Vaticanus (B) came about. In 1940, Kenyon inferred the following:

> During the second and third centuries, a great variety of readings came into existence throughout the Christian world. In some quarters, considerable license was shown in dealing with the sacred text; in others, more respect was shown to the tradition. In Egypt, this variety of texts existed, as elsewhere; but Egypt (and especially Alexandria) was a country of strong scholarship and with a knowledge of textual criticism. Here, therefore, a relatively faithful tradition was preserved. About the beginning of the fourth century, a scholar may well have set himself to compare the best accessible representatives of this tradition, and so have produced a text of which B is an early descendant.[62]

---

[61] Early manuscripts (from before the fourth century) are classified by the Alands as "strict," "normal," or "free." The "normal" text "transmitted the original text with the limited amount of variation." Then, there is the "free" text, "characterized by a greater degree of variation than the 'normal' text." Finally, there was the "strict" text, "which reproduced the text of its exemplar with greater fidelity (although still with certain characteristic liberties), exhibiting far less variation than the 'normal' text." (Aland 1987, 93)

[62] F. Kenyon, "Hesychius and the Text of the New Testament," in *Memorial Lagrange* (1940), 250.

While Kenyon was correct about the manuscripts coming up out of Egypt being a reasonably pure text, he was certainly mistaken when he suggested that Codex Vaticanus was the result of a critical revision by early scribes. P^{75} put this theory to rest. The Agreement between P^{75} and codex B is 92% in John and 94% in Luke. However, Porter has it at about 85% agreement. Zuntz, on the other hand, went a little further than Kenyon did. Kenyon believed that the critical text had been made in the early part of the fourth century, leading to Codex Vaticanus. Zuntz believed similarly but felt that the recension began back in the mid-second-century and was a process that ran up into the fourth-century. Zuntz wrote:

> The Alexander correctors strove, in ever repeated efforts, to keep the text current in their sphere free from the many faults that had infected it in the previous period and which tended to crop up again even after they had been obelized [i.e., marked as spurious]. These labours must time and again have been checked by persecutions and the confiscation of Christian books, and counteracted by the continuing currency of manuscripts of the older type. Nonetheless they resulted in the emergence of a type of text (as distinct from a definite edition) which served as a norm for the correctors in provincial Egyptian scriptoria. The final result was the survival of a text far superior to that of the second century, even though the revisers, being fallible human beings, rejected some of its own correct readings and introduced some faults of their own.[63]

P^{75} and other early, as we can see from the above, influenced the thinking of Kurt Aland. While he said, "We have inherited from the past generation the view that the early text was a 'free' text," he was one of those saying that very thing. However, as he would later say, "Our research on the early papyri has yielded unexpected results that require a change in the traditional views of the early text." P^{75} greatly affected the Alands: "P^{75} shows such a close affinity with the Codex Vaticanus that the supposition of a recension of the text at Alexandria,

---

[63] G. Zuntz, *The Text of the Epistles* (1953), 271–272.

in the fourth century, can no longer be held."[64] Gordon Fee clearly states that there was no Alexandrian recension prior to P[75] (175-225 C.E.) and the time of Codex Vaticanus (350 C.E.), as he commented that P[75] and Vaticanus "seem to represent a 'relatively pure' form of preservation of a 'relatively pure' line of descent from the original text."[65] For many decades now, New Testament textual scholarship has been aware that P[75] is an extremely accurate copy. Of the copyist behind P[75], Colwell said, "his impulse to improve style is for the most part defeated by the obligation to make an exact copy."[66] Colwell went on to comment on the work of that scribe:

> In P[75] the text that is produced can be explained in all its variants as the result of a single force, namely the disciplined scribe who writes with the intention of being careful and accurate. There is no evidence of revision of his work by anyone else, or in fact of any real revision, or check.... The control had been drilled into the scribe before he started writing.[67]

We do not want to leave the reader with the impression that P[75] is perfect, as it is not. On this Comfort says,

> The scribe had to make several corrections (116 in Luke and John), but there was no attempt 'to revise the text by a second exemplar, and indeed no systematic correction at all.'[68] The scribe of P[75] shows a clear tendency to make grammatical and stylistic improvements in keeping with the Alexandrian scriptorial tradition, and the scribe had a tendency to shorten his text, particularly by dropping pronouns. However, his omissions of

---

[64] Kurt Aland, "The Significance of the Papyri for New Testament Research" in *The Bible in Modern Scholarship* (1965), 336.

[65] Gordon Fee, "P75, P66, and Origen: The Myth of Early Textual Recension in Alexandria" in *New Dimensions in New Testament Study* (1974), 19–43.

[66] Ernest C. Colwell, "Method in Evaluating Scribal Habits: A Study of P45, P66, P75," in *Studies in Methodology in Textual Criticism of the New Testament,* New Testament Tools and Studies 9 (Leiden: Brill, 1969), 121.

[67] Ibid., 117

[68] James Ronald Royse, "Scribal Habits in Early Greek New Testament Papyri" (Ph.D. diss., Graduate Theological Union, 1981), 538–39.

text hardly ever extend beyond a word or two, probably because he copied letter by letter and syllable by syllable.[69]

As the early Nestle Greek text moved from edition to edition, the influence of the New Testament papyri increased. It was the son of Eberhard Nestle, Erwin, who added a full critical apparatus in the thirteenth edition of the 1927 Nestle Edition. It was not until 1950 that Kurt Aland began to work on the text that would eventually become known as the Nestle-Aland text. He would begin to add even more evidence from papyri to the critical apparatus of the twenty-first edition. At Erwin Nestle's request, he looked over and lengthened the critical apparatus, adding far more manuscripts. This ultimately led to the 25th edition of 1963. The most significant papyri and recently discovered majuscules, (i.e., 0189), a few minuscules (33, 614, 2814), and rarely also lectionaries were also considered. However, while the critical apparatus was being added to and even altered, the text of the Nestle-Aland was not changed until the 26th edition (1979). Many of these changes to the text were a direct result of the papyri. In the 2012 28th edition of the Nestle Aland Greek Text, there were only 34 changes to the text, all of which were in the General Epistles (James-Jude). The 27th edition of the NA was the same at the 26th edition of 1979, which would mean that in 33 years up unto 2012, with many new manuscript discoveries and much research, very little has needed to be changed, even very little change with the 1881 WH Greek New Testament text. It bears repeating that Robinson[70] has estimated that the 27th edition of the NA Greek New Testament text is 99.5% the same as the 1881 WH Greek New Testament text. Being that there were only 34 changes between 27th edition and the 2012 28th NA Greek New Testament text, the NA is still 99.5% the same as the 1881 WH Greek New Testament text.

The Next chapter will have a little small portion that is repeated for the sake of the context of that chapter. Simply look at it like the book of Proverbs, repetition for emphasis.

---

[69] (Comfort & Barret, The Text of the Earliest New Testament Greek Manuscripts, 2001, p. 506)

[70] Maurice A. Robinson and William G. Pierpont, *The New Testament in the Original Greek: Byzantine Textform*, 2005 (Southborough, MA: Chilton, 2005), 551.

Edward D. Andrews

CHAPTER 6 The Book Writing Process of the New Testament: Authors and Early Christian Scribes

The Place of Writing

When we think of the apostle Paul penning his books that would make up most of the New Testament, some have had the anachronistic tendency to impose their modern way of thinking about him, such as presupposing where he would have written it. As I am writing this page, I am tucked away in my home office, seeking privacy from the hustle and bustle of our modern world. This was not the case in the ancient world, where Paul lived and traveled. People of that time favored a group setting, not isolation. The apostle Paul probably would have been of this mindset. Paul would not have necessarily sought a quiet place to author his letters, to escape the noise of those around him. As for myself, I struggle to get back on track if I am interrupted for more than a couple of minutes.

Most during Paul's day would have been surprised by this way of thinking, i.e., seeking quiet and solitude to focus all of one's energy on the task of writing. Those of Paul's day, including himself, would not have even noticed people talking around them, nor would they have been troubled by what we perceive as interruptions, such as others' discussions, which were neither relevant nor applicable to the subject of their letter writing.

The Scribe of the New Testament Writer

Philip W. Comfort informs us that an **amanuensis** is a "scribe or secretary. In ancient times a written document was first produced by an author who usually dictated the material to an amanuensis. The author would then read the text and make the final editorial adjustments before the document was sent or published. Paul used the writing services of Tertius to write the epistle to the Romans (Rom. 16:22), and Peter was assisted by Silvanus in writing his first Epistle (see 1 Pet. 5:12)."[71]

Dr. Don Wilkins, a Senior Translator for the NASB, also tells us that amanuensis is a "Latin term for a scribe or clerk (plural 'amanuenses'). When used in the context of textual criticism, it refers specifically to a person who served as a secretary to record first-hand the words of a New Testament book if the author chose to use a secretary rather than write down the words himself. Tertius (Rom. 16:22) is our example. The degree to which an amanuensis may have contributed to the content of any particular book of the Bible is a matter of speculation and controversy. At one end of the spectrum is the amanuensis, who merely took dictation (the position preferred here). At the other is the possibility that a New Testament author may have told his amanuensis what he wished to communicate in general terms, leaving it to the amanuensis to actually compose the book." This author would wholeheartedly disagree with the latter view, as the New Testament authors alone were inspired to give us the words of God, and the scribe was merely the vehicle for doing so.

The ancient Greco-Roman society employed secretaries or scribes for various reasons. Of course, the government employed some scribes working for chief administrators. Then, there were the scribes who were used in the private sector. These latter scribes (often slaves) usually were employed by the wealthy. However, even high-ranking slaves and freed slaves employed scribes. Many times, one would find scribes who would write letters for their friends. According to E. Randolph Richards, the skills of these unofficial secretaries "could range from a minimal competency with the language or the mechanics of writing to the highest proficiency at rapidly producing an accurate, proper, and charming letter."[72] Scribes carried out a wide range of administrative, secretarial, and literary tasks, including administrative bookkeeping (keeping records of a business or person), shorthand and taking dictation, letter-writing, and copying literary texts.

The most prominent ways that a scribe would have been used in the first century C.E. would have been as (1) a recorder, (2) an editor, and (3) a secretary for an author. At the very bottom of the writing tasks, he would be

---

[71] Philip Comfort, *Encountering the Manuscripts: An Introduction to New Testament Paleography & Textual Criticism* (Nashville, TN: Broadman & Holman, 2005), 379.

[72] E. Randolph Richards, The Secretary in the Letters of Paul (Heidelberg, Germany: Mohr Siebeck, 1991, 11

used to record information, i.e., as a record keeper. When they were needed or desired, the New Testament scribes were being used as secretaries, writing down letters by dictation. Tertius took down the book of Romans as Paul dictated to him, which was some 7,000+ words. He would have simply written out the very words that the apostle Paul spoke. Some have argued that longhand in dictation was not feasible in ancient times because the author would have to slow down to the point of speaking syllable-by-syllable. They usually cite Cicero as evidence for this argument because of his writings' numerous references to dictation. Cicero stated in a letter to his friend Varro that he had to slow down his dictation to the point of "syllable by syllable" for the sake of the scribe. However, the scribe he was using at that time was inexperienced, not his regular scribe. Of course, it would be challenging to retain one's line of thought in such a dictation process. It should be noted that Cicero had experienced scribes who could take down dictation at an average pace of speaking, even rapid speech.[73] There is evidence that scribes in those days were skilled enough to take down dictation at the average speech rate. Therefore, we should not assume that the apostles would not have had access to such scribes in the persons of Tertius, Silvanus, or even Timothy.

In fact, Marcus Fabius Quintilianus (b. 35 C.E. d. 100 C.E.) complained that a scribe who could write at the speed of everyday speech can make the speaker feel rushed, to the point of not being able to have time to ponder his thoughts.

> On the other hand, there is a fault which is precisely the opposite of this, into which those fall who insist on first making a rapid draft of their subject with the utmost speed of which their pen is capable, and write in the heat and impulse of the moment. They call this their rough copy. They then revise what they have written, and arrange their hasty outpourings. But while the words and the rhythm may be corrected, the matter is still marked by the superficiality resulting from the speed with which it was thrown together. The more correct method is, therefore, to exercise care from the very beginning, and to form the work from the outset in such a manner that it merely requires being chiseled into shape, not fashioned anew. Sometimes, however, we must follow the stream

---

[73] E. Randolph Richards, PAUL AND FIRST-CENTURY LETTER WRITING: Secretaries, Composition and Collection (Downers Grove, IL: IVP Academic, 2004), 29-30; Murphy-O'Connor, *Paul the Letter-Writer*, 9–11; Shorthand references Plutarch, *Cato Minor*, 23.3–5; Caesar, 7.4–5; Seneca, *Epistles*, 14.208.

of our emotions since their warmth will give us more than any diligence can secure. The condemnation which I have passed on such carelessness in writing will make it pretty clear what my views are on the luxury of dictation which is now so fashionable. For, when we write, however great our speed, the fact that the hand cannot follow the rapidity of our thoughts gives us time to think, whereas the presence of our amanuensis hurries us on, and at times we feel ashamed to hesitate or pause, or make some alteration, as though we were afraid to display such weakness before a witness. As a result, our language tends not merely to be haphazard and formless, but in our desire to produce a continuous flow we let slip positive improprieties of diction, which show neither the precision of the writer nor the impetuosity of the speaker. Again, if the amanuensis is a slow writer or lacking in intelligence, he becomes a stumbling-block, our speed is checked, and the thread of our ideas is interrupted by the delay or even perhaps by the loss of temper to which it gives rise.[74]

Therefore, again, we have evidence that some scribes were capable, skilled to the point of writing at the average speed of speech. While Richards says that this is by way of shorthand, saying it was more widespread than initially thought, where the secretary uses symbols in place of words, forming a rough draft that would be written out fully later,[75] this need not be the case. True, there is some evidence that shorthand existed a hundred years before Christ. However, it was still rare, with few scribes having the ability. Whether this was true of the scribes that assisted our New Testament authors is an unknown. It is improbable but not necessarily impossible.

Who in the days of the New Testament authors would use the services of scribes? Foremost would be those who did not know how to read and write. Within ancient contracts and business letters, one can find a note by the scribe (illiteracy statement), who penned it, stating he had done so because his employer could not read or write. For example, an ancient letter concludes with, "Eumelus, son of Herma, has written for him because he does not know letters."[76] It may be that they were able to read but struggled

---

[74] Retrieved Tuesday, February 12, 2019 (Institutio Oratoria, 10.3.17–21)
http://bit.ly/2Zazw2X

[75] E. Randolph Richards, PAUL AND FIRST-CENTURY LETTER WRITING: Secretaries, Composition and Collection (Downers Grove, IL: IVP Academic, 2004), 72.

[76] See examples in Francis Exler, *The Form of the Ancient Greek Letter: A Study In Greek Epistolography* (Washington D.C.: Catholic University of America, 1922), pp. 126-7

with writing. Then again, it may simply be that they wrote slowly and were unwilling to spend the time improving their skills. An ancient letter from Thebes, Egypt, penned for a certain Asklepiades, concludes, "Written for him hath Eumelus the son of Herma ..., being desired so to do for that he writeth somewhat slowly."[77]

On the other hand, whether one knew how to read and write was not always the decisive issue in the use of a secretary. John L. McKenzie writes, "Even people who could read and write did not think of submitting their readers to unprofessional penmanship. It was probably not even a concern for legibility, but rather a concern for beauty, or at least for neatness," (McKenzie 1975, 14) which moved the ancients to turn to the services of a secretary. Although the educated could read and write, some likely felt that writing was tedious, trying, tiring, and frustrating, especially where lengthy and elaborate texts were concerned. It seems that if one could avoid the tremendous task of penning a lengthy letter, entrusting it to a scribe, so much the better.

The apostle Paul had over 100 traveling companions, like Aristarchus, Luke, and Timothy, who served by the apostle's side for many years. Then, there are others such as Asyncritus, Hermas, Julia, or Philologus, of whom we barely know more than their names. Many of Paul's friends traveled for the sake of the gospel, such as Achaicus, Fortunatus, Stephanas, Artemas, and Tychicus. We know that Tychicus was used by Paul to carry at least three letters now included in the Bible canon: the epistles to the Ephesians, the Colossians, and Philemon. Tychicus was not simply some mail carrier. He was a well-trusted carrier for the apostle, Paul. The final greeting from Paul to the Colossians reads,

Colossians 4:7-8 Updated American Standard Version (UASV)

[7] All my affairs Tychicus, my beloved brother and faithful minister and fellow slave in the Lord, will make known to you. [8] I have sent him to you for this very purpose, that you may know how we are and that he may encourage your hearts,

Richards offers the following about a letter carrier, saying he "was often a personal link between the author and the recipients in addition to the written link. . . . [One purpose] for needing a trustworthy carrier was, he often

---

[77] Adolf Deissmann, *LIGHT FROM THE ANCIENT EAST: The New Testament Illustrated by Recently Discovered Texts of the Graeco-Roman World* (New York and London. 1910). 166-7.

carried additional information. A letter may describe a situation briefly, frequently with the author's assessment, but the carrier is expected to elaborate for the recipient all the details."[78] Many of Paul's letters deal with teachings and one crisis after another; the carrier was expected to be aware of these on a much deeper level so that he could orally explain and answer any questions. Therefore, he needed to be a highly trusted messenger who was literate.

As was mentioned, Tertius was the scribe Paul used to pen his letter to the Romans. We cannot assume that all of Paul's companions were proficient readers and writers. However, we can infer that Paul would task coworkers, who were able to carry and read letters and understand the condition of the people or congregation where they were being sent or stationed. Yes, at a minimum, these would have been proficient readers. In addition, the scribes whom Paul used, such as Tertius, would very likely have been semi-professional or professional. It would have been simply senseless to entrust the secretarial work of taking down the monumental words of the book of Romans, for example, to an inexperienced scribe. What skills would Tertius need to carry out the task of penning the book of Romans?

The ordinary coworker of Paul would likely have been able to read proficiently but likely possessed minimum writing skills. Paul would have chosen workers whose skills would have equipped them to carry out their assignments. Again, Tertius would have been the exception to the rule; most likely, he would have been a professional scribe. He would have been able to glue the sheets together if it was to be a roll or stitch the pages together if a codex. He would need to know the appropriate mixture of soot and gum to make ink and to be able to use his knife to make his own reed pen. Richards writes that a professional scribe would also "draw lines on the paper. Small holes were often pricked down each side, and then a straight edge and a lead disk were used to lightly draw evenly spaced lines across the sheet."[79] If Tertius had not been trained as a copyist of documents, he would have made many minor errors because his attention would have been on the sense of what he was penning, as opposed to the exact words, as is typical of the unconscious mind.

---

[78] E. Randolph Richards, The Secretary in the Letters of Paul (Heidelberg, Germany: Mohr Siebeck, 1991, 7.

[79] E. Randolph Richards, PAUL AND FIRST-CENTURY LETTER WRITING: Secretaries, Composition and Collection (Downers Grove, IL: IVP Academic, 2004), 29.

Porter writes, "Textual criticism has also recognized that even original authors may have **revised their work**, and these works have **gone through editions**." Stanley E. Porter (p. 35) *How We Got the New Testament*

Comfort writes, "When I speak of the original text, I am referring to the 'published' text— that is, the text in its **final edited form** as released for circulation in the Christian community."[80]

HOW do you edit the Holy Spirit? If the author was moved along by the Holy Spirit and all original Scripture is inspired, **why the need for editing?**

Some might say, "We believe that the NT authors themselves penned or dictated a one-time, single, and only version of their texts, unedited and uncorrected under the inspiration of the Holy Spirit."

However, I would pause to ponder Paul dictating the book of Romans to Tertius. Tertius was **not** inspired, so is he capable of going without making one single scribal error for 7,000+ words in his human imperfection? Are we removing the Holy Spirit in any way if Paul scratches out a few words that Tertius got wrong and wrote the correct word above it? Or is it the slippery slope to consider this possibility? If we hold fast to "I believe that the NT authors themselves penned or dictated a one-time, single and only version of their texts, unedited and uncorrected under the inspiration of the Holy Spirit," then we have to answer those kinds of questions. We have to raise them ourselves by writing, "some might ask, how is it ..." Peter said, "always being ready to make a defense to everyone who asks you to give an account." – 1 Peter 3:15.

We need to be willing to modify (or clarify) what we said above to include our qualification that Paul would edit the letter to the Romans as was described, as the amanuensis (i.e., Tertius) was not inspired. Paul would **not** change his original dictation in the process, and the outcome would be a single document, corrected, as necessary. We would also say that Paul might not make the actual corrections but might direct the amanuensis to do that as Paul watched. We do not go beyond this, i.e., postulating a fresh copy made from the original before publication, etc.

Did Tertius take Paul's exact dictation, word for word?

Robert H. Mounce writes,

---

[80] Philip W. Comfort (p. 19), The Quest for the Original Text of the New Testament (Grand Rapids: Baker Academic, 1992)

The only legitimate question about authorship relates to the role of Tertius, who in 16:22 writes, "I Tertius, who wrote down this letter, greet you in the Lord." We know that at that time in history an amanuensis [scribe], that is, one hired to write from dictation, could serve at several levels. In some cases he would receive dictation and write it down immediately in longhand. At other times he might use a form of shorthand (tachygraphy [ancient shorthand]) to take down a letter and then later write it out in longhand. In some cases an amanuensis would simply get the gist of what a person wanted to say and then be left on his own to formulate the ideas into a letter.[81]

It might seem quite the task for Tertius to take down Paul's words in longhand. However, this is not to say that it was impossible, just difficult. Paul might have had to speak in a slow to normal speech rate, **but not** syllable-by-syllable. Tertius would indeed have been writing on a papyrus sheet with a reed pen, intending to be legible; however, he would have been very skilled in his trade. Then again, there is the **slight possibility** of Tertius taking it down in shorthand and after that making out a complete draft, which would have been reviewed by both Paul and Tertius. This is only the case if it is comparable to what a modern-day court reporter does. In some sense, they are taking down whoever is speaking down in shorthand. Imagine a courtroom where you have a witness talking fast, the prosecution interrupts, the defense jumps in with his rebuttal, and the judge snaps his ruling, and the witness resumes their account of things. All of that is taken down explicitly word for word in shorthand, and if ever turned into longhand, it would be precisely what was said, down to the uh and um common in speech. So, if the shorthand of the day had that kind of capability; then, it is conceivable. We must remember these are the Bible author's dictated words to the scribe based on their inspiration, not the scribe's word choice or writing style.

The last option by Mounce in the above is contrary to the attitudes that both the scribes and the New Testament authors would have had. Paul and Tertius knew that Paul's words were Spirit-inspired, that is, God's words. God chose to convey a message through Matthew, Mark, Luke, John, Peter, Jude, James, and Paul, not Tertius and Silvanus, Timothy, or others. We cannot say with any certainty whether Tertius or Silvanus took their authors' words down in shorthand or longhand. However, we can say that the human

---

[81] Robert H. Mounce, *Romans*, vol. 27, The New American Commentary (Nashville: Broadman & Holman Publishers, 1995), 22.

author was dictating the Word of God to the scribe, and in no way was it composed by the scribe. Yes, it is true that the Spirit-inspired author, who is literally moved along by the Holy Spirit, retained their style of expressing the message but not the scribe. Mark's writing style is concise, even abrupt at times. His Gospel contains rapid changes of thought. The style of writing of First and Second Timothy is the same as Titus, which adds authenticity to the letter to Titus.

Inspiration and Inerrancy in the Writing Process

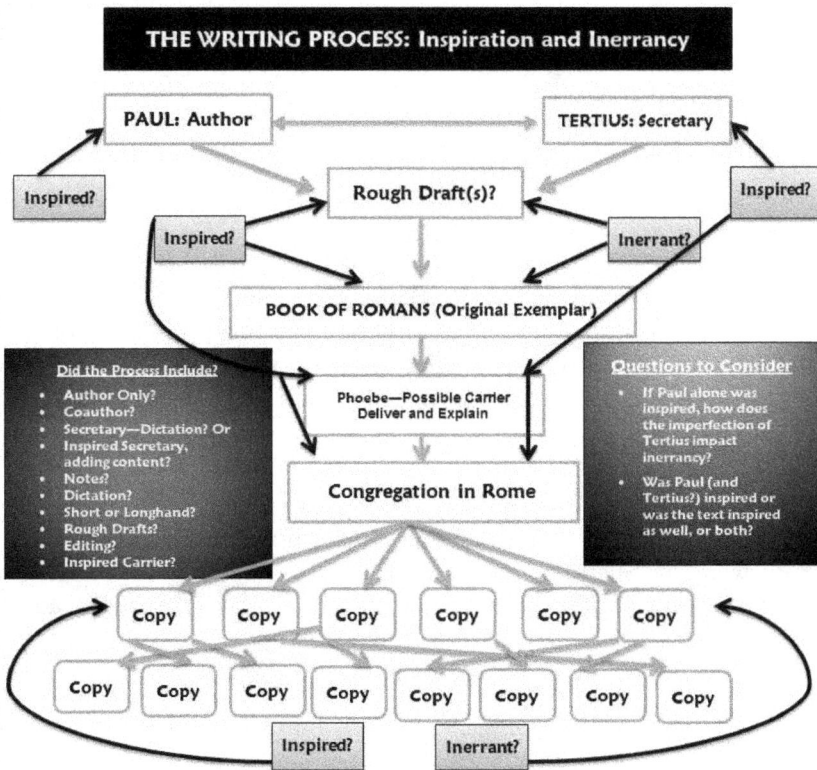

THE WRITING PROCESS: Inspiration and Inerrancy

PAUL: Author — TERTIUS: Secretary

Inspired?

Rough Draft(s)?

Inspired?

Inspired?

Inerrant?

BOOK OF ROMANS (Original Exemplar)

Did the Process Include?
- Author Only?
- Coauthor?
- Secretary—Dictation? Or
- Inspired Secretary, adding content?
- Notes?
- Dictation?
- Short or Longhand?
- Rough Drafts?
- Editing?
- Inspired Carrier?

Phoebe—Possible Carrier Deliver and Explain

Questions to Consider
- If Paul alone was inspired, how does the imperfection of Tertius impact inerrancy?
- Was Paul (and Tertius?) inspired or was the text inspired as well, or both?

Congregation in Rome

Copy | Copy | Copy | Copy | Copy | Copy

Copy | Copy | Copy | Copy | Copy | Copy | Copy | Copy

Inspired?

Inerrant?

All Scripture is Inspired by God

In this context, inspiration is **the state** of a human being moved by the Holy Spirit, which results in an inspired, fully inerrant written Word of God.

Chicago Statement on Biblical Inerrancy ICBI

Article VII

We affirm that **inspiration** was the work in which God by His Spirit, through human writers, gave us His Word. The origin of Scripture is divine. The mode of divine **inspiration** remains largely a mystery to us. We deny that **inspiration** can be reduced to human insight, or to heightened states of consciousness of any kind.

Article VIII

We affirm that God in His Work of **inspiration** utilized the distinctive personalities and literary styles of the writers whom He had chosen and prepared. We deny that God, in causing these writers to use the very words that He chose, overrode their personalities. ["I would argue that if by human imperfection an author was going to choose an inappropriate word that would fail to communicate the meaning intended by God that the Holy Spirit would then override that word choice." – Edward D. Andrews]

Article IX

We affirm that **inspiration**, though not conferring omniscience, guaranteed true and trustworthy utterance on all matters of which the Biblical authors were moved to speak and write. We deny that the finitude or fallenness of these writers, by necessity or otherwise, introduced distortion or falsehood into God's Word.

Article X

We affirm that **inspiration**, strictly speaking, applies only to the autographic text of Scripture, which in the providence of God can be ascertained from available manuscripts with great accuracy. We further affirm that copies and translations of Scripture are the Word of God to the extent that they faithfully represent the original. We deny that any essential element of the Christian faith is affected by the absence of the autographs. We further deny that this absence renders the assertion of Biblical **inerrancy** invalid or irrelevant. [There is no miracle of preservation, but rather, it is preservation by restoration. Today, what we have, thanks to hundreds of textual scholars over a few hundred years, is a 99.99% restored original language text. – Edward D. Andrews]

Article XI

We affirm that Scripture, having been given by divine inspiration, is infallible, so that, far from misleading us, it is true and reliable in all the matters it addresses. We deny that it is possible for the Bible to be at the same time infallible and errant in its assertions. Infallibility and inerrancy may be distinguished, but not separated.

Inerrancy of Scripture

Inerrancy of Scripture is **the result** of the state of a human being moved by the Holy Spirit from God, which results in an inspired, fully inerrant written Word of God.

Article XII

We affirm that Scripture in its entirety is **inerrant**, being free from all falsehood, fraud, or deceit. We deny that Biblical infallibility and **inerrancy** are limited to spiritual, religious, or redemptive themes, exclusive of assertions in the fields of history and science. We further deny that scientific hypotheses about earth history may properly be used to overturn the teaching of Scripture on creation and the flood.

Article XIII

We affirm the propriety of using **inerrancy** as a theological term with reference to the complete truthfulness of Scripture. We deny that it is proper to evaluate Scripture according to standards of truth and error that are alien to its usage or purpose. We further deny that **inerrancy** is negated by Biblical phenomena such as a lack of modern technical precision, irregularities of grammar or spelling, observational descriptions of nature, the reporting of falsehoods, the use of hyperbole and round numbers, the topical arrangement of material, variant selections of material in parallel accounts, or the use of free citations.

Article XV

We affirm that the doctrine of **inerrancy** is grounded in the teaching of the Bible about **inspiration**. We deny that Jesus' teaching about Scripture may be dismissed by appeals to accommodation or to any natural limitation of His humanity.

Article XVI

We affirm that the doctrine of **inerrancy** has been integral to the Church's faith throughout its history. We deny that inerrancy is a doctrine invented by Scholastic Protestantism, or is a reactionary position postulated in response to negative higher criticism.

Authoritative Word of God

The **authoritative** aspect of Scripture is that God by way of inspiration gives the words the authors chose to use power and authority, so that the outcome (i.e., originals) is the very Word of God, as though God were speaking to us himself.

Article I

We affirm that the Holy Scriptures are to be received as the **authoritative** Word of God. We deny that the Scriptures receive their authority from the Church, tradition, or any other human source.

2 Timothy 3:16-17 Updated American Standard Version (UASV)

16 All Scripture is inspired by God and profitable for teaching, for reproof, for correction, for training in righteousness; 17 so that the man of God may be fully competent, equipped for every good work.

What does this mean? The phrase "inspired by God" (Gr., *theopneustos*) literally means, "Breathed out by God." A related Greek word, *pneuma*, means "wind," "breath," life, "Spirit." Since *pneuma* can also mean "breath," the process of "breathing out" can rightly be said to be the work of the Holy Spirit inspiring the Scriptures. The result is that the originals were accurate, fully inerrant, and authoritative. Thus, the Holy Spirit moved human writers so that the result can truthfully be called the Word of *God*, not the word of man.

2 Peter 1:21 Updated American Standard Version (UASV)

21 for no prophecy was ever produced by the will of man, but men carried along by the Holy Spirit spoke from God.

The Greek word here translated "men carried along by," "men moved by" (NASB)," (φέρω pherō), is used in another form at Acts 27:15, 17, which describes a ship that was driven along by the wind. So, the Holy Spirit, by analogy, 'navigated the course' of the Bible writers. While the Spirit did not give them each word by dictation,[82] it certainly kept the writers from inserting any information that did not convey the will and purpose of God.

The heart of what the International Council on Biblical Inerrancy (ICBI) stood for is apparent in "A Short Statement," produced at the Chicago conference in 1978:

A SHORT STATEMENT

1. God, who is Himself Truth and speaks truth only, has inspired Holy Scripture in order thereby to reveal Himself to lost mankind through Jesus Christ as Creator and Lord, Redeemer and Judge. Holy Scripture is God's witness to Himself.

2. Holy Scripture, being God's own Word, written by men prepared and superintended by His Spirit, is of infallible divine authority in all matters upon which it touches: it is to be believed, as God's instruction, in all that it affirms, obeyed, as God's command, in all that it requires; embraced, as God's pledge, in all that it promises.

3. The Holy Spirit, Scripture's divine Author, both authenticates it to us by His inward witness and opens our minds to understand its meaning.

4. Being wholly and verbally God-given, Scripture is without error or fault in all its teaching, no less in what it states about God's acts in creation, about the events of world history, and about its own literary origins under God, than in its witness to God's saving grace in individual lives.

5. The **authority of Scripture** is inescapably impaired if this total divine **inerrancy** is in any way limited or disregarded or made relative to a view of truth contrary to the Bible's own; and such lapses bring serious loss to both the individual and the Church.

---

[82] Dr. Don Wilkins, Senior Translator of the NASB writes, "Exactly how the Spirit guided the writers is a mystery, and the words "thus says the Lord" in prophecy most likely do introduce a dictated message. However, those familiar with Greek can easily see stylistic differences between the NT writers which seem to reflect different personalities and rule out verbatim dictation from a single source."

Questions to Consider

We have been using the book of Romans as our example, so we will continue with it. We know that Paul was the author who gave us the inspired content of Romans, Tertius was the secretary who recorded Romans, and Phoebe was likely the one who carried the letter to Rome or else accompanied the one who did. Thus, we have at least three persons: the author, the secretary (amanuensis; scribe), and the carrier.

What is inspiration?

Inspiration is a "theological concept encompassing phenomena in which human action, skill, or utterance is immediately and extraordinarily supplied by the Spirit of God. Although various terms are employed in the Bible, the basic meaning is best served by Gk. *theopneustos* "God-breathed." (2 Tim. 3:16) This means "breathed forth by God" rather than "breathed into by God" (Warfield)." (Myers 1987, 524) **Verbal plenary inspiration** holds that "every word of Scripture was God-breathed." Human writers played a significant role. Their individual backgrounds, personal traits, and literary styles were authentically theirs but had been providentially prepared by God for use as his instrument in producing Scripture. "The Scriptures had not been dictated, but the result was as if they had been (A. A. Hodge, B. B. Warfield)."[83]

World-Renowned Bible Scholars Define Inspiration

Benjamin B. Warfield: "Inspiration is, therefore, usually defined as a supernatural influence exerted on the sacred writers by the Spirit of God, by virtue of which their writings are given Divine trustworthiness."[84]

Edward J. Young: "Inspiration is a superintendence of God the Holy Spirit over the writers of the Scriptures, as a result of which these Scriptures possess Divine authority and trustworthiness and, possessing such Divine authority and trustworthiness, are free from error."[85]

---

[83] Allen C. Myers, *The Eerdmans Bible Dictionary* (Grand Rapids, MI: Eerdmans, 1987), 525.

[84] B. B. Warfield, *The Inspiration and Authority of the Bible* (Philadelphia, PA: Presbyterian and Reformed Pub. Co., 1948), p. 131.

[85] Edward J. Young, *Thy Word Is Truth* (Grand Rapids: Eerdmans, 1957), p. 27.

Charles C. Ryrie: "Inspiration is … God's superintendence of ˈ human authors so that, using their own individual personalities, tl composed and recorded without error His revelation to man in the words the original autographs."[86]

Paul P. Enns: "There are several important elements that belong i proper definition of inspiration: (1) the divine element—God the Holy Sɟ superintended the writers, ensuring the accuracy of the writing; (2) the hur element—human authors wrote according to their individual styles personalities; (3) the result of the divine-human authorship is the recorɗ of God's truth without error; (4) inspiration extends to the selection of wɡ by the writers; (5) inspiration relates to the original manuscripts."[87]

Were both Paul and Tertius inspired, or just Paul?

Only Paul and other Old and New Testament authors were inspɪ First, as was stated above, **Verbal plenary inspiration** holds that "e word of Scripture was God-breathed." However, God **did not**, gene speaking, dictate the books of the Bible word by word to the Bible autˈ as if they were dictating machines.

As the apostle Paul states, God spoke "in many ways" to his serv before the arrival of Jesus Christ. (Heb. 1:1-2) We do have one spɡ circumstance: The Ten Commandments, wherein the information divinely provided in written form. Therefore, a scribe would only haˈ copy them into the scrolls created by Moses. (Ex. 31:18; Deut. 10:1-ˈ other times, information was communicated by verbal dictation, litɡ word for word. When introducing the large number of laws and statut the covenant with Israel, "Jehovah said to Moses: 'Write these words, f accordance with these words I have made a covenant with you and Israel.'" (Ex. 34:27) And on other occasions, the prophets also frequently given precise messages that were to be delivered. These were recorded after that, which then became part of the inspired, fully inɡ Scriptures. – 1 Kings 22:14; Jeremiah 1:7; 2:1; 11:1-5; Ezekiel 3:4; 11:5.

2 Thessalonians 3:17 Updated American Standard Version (UAS

17 The greeting is by my hand, Paul's,[88] which is a sign in every letteɪ is the way I write.

---

[86] Charles C. Ryrie, *A Survey of Bible Doctrine* (Chicago: Moody, 1972), p. 38.
[87] Paul P. Enns, *The Moody Handbook of Theology* (Chicago: Moody Press, 1989), p.
[88] Lit *the greeting by my hand of Paul*

An appended note to every letter with his signature "distinguishing mark" is like a boss signing a letter that he dictated to a secretary. It is unthinkable that Paul would sign or make a distinguishing mark on anything without reading through it and, after that, making any necessary corrections or having Tertius makes the corrections. This supposes that Paul looked over all of his letters, which would also suppose that the scribe could not have been inspired because if he were, then there would have been no mistakes in the document, which means it would not have been needed to be looked over let alone corrected. So again, there would have been no need for Paul to check the work of an inspired secretary. Again, more plainly, if Tertius had been inspired, Paul would have had no need to look the text over the moment he set the pen down. There is no need to read into silence and suggest that the secretary was inspired. While Tertius was likely a professional scribe and indeed engaged in his work, they were also coworkers and traveling companions. As was stated earlier, in a small percentage of cases, information was transmitted by verbal dictation, word for word from God by way of the Holy Spirit to the author. For example, when God delivered the large body of laws and statutes of his covenant with Israel, Jehovah instructed Moses: "Write for yourself these words." (Ex 34:27) In another example, the prophets were often given specific messages to deliver. (1 Ki 22:14; Jer. 1:7; 2:1; 11:1-5; Eze. 3:4; 11:5) Additionally, the Bible authors did dictate word for word what they received under inspiration to their secretaries, i.e., amanuenses/scribes. In other words, any word choices or writing styles belonged to the Bible author.

Jeremiah 36:4 Updated American Standard Version (UASV)

4 Then Jeremiah called Baruch the son of Neriah, and Baruch wrote on a scroll at the **dictation of Jeremiah** all the words of Jehovah that he had spoken to him. (Bold mine)

If Paul alone was inspired, how does the imperfection of Tertius affect inerrancy?

First, we should state that just because Paul used Tertius, Peter used Silvanus, or Jeremiah used Baruch to pen the Word of God, they did not thereby detract from or weaken the authority of God's Word or the inerrancy of Scripture. The dictation that Paul gave Tertius was the result of divine inspiration as he, Paul, was moved along by the Holy Spirit. Tertius merely recorded Paul's dictation, word by word. Whether Tertius was a professional scribe[89] or had the skills of a semi-professional scribe, he must have made at

---

[89] In the strictest sense, a professional scribe is one who was specifically trained in that vocation and was paid for his services.

least a few slips of the pen, as the epistle to the Romans was some 7,000 words, and writing conditions were challenging. Afterward, however, Paul would have reviewed the document with Tertius, correcting any errors before publishing the official, authoritative text.

What about Phoebe? What role did the carrier have in the process?

Those used by New Testament authors to deliver the Word of God to people or congregations would have been some of Paul's most trusted, competent coworkers. Paul had over one hundred of these. Indeed, in the case of congregations contacting Paul with questions and concerns, Paul responded with an inspired letter, the carrier would be made aware of those questions and concerns. Paul would have spoken to the carrier at length about these matters, going over what he meant by the words he had used. This would have provided the carrier sufficient knowledge; if the person or congregation had any question(s) that the carrier could address. This process is not indicated within the Scriptures. Are we to believe God and Paul, for that matter, would send a simple carrier who was left in the dark as to what he was carrying? And that no congregational leader would have follow-up questions, which God would have foreseen? Hardly.

The Publishing, Copying, and Distributing Process

In the above, we spoke of the initial aspect of the publishing process, i.e., the moment Paul decided to pen a letter to a congregation like the Romans, the Ephesians, the Colossians, or a person such as Philemon. We discussed the process that Paul went through with his secretary (e.g., Tertius), to the carrier (e.g., Phoebe, Tychicus), and the recipients (e.g., Roman congregation). Now we turn to the circulation aspect, i.e., getting the book out to more readers. Harry Y. Gamble says the following in *The Publication and Early Dissemination of Early Christian Books*:

> The letters of Paul to his communities, the earliest extant Christian texts, were dictated to scribal associates (presumably Christian), carried to their destinations by a traveling Christian, and read aloud to the congregations.[90] But Paul also envisioned the circulation of some of his

---

[90] On the dictation of Paul's letters to a scribe, see E. R. Richards, The Secretary in the Letters of Paul (WUNT 42; Tubingen: Mohr, 1991), 169–98; for couriers see Rom. 16: 1, 1 Cor. 16: 10, Eph. 6: 21, Col. 4: 7, cf. 2 Cor. 8: 16–17. Reference to their carriers is common in

letters beyond a single Christian group (cf. Gal. 1: 2, 'to the churches of Galatia', Rom. 1:7 'to all God's beloved in Rome'—dispersed among numerous discrete house churches, Rom. 16: 5, 10, 11, 14, 15), and the author of Colossians, if not Paul, gives instruction for the exchange of Paul's letters between different communities (Col. 4: 16), which must indeed have taken place also soon after Paul's time.[91] The gospel literature of early Christianity offers only meager hints of intentions or means of its publication and circulation. The prologue to Luke/Acts (Luke 1: 1–4) provides a dedication to 'Theophilus', who (whether or not a fictive figure) by that convention is implicitly made responsible for the dissemination of the work by encouraging and permitting copies to be made. The last chapter of the Gospel of John, an epilogue added by others after the original conclusion of the Gospel (20: 30–1), aims at least in part (21: 24–5) to insure appreciation of the book and to promote its use beyond its community of origin. To take another case, the Apocalypse, addressed to seven churches in western Asia Minor, was almost surely sent in separate copy to each. Even so, the author anticipated its wider copying and dissemination beyond those original recipients, and so warned subsequent copyists to preserve the integrity of the book, neither adding nor subtracting, for fear of religious penalty (Rev. 22:18–19). The private Christian copying and circulation that is presumed in these early writings continued to be the means for the publication and dissemination of Christian literature in the second and third centuries. It can be seen, for example, in the explicit notice in The Shepherd of Hermas (Vis. 2.4.3) that the book was to be published or released in two final copies, one for local use in Rome, the other for the transcription of further copies to be sent to Christian communities in 'cities abroad'. It can also be seen when Polycarp, bishop of Smyrna, had the letters of Ignatius copied and sent to the Christian community in Philippi, and had copies of letters from them and other churches in Asia Minor sent to Syrian Antioch (Phil. 13). It is evident too in the scribal colophons of the Martyrdom of Polycarp (22.2–4), and

other early Christian letters (e.g., 1 Pet. 5: 12, 1 Clem. 65: 1, Ignatius, Phil. 11.2, Smyr. 12.1, Polycarp, Phil. 14.1). For the general practice see E. Epp, 'New Testament Papyrus Manuscripts and Letter Carrying in Greco-Roman Times', in B. A. Pearson (ed.), The Future of Early Christianity (Minneapolis: Fortress, 1991), 35–56. Reading a letter aloud to the community, which seems to be presupposed by all the letters, is stipulated only in 1 Thess. 5: 27.

[91] This is shown for an early time by the generalization of the original particular addresses of some of Paul's letters (Rom. 1: 7, 15; 1 Cor. 1: 2; cf. Eph. 1: 1).

must be assumed also in connection with the letters of Dionysius, bishop of Corinth (fl. 170 ce; Eusebius, H.E. 4.23.1–12).

From another angle, the physical remains of early Christian books show that they were produced and disseminated privately within and between Christian communities. Early Christian texts, especially those of a scriptural sort, were almost always written in codices or leaf books—an informal, economical, and handy format—rather than on rolls, which were the traditional and standard vehicle of all other books. This was a sharp departure from convention, and particularly characteristic of Christians. Also distinctive to Christian books was the pervasive use of nomina sacra, divine names written in abbreviated forms, which was clearly an in-house practice of Christian scribes. Further, the preponderance in early Christian papyrus manuscripts of an informal quasi-documentary script rather than a professional bookhand also suggests that Christian writings were privately transcribed with a view to intramural circulation and use.[92]

If Christian books were disseminated in roughly the same way as other books, that is, by private seriatim copying, we might surmise that they spread slowly and gradually in ever-widening circles, first in proximity to their places of origin, then regionally, and then transregionally, and for some books this was doubtless the case. But it deserves notice that some early Christian texts appear to have enjoyed surprisingly rapid and wide circulation. Already by the early decades of the second century Papias of Hierapolis in western Asia Minor was acquainted at least with the Gospels of Mark and Matthew (Eusebius, H.E. 3.39.15–16); Clement of Rome, Ignatius of Antioch, and Polycarp of Smyrna were all acquainted with collections of Paul's letters; and papyrus copies of various early Christian texts were current in Egypt.[93] The Shepherd of Hermas, written in Rome near the mid-second century, was current and popular in Egypt not long after.[94] Equally interesting, Irenaeus' Adversus haereses, written about 180 in Gaul, is shown by papyrus fragments to have found its way to Egypt by

---

[92] On these features see H. Gamble, Books and Readers in the Early Church (New Haven: Yale University Press, 1995), 66–81, and L. Hurtado, The Earliest Christian Artifacts (Grand Rapids: Eerdmans, 2006).

[93] For Clement, Ignatius, and Polycarp, see A. F. Gregory and C. M. Tuckett, eds., The Reception of the New Testament in the Apostolic Fathers (Oxford: OUP, 2005), 142–53, 162–72, 201–18, 226–7. For early Christian papyri in Egypt see Hurtado, Earliest Christian Artifacts, appendix 1 (209–29). The most notable case is P52 (a fragment of the Gospel of John, customarily dated to the early 2nd cent.).

[94] Some papyrus fragments of Hermas are 2nd cent. (P.Oxy. 4706 and 3528, P.Mich. 130, P.Iand. 1.4).

the end of the second century, and indeed also to Carthage, where it was used by Tertullian.[95]

The brisk and broad dissemination of Christian books presumes not only a lively interest in texts among Christian communities but also efficient means for their reproduction and distribution. Such interest and means may be unexpected, given that the rate of literacy within Christianity was low, on average no greater than in the empire at large, namely in the range of 10–15 percent.[96] Yet there were some literate members in almost all Christian communities, and as long as texts could be read aloud by some, they were accessible and useful to the illiterate majority. Christian congregations were not reading communities in the same sense as elite literary or scholarly circles, but books were nevertheless important to them virtually from the beginning, for even before Christians began to compose their own texts, books of Jewish scripture played an indispensable role in their worship, teaching, and missionary preaching. Indeed, Judaism and Christianity were the only religious communities in Greco-Roman antiquity in which texts had any considerable importance, and in this, as in some other respects, Christian groups bore a greater resemblance to philosophical circles than to other religious traditions.[97]

If smaller, provincial Christian congregations were not well-equipped or well-situated for the tasks of copying and disseminating texts, larger Christian centers must have had some scriptorial capacity: already in the second century: Polycarp's handling of Ignatius' letters and letters from other churches shows its presence in Smyrna; the instruction about the publication of Hermas' The Shepherd suggests it for Rome; and it can hardly be doubted for Alexandria, since even in a provincial city like

---

[95] For the A.H. in Egypt: P.Oxy. 405; for Tertullian's use of A.H. in Carthage, see T. D. Barnes, Tertullian (Oxford: Clarendon, 1971), 127–8, 220–1.

[96] The fundamental study of literacy in antiquity is still W. V. Harris, Ancient Literacy (Cambridge, Mass.: Harvard University Press, 1989); see now also the essays in J. H. Humphrey, ed., Literacy in the Roman World (Journal of Roman Archaeology, suppl. ser. 3; Ann Arbor: University of Michigan, 1991), and in W. A. Johnson and H. N. Parker, eds., Ancient Literacies (Oxford: OUP, 2009).

[97] M. Beard, 'Writing and Religion: Ancient Religion and the Function of the Written Word in Roman Religion', in Humphrey, Literacy in the Roman World, 353–8, argues that texts played a relatively large role in Greco-Roman religions, yet characterizes that role as 'symbolic rather than utilitarian', which was clearly not the case in early Christianity. The kind of careful reading, interpretation, and exposition of texts that we see in early Christianity and in early Judaism (whether in worship or school settings) provides, mutatis mutandis, an interesting analogy to the activity of elite literary circles.

Oxyrhynchus many manuscripts of Christian texts were available.[98] The early third-century Alexandrian scriptorium devised for the production and distribution of the works of Origen (Eusebius, H.E. 6.23.2), though unique in its sponsorship by a private patron and its service to an individual writer, surely had precursors, more modest and yet efficient, in other Christian communities. It also had important successors, not the least of which was the library and scriptorium that flourished in Caesarea in the second half of the third century under the auspices of Pamphilus.[99] Absent such reliable intra-Christian means for the production of books, the range of texts known and used by Christian communities across the Mediterranean basin by the end of the second century would be without explanation.[100]

When we think of publishing a book today, there are some similarities to the ancient process, but it was not the same for Christian communities in the ancient world of the Roman Empire. Paul dispatched Tychicus as a carrier with a letter to the Ephesians, the Colossians, and Philemon and a potential fourth letter to the Laodiceans. Tychicus was competent, trusted, and a skilled coworker who delivered these letters hundreds of miles from an imprisoned Paul, with enough information to bring God's Word to the first-century Christian congregations. However, in the letter to the Colossians, Paul said, "When this letter has been read among you, have it also read in the church of the Laodiceans; and see that you also read the letter from Laodicea." (Col. 4:16) In other words, it was to be a circuit letter. Paul had also stated to the Thessalonians in a letter to them, "I put you under oath

---

[98] On the question of early Christian scriptoria (the term may be variously construed), see Gamble, Books and Readers, 121–6. Hurtado, Earliest Christian Artifacts, 185–9, rightly calls attention to corrections by contemporary hands in early Christian papyri as pointing to at least limited activity of a scriptorial kind.

[99] The role of Pamphilus and the Caesarean library/scriptorium in the private production and dissemination of early Christian literature, esp. of scriptural materials, was highlighted by Eusebius in his Life of Pamphilus, as quoted by Jerome in his Apology against Rufinus (1.9).

[100] Charles E. Hill; Michael J. Kruger, *THE EARLY TEXT OF THE NEW TESTAMENT* (Oxford, United Kingdom: Oxford University Press, 2012), 32-35.

Beyond the uses of Christian texts in congregational settings, there were already in the 2nd cent. some Christian circles that pursued specialized and technical engagements with texts, usually in the service of theological arguments and exegetical agendas. The 'school-settings' of teachers such as Valentinus and Justin, and a little later of Theodotus, Clement, and Origen, were Christian approximations to the kinds of literary activity associated with 'elite' reading communities in the early empire.

before the Lord to have this letter read to all the brothers." (1 Thess. 5:27) Paul encouraged the distribution of his letters.

Remember the process from the above; the book would be shared with friends of similar interests, and then the circles grew wider and wider to friends of friends and others. First, Paul's primary level of friends would be his more than one hundred traveling companions and fellow workers, some being the carriers who delivered the books. Second, the friends in the Christian congregation would have the letter read to them, who would then share it with other fellow congregations. In the secular (non-Christian) circle of friends, interested readers who wished to have a copy would have their slaves (i.e., scribes) make a copy or copies of a book. The same would have been valid within the Christian congregation. When the Laodiceans read the letter that Paul had sent to the Colossians, they would have had one of their wealthy members use his literate and trained scribe to make a copy for their congregation and maybe even a few copies for other members. The same would hold true when the Colossians received the letter written to the Laodiceans. Eventually, Paul's letters would have been gathered in one codex to circulate as a group, such as P[46]. Papyrus 46 is an early Greek New Testament manuscript written on papyrus. Its most probable date between 100 and 150 C.E. Michael Marlowe says that P[46] contains (in order) "the last eight chapters of Romans; all of Hebrews; virtually all of 1–2 Corinthians; all of Ephesians, Galatians, Philippians, Colossians; and two chapters of 1 Thessalonians. All of the leaves have lost some lines at the bottom through deterioration."

The scriptorium was a room for copying manuscripts, where a lector would read aloud from his exemplar, with a room full of copyists taking down his dictation. Recent scholarship has suggested that we remove the concept of the scriptorium in the time of Jesus and the apostles of the first century C.E. because this was not a practice until the fourth century C.E. Harry Y. Gamble addresses this effectively when he writes,

> It is difficult to determine just when Christian scriptoria came into existence. The problem is partly of definition, partly of evidence. If we think of the scriptorium as simply a writing center where texts were copied by more than a single scribe, then any of the larger Christian communities, such as Antioch or Rome, may have already had scriptoria in the early second century, and in view of Polycarp's activity something of the kind can be imagined for Smyrna. If we think instead of a scriptorium as being more structured, operating, for example, in a specially designed and

designated location; employing particular methods of transcription; producing certain types of manuscripts; or multiplying copies on a significant scale, then it becomes more difficult to imagine that such institutions developed at an early date.[101]

Gamble goes on to inform us that Origen's scriptorium of about 230 C.E. was an exception. Just a few short years later, the scriptorium of Cyprian was a more official version of what we think of when picturing scriptoria. Then, there is the scriptorium that was attached to the Christian library in Caesarea, which we know was commissioned to produce fifty New Testament manuscripts in short order. It may even have been added in the third century when Pamphilus (latter half of the 3rd century–309 C.E.) built the library. A more official type of scriptorium could likely be found in this period at other Christian epicenters, such as Rome, Jerusalem, and Alexandria. Comfort tells us that "church history and certain manuscript discoveries from other parts in Egypt suggest that Alexandria had a Christian scriptorium or writing center."[102] Gamble adds, "It was only during the fourth and fifth centuries that the scriptoria on monastic communities came into their own, also in association with monastic libraries."[103]

While it is challenging, if not impossible, to identify a specific Alexandrian scriptorium for our early manuscripts of the second century, or even if they were produced in a scriptorium at all, we do know that professional scribes produced them. There are many possibilities: (1) the professional scribe could have produced them in a Christian scriptorium. On the other hand, (2) the professional scribe could have been a Christian who worked for a scriptorium, who then used his skills to produce copies. Then again, (3) it could have been that the scribe formerly worked in a scriptorium but now was the private scribe of a wealthy Christian who used his skills to make copies. We know that about a million Christians spread throughout the Roman Empire at the beginning of the second century (c. 130 C.E.). Therefore, the copying of manuscripts could very well have been within the Christian community, i.e., from the Christian congregation to the Christian

---

[101] Henry Y. Gamble, *Books and Readers in the Early Church: A History of Early Christian Texts* (New Haven, CT, New Haven University Press, 1995), 121.

[102] Philip Comfort, *Encountering the Manuscripts: An Introduction to New Testament Paleography & Textual Criticism* (Nashville, TN: Broadman & Holman, 2005), 22.

[103] Henry Y. Gamble, *Books and Readers in the Early Church: A History of Early Christian Texts* (New Haven, CT, New Haven University Press, 1995), 121-2.

congregation and wealthy Christians acquiring personal copies for themselves.

We have several early manuscripts that evidence that they were very likely produced in a scriptorium, even if it was simply a room attached to a Christian library, which had a handful of copyists. For example, a professional scribe undoubtedly did P46 (100-150 C.E.) because it contained stichoi marks, which are notes at the end of sections, stating how many lines were copied. This was a means of calculating how much a scribe should be paid. It is likely that an employee of the scriptorium numbered the pages, indicating the stichoi marks. Moreover, this same scribe made corrections as he went. Another example would be P66 (also c. 100-150 C.E.) according to Comfort:

> It is also fairly certain that P66 was the product of a scriptorium or writing center. The first copyist of this manuscript had his work thoroughly checked by a diorthotes [corrector], according to a different exemplar—just the way it would happen in a scriptorium. Of course, it can be argued that an individual who purchased the manuscript made all the corrections, which was a common practice in ancient times. But the extent of corrections in P66 and the fact that the paginator (a different scribe) made many of the corrections speaks against this (see description of P66 in chap. 2). It was more the exception than the rule in ancient times that a manuscript would be fully checked by a diorthotes. P66 has other markings of being professionally produced. The extant manuscript still shows the pinpricks in the corners of each leaf of the papyri; these served as a guide for left hand justification and right hand. The manuscript also exhibits a consistent set of marginal and interlinear correction signs. Another sign of professionally produced manuscript is the use of the diple (>) in the margin, which was used to signal a correction in the text and/or the need for a correction in the text. There are very few of these in the extant New Testament manuscripts.[104]

The production and distribution of New Testament manuscripts were carried out at the congregation and individual Christian levels in the early days of Christianity.

---

[104] Philip W. Comfort, *New Testament Text and Translation Commentary: Commentary on the Variant Readings of the Ancient New Testament Manuscripts and How They Relate to the Major English Translations* (Carol Stream, IL: Tyndale House Publishers, Inc., 2008), 26.

Moreover, this process did not negate the use of professional scribes. Just as Paul would not have used an inexperienced scribe to produce the epistle to the Romans. Congregations and wealthy Christians would have likely used professional scribes to make copies. Of course, there are exceptions to the rule, and some congregations may not have had access to a professional scribe, so they would have to have chosen to use the best person available to them. Nevertheless, if a congregation had access to a person experienced at making documents or a semi-professional or professional scribe, they would have lacked good sense or practicality not to take advantage of such a person. Think of anything we want to have done in our Christian congregation today: would we not seek a professional if we had access to one as a member, be it plumbing, wiring, teaching, or computer technology? We naturally look to the most skilled person that we can find, even if we have a clogged-up commode. Would we do any less if we were in the first century and had just received a letter from the apostle Paul, who was imprisoned hundreds of miles away in Rome?

Why Would the Holy Spirit Miraculously Inspire 66 Fully Inerrant Texts and Then Allow Variant Errors in the Copies?

Agnostic New Testament textual and early Christianity scholar Dr. Bart D. Ehrman states, "For the only reason (I came to think) for God to inspire the Bible would be so that his people would have his actual words; but if he really wanted people to have his actual words, surely he would have miraculously preserved those words, just as he had miraculously inspired them in the first place. Given the circumstance that he didn't preserve the words, the conclusion seemed inescapable to me that he hadn't gone to the trouble of inspiring them."[105]

New Testament textual scholar Dr. Dirk Jongkind offers a brief response, "God chose not to give us exhaustive knowledge of every detail of the text, though he could have done so. Still, he has given us abundant access to his words. In other words, to say that God inspired the words of the New Testament does not mean that God is therefore under an obligation to preserve for us each and every detail."[106]

---

[105] Misquoting Jesus: The Story Behind Who Changed the Bible and Why (San Francisco: HarperSanFrancisco, 2005), 211.

[106] An Introduction to the Greek New Testament, Produced at Tyndale House, Cambridge, Crossway.

Why didn't God inspire the copyists? Some have become anxious because this question has plagued them, or some Bible critic has challenged them. Therefore, they are looking for the silver bullet to quench their personal concern or have a ready, quick response for the Bible critic. Draw comfort in that there are hundreds, if not thousands, of great responses to attacks from Bible critics that will cause them to move onto another victim in their quest to stumble God's people. However, there are good reasons, rational responses to some questions that will not be fully answered until the second coming of Jesus Christ. What lies below is the latter. Before delving into the rational, reasonable reasons why God would inspire the authors but not the copyists, let's talk a little about what we do have.

Some people have unreceptive hearts and minds. They are Pharisaical because they are not interested in an answer, and the Word of God, reason, and logic will not get through their callused hearts. Suppose I have only taught one thing in my 32 years. In that case, it is this, identify these people fast, or you will waste much of your life, giving reasonable, rational responses to then have the person reject it out of hand and move onto something else as though they never brought it up. Mind you, an angry person, a person with doubts, is not necessarily a Pharisaical person. There are reasons for some to doubt. There are reasons for some to be angry. If the person is treating you with disdain, mocking, talking down to you, these and other things are indications of a Pharisaical attitude.

Christian Bible students need to be familiar with Old and New Testament textual studies as the two are essential foundational studies. Why? If we fail to establish what was originally authored with reasonable certainty, how are we to translate or even interpret what we think is God's actual Word? We are fortunate that there are far more existing New Testament manuscripts today than any other book from ancient history. Some ancient Greek and Latin classics are based on one existing manuscript, while with others, there are just a handful and a few exceptions that have a few hundred available. However, the New Testament has over 5,898 Greek New Testament manuscripts that have been cataloged (As of January 2021),[107] 10,000 Latin

---

[107] While at present here in 2020, there are 5,898 manuscripts. There are **140 listed Papyrus** manuscripts, 323 Majuscule manuscripts, 2,951 Minuscule manuscripts, and 2,484 Lectionary manuscripts, bringing the total cataloged manuscripts to 5,898 manuscripts. However, you cannot simply total the number of cataloged manuscripts because, for example, $P^{11/14}$ are the same manuscript but with different catalog numbers. The same is true of $P^{33/5}$, $P^{4/64/67}$, $P^{49/65}$ and $P^{77/103}$. Now this alone would bring our 140 listed papyrus manuscripts down to 134. Then, we turn to one example from our majuscule manuscripts where clear 0110, 0124, 0178, 0179, 0180, 0190, 0191, 0193, 0194, and 0202 are said to be part of 070. A

manuscripts, and an additional 9,300 other manuscripts in such languages as Syriac, Slavic, Gothic, Ethiopic, Coptic, and Armenian. This gives New Testament textual scholars vastly more to work within establishing the original words of the text.

The other difference between the New Testament manuscripts and those of the classics is that the existing copies of the New Testament date much closer to the originals. In the case of the Greek classics, some of the manuscripts are dated about a thousand years after the author had penned the book. Some of the Latin classics are dated from three to seven hundred years after the time the author wrote the book. When we look at the Greek copies of the New Testament books, some portions are within decades of the original author's book. Seventy-nine Greek papyri, along with five majuscules,[108] date from 110 C.E. to 300 C.E.

Distribution of Greek New Testament Manuscripts

- The **Papyrus** is a copy of a portion of the New Testament made on papyrus. At present, we have 141 cataloged New Testament papyri, many dating between 110-350 C.E., but some as late as the 6th century C.E.

- The **Majuscule** or **Uncial** is a script of large letters commonly used in Greek and Latin manuscripts written between the 3rd and 9th centuries C.E. that resembles a modern capital letter but is more rounded. At present, we have 323 cataloged New Testament Majuscule manuscripts.

---

minuscule manuscript was listed with five separate catalog numbers for 2306, which then have the letters a through e. Thus, we have the following GA numbers: 2306 for 2306a, and 2831-2834 for 2306b-2306e.' – (Hixon 2019, 53-4) The problem is much worse when we consider that there are 323 Majuscule manuscripts and then far worse still with a listed 2,951 Minuscule and 2,484 Lectionaries. Nevertheless, those who estimate a total of 5,300 (Jacob W. Peterson, Myths and Mistakes, p. 63) 5,500 manuscripts (Dr. Ed Gravely / ehrmanproject.com/), 5,800 manuscripts (Porter 2013, 23), it is still a truckload of evidence far and above the dismal number of ancient secular author books.

[108] Large lettering, often called "capital" or uncial, in which all the letters are usually the same height.

- The **Minuscule** is a small cursive style of writing used in manuscripts from the 9th to the 16th centuries, now having 2,951 Minuscule manuscripts cataloged.

- The **Lectionary** is a schedule of readings from the Bible for Christian church services during the year, in both majuscules and minuscules, dating from the 4th to the 16th centuries C.E., now having 2,484 Lectionary manuscripts cataloged.

Distribution of Papyri by Century and Type				
DATE	**ALEX**	**WEST**	**CAES**	**BYZ**
100-150/175 C.E.	7Q4? 7Q5? P4/64/67 P32 P46 P52 P66 P75 P77/103 P87 P90 P98 (bad shape, differences) P101 P109 (too small) P118 (too small) P137 0189 P. Oxyrhynchus 405 P. Egerton 2	P104	0	0
175-250 C.E.	P1 P5 P13 P20 P23 P27 P30 P35 P39 P40 P45 P47 P49/65 P71 P72 P82 P85 P95 P100 P106 P108 P110 P111 P113 P115 P121 (too small) P125 P126 (too small) P133 P136 P141 0220 0232 P. Oxyrhynchus 406 P. Egerton 3	P29 (Metzger Western & Aland Free; too small to be certain) P38 P48 P69 0171 0212 (mixed) P107 (Independent)	0	0
250-300 C.E.	P8 P9 P12 P15 P16 P17 P18 P19 P24 P28 P50 P51 P53 P70 P78 P80 P86 P88 P89 (too small) P91 P92 P114 P119 P120 P129 (too small) P131 P132 too small) P134 0162 0207 0231 P. Antinoopolis 54	P37 (Free, mostly Western)	0	0

290-390 C.E.	P3 P6 P7 P10 P21 P54 P62 P81 P93 P94 P102 (too small) P117 (too small) P122 (too small) P123 P130 (too small) P139 (too small) 057 058 059 / 0215 071 0160 0163 0165 0169 0172 0173 0175 0176 0181 0182 0185 0188 0206 0214 0217 0218 0219 0221 0226 0227 0228 0230 0242 0264 0308 0312 P. Oxyrhynchus 4010 P. Oxyrhynchus 5073	P21 (mixed) P25 (independent) P112 (independent) P127 (independent; like no other)	0	0
4th / 5th Century C.E.	P11 P14 P33/P58 P56 P57 P63 P105 (too small) P124 0254			069 P. Oxyrh ynchus 1077?

We should clarify that of the approximate 24,000 total manuscripts of the New Testament, not all are complete books. There are fragmented manuscripts with just a few verses, manuscripts containing an entire book, others that include numerous books, and some that have the whole New Testament, or nearly so. This is expected since the oldest manuscripts we have were copied in an era when reproducing the entire New Testament was not the norm, but rather a single book or a group of books (i.e., the Gospels or Paul's letters). This still does not negate the vast riches of manuscripts that we possess.

What can we conclude from this short introduction to New Testament textual studies? There is some irony here: secular scholars have no problem accepting classic authors' wording with their minuscule amount of evidence. However, they discount the treasure trove of evidence that is available to the New Testament textual scholar. Still, this should not surprise us, as the New Testament has always been under-appreciated and attacked in some way, shape, or form over the past 2,000 years.

On the contrary, in comparison to classical works, we are overwhelmed by the quantity and quality of existing New Testament manuscripts. We should also keep in mind that seventy-five percent[109] of the New Testament does not require textual scholars' help because that much of the text is unanimous, and thus, we know what it says. Of the other twenty-five percent, about twenty percent make up trivial scribal mistakes that are easily corrected. Therefore, textual criticism focuses mainly on a small portion of the New Testament text. The facts are clear: the Christian, who reads the New Testament, is fortunate to have so many manuscripts, with so many dating so close to the originals, with 500 hundred years of hundreds of textual scholars who have established the text with a level of certainty unimaginable for ancient secular works.

After discussing the amount of New Testament manuscripts available, Atheist commentator Bob Seidensticker, writes, "The first problem is that more manuscripts at best increase our confidence that we have the original version. That does not mean the original copy was history ...."[110] That is, Seidensticker is forced to acknowledge the reliability of the New Testament text as we have it today and can only try to deny what it says. He also tells us of the New Testament, "Compare that with 2000 copies of the Iliad, the second-best represented manuscript."[111] Of those 2,000 copies of the Iliad, how far removed are they from the alleged originals? The Iliad is dated to about 1260–1180 B.C.E. The most notable Iliad manuscripts are from the 9th, 10th, and 11th centuries C.E. That would make these manuscripts over 2,000 years removed from their original.

The Range of Textual Criticism

The Importance and scope of New Testament textual criticism could be summed up in the few words used by J. Harold Greenlee; it is "the basic biblical study, a prerequisite to all other biblical and theological work. Interpretation, systemization, and application of the teachings of the NT cannot be done until textual criticism has done at least some of its work. It is, therefore, deserving of the acquaintance and attention of every serious student of the Bible."[112]

---

[109] The numbers in this paragraph are rounded for simplicity purposes.

[110] 25,000 New Testament Manuscripts? Big Deal. – Patheos,

http://www.patheos.com/blogs/crossexamined/2013/11/25000-new-testament-manuscrip (Retrieved Monday, August 10, 2020).

[111] Ibid

[112] J. Harold Greenlee, Introduction to New Testament Textual Criticism (Grand Rapids, MI: Baker Academic, 1995), 8-9.

It is only reasonable to assume that the Old Testament's original 39 books and the 27 books written first-hand by the New Testament authors have not survived. Instead, we only have what we must consider being imperfect copies. **Why the Holy Spirit would miraculously inspire 66 fully inerrant texts and then allow human imperfection into the copies.** This is not explained for us in Scripture. We do know that imperfect humans have tended to worship relics where traditions hold to have been touched by the miraculous powers of God or to have been in direct contact with one of his special servants of old. Ultimately, though, all we know is that God had his reasons for allowing the Old and New Testament autographs to be worn out by repeated use. From time to time, we hear of the discovery of a fragment possibly dated to the first century, but even if such a fragment is eventually verified, the dating alone can never serve as proof of an autograph; it will still be a copy in all likelihood.

Pondering: If we ask why didn't God inspire copyists, then it will have to follow, why didn't God inspire translators, why didn't God inspire Bible scholars that author commentaries on the Bible, and so on? Suppose God's initial purpose was to give us a fully inerrant, authoritative, authentic and accurate Word. Why not adequately protect the Scriptures in all facets of transmission from error: copy, translate, and interpret? If God did this, and people were moved along by the Holy Spirit, it would soon become noticeable that when people copy the texts, they would be unable to make an error or mistake or even willfully change something.

Where would it stop? Would this being moved along by the Holy Spirit apply to anyone who decided to make themselves a copy, testing to see if they too would be inspired? In time, this would prove to be actual evidence for God. This would negate the reasons why God has allowed sin, human imperfection to enter into humanity in the first place, to teach them an **object lesson**, man cannot walk on his own without his Creator. God created perfect humans, giving them a perfect start, and through the abuse of free will, they rejected his sovereignty. He did not just keep creating perfect humans again and again, as though he got something wrong. God gave us his perfect Word and has again chosen to allow us to continue in our human imperfection, learning our **object lesson**. God has stepped into humanity many hundreds of times in the Bible record, maybe tens of thousands of times unbeknownst to us over the past 6,000+ years, to tweak things to get the desired outcome of his will and purposes. However, there is no aspect of life where his stepping in for any particular point was to be continuous until the return of the Son. Maybe God gave us a perfect copy of sixty-six books.

Then like everything else, he placed the responsibility of copying, translating, and interpreting on us, just as he gave us the Great Commission of proclaiming that Word, explaining that Word, to make disciples. – Matthew 24:14;28-19-20; Acts 1:8.

Reflecting: Some Bible critics seem, to begin with, the belief that if God inspired the originals and fully inerrant, the subsequent copies must continue to be inerrant for the inerrancy of the originals to have value. They seem to be asking, "If only the originals were inspired, and the copies were not inspired, and we do not have the originals, how are we to be certain of any passage in Scripture?" In other words, God would never allow the inspired, inerrant Word to suffer copying errors. Why would he perform the miracle of inspiring the message to be fully inerrant and not continue with the miracle of inspiring the copyists throughout the centuries to keep it inerrant? First, we must acknowledge that God has not given us the specifics of every decision he has made about humans. If we begin asking, "Why did God not do this or do that," where would it end? For example, why didn't God just produce the books himself and miraculously deliver them to people as he gave the commandments to Moses? Why not use angelic messengers to pen the message or produce the message miraculously instead of using humans? God has chosen not to tell us why he did not move the copyists along by the Holy Spirit to have perfect copies, and it remains an unknown. However, I would note that if we can restore the text to its original wording through the art and science of textual criticism, i.e., to an exact representation thereof, we have, in essence, the originals. This is the preservation of Scripture through the restoration of Scripture.

As for errors in all the copies that we have, however, we can say that the vast majority of the Greek text is not affected by errors. The errors occur in variant readings, i.e., portions of the text where different manuscripts disagree. Of the **small amount** of the text affected by variant readings, the vast majority of these are minor slips of the pen, misspelled words, etc., or intentional but quickly analyzed changes, and we are certain what the original reading is in these places. A **far smaller number** of changes present challenges to establishing the original reading. It has always been said and remains true that no central doctrine is affected by a textual problem. Only rarely does a textual issue change the meaning of a verse.[113] Still, establishing

---

[113] Leading textual scholar Daniel Wallace tells us, after looking at all of the evidence, that the percentage of instances where the reading is uncertain and a well-attested alternative reading could change the meaning of the verse is a quarter of one percent, i.e., 0.0025%

the original text wherever there are variant readings is vitally important. Every word matters!

It is true that the Jewish copyists and the later Christian copyists were not led along by the Holy Spirit, and therefore their manuscripts were not inerrant, infallible. Errors (textual variants) crept into the documents unintentionally and intentionally. However, the vast majority of the Hebrew Old Testament and Greek New Testament has not been infected with textual errors. The portions impacted by textual errors are the many tens of thousands of copies that we have to help us weed out the errors. How? Well, not every copyist made the same textual errors. Hence, by comparing the work of different copyists and manuscripts, textual scholars can identify the textual variants (errors) and remove those, leaving us with the original content.

Yes, it would be the most significant discovery of all time if we found the original five books penned by Moses himself, Genesis through Deuteronomy, or the original Gospels of Matthew, Mark, Luke, and John. However, first, there would be no way of establishing that they were the originals. Second, we do not need the originals. Third, we do not need those original documents. What is so important about the documents? It is the content on the original documents that we are after. And truly, miraculously, we have more copies than needed to do just that. We do not need miraculous preservation because we have miraculous restoration. We now know beyond a reasonable doubt that the Hebrew Old Testament and the Greek New Testament critical texts are a 99% reflection of the content in those ancient original manuscripts.

How did God inspire the Bible Authors? How Were They Moved Along by the Holy Spirit? How Did Jesus Bring Remembrance to the Apostles?

Biblical inspiration is the quality or state of being moved along or by or under the Holy Spirit's direction from God.

2 Timothy 3:16 Updated American Standard Version (UASV)	**2 Peter 1:21** Updated American Standard Version (UASV)	**John 14:26** Updated American Standard Version (UASV)
16 All Scripture is **inspired by** God and profitable for teaching, for reproof, for correction, for training in righteousness;	21 for no prophecy was ever produced by the will of man, but men **carried along by** the Holy Spirit spoke from God.	26 But the Helper,[114] the Holy Spirit, whom the Father will send in my name, that one will teach you all things and **bring to your remembrance** all that I have said to you.

How Were the Bible Authors Inspired By God, That Is, Given Divine Direction?

Inspired By θεόπνευστος (theopneustos)

The Greek phrase "inspired by God" translates the compound Greek word θεόπνευστος (theopneustos), which literally means, literally, "God-breathed" or "breathed by God." The Greek phrase here needs to be nuanced so at not to be less than what was meant or go beyond what was meant. The Bible author was under God's influence, to the extent that he was guided or directed by God but not to the extent of dictation. To a lesser extent, Christians are guided by the inspired Word of God if they have an accurate understanding and apply it correctly in their lives. The Bible author was allowed to convey God's Word within their own writing style but would be controlled or guided to the point that he would not choose words, phrases, sentences that would miscommunicate the wrong message.

Carried Along By φερόμενοι (pheromenoi)

The Greek word φερόμενοι (pheromenoi) literally means to **cause** the Bible author to be carried along or moved along by the Holy Spirit. It means to guide, direct, lead.

Bring to Remembrance ὑπομνήσει (hupomnēsei)

The Greek word ὑπομνήσει (*hupomnēsei*) literally means to God put in the mind of the Gospel authors. God **caused** the Gospel authors (Matthew and John, Mark by way of Peter, Luke by Peter, research, and others) to recall in detail what they had formerly experienced.

---

114 Or, *Advocate.* Or, *Comforter.* Gr., *ho … parakletos,* masc.

The apostle Paul says that God spoke "in many ways" to his servants in Old Testament times before Christ coming. (Heb 1:1-2) The Ten Commandments were divinely provided in written form. Scribes, thereafter, would have had to merely copy it into the scrolls used by Moses. (Ex. 31:18; Deut. 10:1-5) In some very special cases, the words put into Scripture by a Bible author inspired by God, moved along by the Holy Spirit, would have been transmitted by verbal dictation, literally word for word. This would have likely been the case in situations such as the Mosaic Law given to Israel. Jehovah commanded Moses: "**Write these words**, for in accordance with these words I have made a covenant with you and with Israel." (Ex 34:27) The prophets who would author Bible books were also frequently given precise messages from God that they were to deliver, and then God put these same words in the mind of the prophetic authors. God **caused** the prophet (Isaiah, Jeremiah, Ezekiel, Daniel, and others) to recall in detail what they had formerly delivered to others, now becoming Scriptures. – 1 Kings 22:14; Jeremiah 1:7; 2:1; 11:1-5; Ezekiel 3:4; 11:5.

There are other ways that the Bible authors, such as dreams and visions. We are told, "Then the mystery was revealed to Daniel in a **vision of the night**. Then Daniel blessed the God of heaven." (Dan. 2:19) "In the first year of Belshazzar king of Babylon, Daniel saw a **dream and visions** of his head as he lay in his bed. Then he wrote down the dream and told the sum of the matter." (Dan. 7:1) Readers might not know that Bible authors were more often given visions while they were awake, fully conscious, giving the author the thoughts of God directly to his mind. "In the thirtieth year, in the fourth month, on the fifth day of the month, as I was among the exiles by the Chebar canal, the heavens were opened, and **I saw visions** of God." (Eze 1:1) "In the third year of the reign of King Belshazzar **a vision appeared to me**, Daniel, after that which appeared to me at the first." (Dan. 8:1) "And this is how I saw the horses in **my vision** and those who rode them: they wore breastplates the color of fire and of sapphire and of sulfur, and the heads of the horses were like lions' heads, and fire and smoke and sulfur came out of their mouths." (Rev. 9:17) Other visions were given to the Bible author when he was in a trance. Even though the author was clearly awake and conscious, he was extremely, deeply absorbed by what he saw, blocking out all else around him. – Ac 10:9-17; 11:5-10; 22:17-21.

Another way Bible authors received the Word of God was through angelic messengers. "For if the word spoken through angels proved reliably certain, and every transgression and disobedience received a just penalty." (Heb 2:2) "You who received the law as delivered **by angels** and did not keep it." (Ac 7:53) "Why, then, the Law? It was added because of transgressions, until the seed should arrive to whom the promise had been made; and it was **transmitted through angels** by the hand of a mediator." (Gal. 3:19) The angelic representatives spoke in God's name. Therefore, the message they delivered could therefore correctly be called "the word of Jehovah." – Gen 22:11-12, 15-18; Zech. 1:7, 9.

Regardless of how the Bible author received the Word of God, be it, dictation, God directly putting words in the minds of the author, perfect recall, dreams, visions, angelic representatives, being led along by the Holy Spirit, it was all inspired by God or "God-breathed."

Authors evidenced individuality that is still compatible with the Bible's being inspired by God.

The Bible authors were not merely robots who put down dictated words, literally word for word. "The revelation of Jesus Christ, which God gave him to show to his servants the things that must soon take place. He made it known by sending his angel to his servant John, who bore witness to the word of God and to the testimony of Jesus Christ, even to all that he saw." (Rev. 1:1-2) The "God-breathed" revelation was given to him through an angel, which John then conveyed in his own words. Like many things, God allowed humans to use their God's given minds, and in the case of His Word, in choosing words and expressions (Hab. 2:2), he allowed them to use their own style, but he always maintained adequate control and guided them so that the Bible book would be accurate and true. In addition, it would also be according to God's will and purposes. (Prov. 30:5-6) This concept is even conveyed in Scripture itself. "Besides being wise, the Preacher also taught the people knowledge, weighing and studying and arranging many proverbs with great care. The Preacher sought to find words of delight, and uprightly he wrote words of truth." – See also Lu 1:1-4.

This is why every Bible commentary volume explains to its reader the style of that particular author and the background of the individual author. The ones chosen to be Bible authors were not only qualified to do so but had qualities and characteristics that moved God to choose them. In some cases, God likely got them ready before having to serve this particular purpose of being a Bible author. Matthew was a tax collector before being chosen as a disciple, so we note that he makes many particular references to numbers and money amounts. (Matt. 17:27; 26:15; 27:3) On the other hand, Luke was a "physician" (Col 4:14), so we find him using unique expressions that show that he had a medical background. – Lu 4:38; 5:12; 16:20.

In many cases where the Bible speaks about the Bible author receiving "the word of Jehovah" (UASV) or things that were said, it is likely that this was given, not word for word, but rather the author was given an image in his mind of God's purpose. After that, the author would put it in his own words. This can be inferred by the author's sating he 'saw' things rather than his 'hearing' what God said or "the word of Jehovah." – Isaiah 13:1; Micah 1:1; Habakkuk 1:1; 2:1-2.

The authors of God's Word express it that "God has given me the tongue of those who are taught, that I may know how to sustain with a word him who is weary. Morning by morning he awakens; he awakens my ear to hear as those who are taught. Jehovah God has opened my ear, and I was not rebellious; I turned not backward." (Isa 50:4-5) These authors were ready and submissive to being guided by God. Isaiah was eager to do God's will and sought to be led. "My soul yearns for you in the night; my spirit within me earnestly seeks you. For when your judgments are in the earth, the inhabitants of the world learn righteousness." (Isa 26:9) In the case of Luke, he had specific objectives that he sought to carry out. (Lu 1:1-4) In many cases, Paul was writing to fill a need. (1 Cor. 1:10-11; 5:1; 7:1) God guided these authors so that their words in their style went along with his purpose. (Prov. 16:9) These men were chosen because their hearts and minds were already in harmony with God's will and purposes. In fact, they already 'had the mind of Christ.' They were not interested in human wisdom nor in "speak[ing] visions of their own minds," as was the case with the false prophets, "who follow their own spirit." – 1 Corinthians 2:13-16; Jeremiah 23:16; Eze 13:2-3, 17.

As to the being led along by the Holy Spirit, "there are varieties of activities" that would come upon these Bible authors. (1 Cor 12:6) Much information was already at the fingertips of the authors. In other words, it already existed in manuscript evidence, such as genealogies and specific historical accounts. (Lu 1:3; 3:23-38; Num. 21:14, 15; 1 Kings 14:19, 29; 2 Kings 15:31; 24:5) In the case of using historical records, the Holy Spirit would serve as a protection against inaccurate information being part of the Bible author's book. Not everything said by other persons that would end up in the Word of God was inspired by God, but the Holy Spirit guided the author to make it part of the Scriptures and record it accurately. (Gen. 3:4-5; Job 42:3; Matt. 16:21-23) We end up with clear evidence of why it is good to heed God's Word and apply it correctly in our lives. Doing or saying what we think, feel, or believe, ignoring God's Word, or being ignorant of God and his message leads to much heartache.

Then, again, there is information in the Bible that is far beyond human abilities to acquire. We can consider what happened before the creation of the heavens and the earth, as well as man. (Gen. 1:1-26) Humans are also oblivious to what happens in the spiritual heavens as well. (Job 1:6-12, etc.) Then, we have prophecies that foretell events that are to take place decades, centuries, or millenniums after the prophets penned them. We also have revelations as to what God's will and purposes are for humanity. When we think of Solomon's wise sayings, he certainly had much life experience to share. Others had vast knowledge of the Scriptures themselves, not to mention their experience at living by God's Word. They still needed to be moved along by the Holy Spirit, so that the information that they conveyed would be "living and active and sharper than any two-edged sword and piercing as far as the division of soul and spirit, of both joints and marrow, and able to judge the thoughts and intentions of the heart." – Hebrews 4:12.

There are times that Paul said things that were not taken from anything that Jesus had taught. "To the rest, I say (**I, not the Lord**) that if any brother has a wife who is an unbeliever, and she consents to live with him, he should not divorce her." (1 Corinthians 7:12-15) The first thing to notice is Paul saying, God inspires me, so I can say this and the Lord (Jesus), did not touch on this, but I am. Let us take a look at the context and historical setting. Paul says, "Now concerning virgins I do not have a command from the Lord, but I am giving an opinion as one shown mercy by the Lord to be trustworthy." (1 Cor. 7:25) "But in my opinion she is happier if she remains as she is, and I think that I too have the Spirit of God." (1 Cor. 7:40) Paul's point is clear; he, too, is inspired and moved along by the Holy Spirit. Paul's direction was "God-breathed" and so was Scripture, having the same authority as the rest of those Scriptures. – 2 Peter 3:15-16.

CHAPTER 7 What Are Textual Variants and How Many Are There?

The first part of this chapter will cover the gist of what is most often discussed in New Testament textual criticism today. After that, we will discuss what should be the primary focus of NTTC (New Testament Textual Criticism). It would seem that Bart D. Ehrman and other Bible critics of his persuasion have sent many textual scholars on a quest. These scholars have become obsessed with discussing how many variants there are, how to count the textual variants, and whether they are significant or insignificant. Below, we will cover what is being said about variants and whether some are more significant than others, and then close the chapter with what actually is the most important mission in NTTC.

Some Bible critics seem, to begin with, the belief that if God inspired the originals and they were fully inerrant, the subsequent copies must continue to be inerrant for the inerrancy of the originals to have value. They seem to be asking, "If only the originals were inspired, and the copies were not inspired, and we do not have the originals, how are we to be certain of any passage in Scripture?" In other words, God would never allow the inspired, inerrant Word to suffer copying errors. Why would he perform the miracle of inspiring the message to be fully inerrant and not continue with the miracle of inspiring the copyists throughout the centuries to keep it inerrant? First, we must acknowledge that God has not given us the specifics of every decision he has made in reference to humans. If we begin asking, "Why did God not do this or do that," where would it end? For example, why didn't God just produce the books himself and miraculously deliver them to people as he gave the commandments to Moses? Instead of using humans, why did he not use angelic messengers to pen the message, or produce the message miraculously? God has chosen not to tell us why he did not move the copyists along with the Holy Spirit, so as to have perfect copies, and it remains an unknown. However, it should be noted that if we can restore the text to its original wording through the science of textual criticism, i.e. to an exact representation thereof, we have, in essence, the originals.

We do know that the Jewish copyists and later Christian copyists were not infallible as were the original writers. The Holy Spirit inspired the original writers, while the most that can be said about the copyists is that the Holy

Spirit **guided** them. However, do we not have a treasure-load of evidence from centuries of copies, unlike ancient secular literature? Regardless of the recopying, do we not have the Bible in a reliable critical text and trustworthy translations, with both improving all the time? It was only inevitable that imperfect copyists, who were not under inspiration, would cause errors to creep into the text. However, the thousands of copies that we have enable textual scholars to identify and reject these errors. How? For one thing, different copyists made different errors. Therefore, the textual scholar compares the work of different copyists. He is then able to identify their mistakes.

A Simple Example

Suppose 100 people were invited or hired to make a handwritten copy of Matthew's Gospel, with 18,345 words. Further, suppose that these people fit in one of four categories as writers: **(1)** struggle to write and have no experience as a document maker; **(2)** skilled document makers (recorders of events, wills, business, certificates, etc.); **(3)** trained copyists of literature; and **(4)** the professional copyists. There is little doubt that these copyists would make some copying errors, even the professionals. However, it would be impossible that they would all make the same errors. Suppose a trained textual scholar with many years of religious education, including textual studies and decades of experience, was to compare the 100 documents carefully. In that case, he could identify the errors and restore the text to its original form, even if he had never seen that original.

The textual scholars of the last 250 years, especially the last 70 years, have had 5,000+ and now over 5,898 Greek manuscripts at their disposal. A number of the manuscripts are portions dating to the second and third centuries C.E. Moreover, more manuscripts are always becoming known; technology is ever advancing, and improvements are always being made.

Hundreds of scholars throughout the last three centuries have produced what we might call a master text through lifetimes of hard work and careful study. Are there places where we are not certain of the reading? Yes, of course. However, we are considering very infrequent places in the Greek NT text containing about 138,020 words, which would be considered difficult to arrive at what the original reading was. In all these places, the alternative readings are provided in the apparatus. Bible critics who exaggerate the extent of errors are misleading the public on several fronts. First, some copies are almost error-free and negate the critics, who claim, "We have only error-ridden copies."[115] Second, the vast majority of the Greek New Testament has no scribal errors. Third, textual scholarship can easily identify and correct the majority of the scribal errors. In addition, of the remaining errors, we can still say most are solved with satisfaction. Of the small number of scribal errors remaining, we can say that most are solved with some difficulty, and there remain very few errors of which textual scholarship continues to be uncertain about the original reading at this time.

400,000 to 500,000 Supposed Variants in the Manuscripts

With this abundance of evidence, what can we say about the total number of variants known today? Scholars differ significantly in their estimates—some say there are 200,000 variants known, some say 300,000, some say **400,000 or more!** We do not know for sure because, despite impressive developments in computer technology, no one has yet been able to count them all. Perhaps, as I indicated earlier, it is best simply to leave the matter in comparative terms. There are more variations among our manuscripts than there are words in the New Testament.[116]

Bart D. Ehrman has some favorite, unprofessional ways of describing the problems, which he stresses without qualification, in every interview he has for a lay audience or seminary students. Below are several, the first two from the quotation above:

- Scholars differ significantly in their estimates—some say there are 200,000 variants known, some say 300,000, some say **400,000 or more!**

- There are **more variations** among our manuscripts **than there are words** in the New Testament.

- We have only **error-ridden copies,** and the vast majority of these are centuries removed from the originals and different from them, evidently, in thousands of ways. (*Whose Word is It,* 7)

- We don't even have copies of the copies of the originals, or **copies of the copies of the copies of the originals.** (*Misquoting Jesus,* 10)

---

[115] (Bart D. Ehrman, Misquoting Jesus: The Story Behind Who Changed the Bible and Why 2005, 7)

[116] Ibid., 89-90

- **In the early Christian centuries, scribes were amateurs** and as such were more inclined to alter the texts they copied. (*Misquoting Jesus*, 98)

- **We could go on nearly forever** talking about specific places in which the texts of the New Testament came to be changed, either accidentally or intentionally. (*Misquoting Jesus*, 98)

- The Bible began to appear to me as a very **human book**. (*Misquoting Jesus*, 11)

Each of the bullet points above claimed by Ehrman can be categorized as an exaggeration, misinformation, misleading, or just a failure to be truthful. Many laypersons-churchgoers have been spiritually shipwrecked in their faith by such unexplained hype. What the uninformed person hears is that we can never get back to the originals or even close, that there are hundreds of thousands of significant variants that have so scarred the text, we no longer have the Word of God, and it is merely the word of man. How such a knowledgeable man cannot know the impact his words are having is beyond this author.

Miscounting Textual Variants

In 1963, Neil R. Lightfoot penned a book that has served to help over a million readers, *How We Got the Bible*. It has been revised two times since 1963, once in 1988, and again in 2003. There is a "miscalculation" in the book which has contributed to a misunderstanding in how textual variants are counted. In fact, there are several other books repeating it. A leading textual scholar, Daniel B. Wallace, has brought this to our attention in an article entitled, *The Number of Textual Variants an Evangelical Miscalculation*.[117] World-renowned Bible apologist Norman L. Geisler has commented on it as well.

Lightfoot wrote,

From one point of view, it may be said that there are 200,000 scribal errors in the manuscripts. Indeed, the number may well considerably exceed this and obviously will grow, as more and more manuscripts become known. However, it is wholly misleading and untrue to say that there are 200,000 errors in the text of the New Testament. (Actually, textual critics consciously

---

[117] http://bible.org/article/number-textual-variants-evangelical-miscalculation

avoid the word "error;" they prefer to speak of "textual variants.") This large number is gained by counting all the variations in all of the manuscripts (5,898). This means that if, for example, one word is misspelled in 4,000 different manuscripts, and it amounts to 4,000 "errors." Actually, in a case of this kind, only one slight error has been made, and it has been copied 4,000 times. But this is the procedure which is followed in arriving at the large number of 200,000 "errors."[118]

Wallace makes this observation in his article:

In other words, Lightfoot was claiming that textual variants are counted by the number of manuscripts that support such variants, rather than by the wording of the variants. This book has been widely influential in evangelical circles. I believe over a million copies of it have been sold. And this particular definition of textual variants has found its way into countless apologetic works." He goes on to clarify just what a textual variant is, "The problem is, the definition is wrong. Terribly wrong. A textual variant is simply any difference from a standard text (e.g., a printed text, a particular manuscript, etc.) that involves spelling, word order, omission, addition, substitution, or a total rewrite of the text. No textual critic defines a textual variant the way that Lightfoot and those who have followed him have done.

Geisler writes,

Some have estimated there are about 200,000 of them. First of all, these are not "errors" but variant readings, the vast majority of which are strictly grammatical. Second, these readings are spread throughout more than 5300 manuscripts, so that a variant spelling of one letter of one word in one verse in 2000 manuscripts is counted as 2000 "errors."[119]

Lightfoot evidently was thought to have erred by counting manuscripts rather than the variants in the text. In fairness to Lightfoot, it should be pointed out that he deplored the system of counting "errors" by the number of manuscripts, as the quotation above reveals. He was simply saying that critics were doing this, not that it was proper. It is difficult to see why Wallace

---

[118] *How We Got the Bible* (Grand Rapids: Baker, 2003; p). Lightfoot says (53-54)

[119] *Baker Encyclopedia of Christian Apologetics*, by Norm Geisler (Grand Rapids: Baker, 1998; p. 532)

would attribute responsibility for the system to Lightfoot. Also, Wallace cited Lightfoot's 1963 edition that did not include the distinction between "error" and "textual variant."

Let me offer the reader an example for our purposes. First, we should underscore a few important points raised: 1) we have so many variants because we have so many manuscripts. 2) We do *not* count the manuscripts; we count the variants. 3) A variant is any portion of the text that exhibits variations in its reading between two or more different manuscripts. This is more precisely called a **variation unit**. It is important to distinguish variation units from variant readings. Variation units are the places in the text where manuscripts disagree, and each variation unit has at least two variant readings. Setting the limits and range of a variation unit is sometimes difficult or even controversial because some variant readings affect others nearby. Such variations may be considered individually or as elements of a longer single reading.

We should also note that the terms "manuscript" and "witness" may appear to be used interchangeably in this context. Strictly speaking, "witness" (see below) only refers to the content of a given manuscript or fragment, so the witness predates the physical manuscript on which it is written to a greater or lesser extent. However, the only way to reference the "witness" is by referring to the manuscript or fragment that contains it. In this book, we have sometimes used the terminology "witness *of* x or y manuscript" to distinguish the content in this way.

We begin by choosing our "base" or "standard text." We are primarily using the *standard text* (critical or master text), **N**estle-Aland (NA) Greek Text (28th edition), and the **U**nited Bible Society (UBS) Greek Text (5th edition). These two critical texts are the same. However, we also include the 1881 **W**estcott and **H**ort (WH) critical text. Therefore,

Note: When the acronym **NU** is used, **N** stands for **N**estle-Aland, the **U** for **U**nited Bible Societies, since the texts are the same. The apparatuses are different, and the UBS version is designed primarily for translators (more on this below). The acronym **WH** is for Westcott and Hort Greek text. Here is another opportunity to emphasize the documentary approach in making textual decisions, which is shown in the fact that about 155 variant decisions were made by the editors of the NU text when the preferred reading is found in the WH text. When we consider the WH NU texts, we can argue that we have a critical text that is a 99.99% reflection of the original.

In this writer's opinion, the critical WH NU texts are as close as we can get to what the original would have been like.[120] Therefore, we can use the reading in the critical text as the original reading, and anything outside of that in the manuscript history is a variant: spelling, word order, omission, addition, substitution, or a total rewrite of the text. Any difference in two different manuscripts is a variant, technically speaking.

Before going to our example, I want to emphasize that Bible critics, who grumble and repeat over and over again how there are 400,000+ variants in the text of the New Testament, have only one agenda: they want to discredit the Word of God. They use the issue of variants as a misrepresented excuse for their having lost their faith, having shipwrecked their faith, or having had no faith from the start. These Bible critics are no different from the religious leaders Jesus dealt with in the first century. Jesus said of them, "Blind guides! You strain out a gnat yet gulp down a camel!" (Matt. 23:24). They thrust aside 99.99 percent because 0.01 of one percent is not absolutely certain! Now let's turn to our example, which comes from the Apostle Paul's letter to the Colossians.

Example of a Textual Variant

Colossians 2:2 Updated American Standard Version (UASV)

² that their hearts may be comforted, having been knit together in love, and into all riches of the full assurance of understanding, and that they may have a complete knowledge[121] of the mystery **of God**, namely **Christ**, [τοῦ θεοῦ Χριστοῦ; tou theou Christou]

See the chart below.

---

[120] It is true that some scholars, such as Philip Comfort, argue that the NU could be improved upon because in many cases it is too dependent on internal evidence, when the documentary evidence should be more of a consideration in choosing readings. It should be pointed out, however, that this is in only a relative handful of places, when one considers 138,020 words in the Greek New Testament, and it is hardly consequential. I would also mention that this writer would agree with Comfort in the matter of giving more weight to documentary evidence.

[121] *Epignosis* is a strengthened or intensified form of *gnosis* (*epi,* meaning "additional"), meaning, "true," "real," "full," "complete" or "accurate," depending upon the context. Paul and Peter alone use *epignosis.*

Variants	Variant	MSS or Versions
NU[122]	of the God of Christ	Standard Text
1	of the God	10 MSS[123]
2	of the Christ	1 MS
3	of the God who is Christ	4 MSS
4	of the God who is concerning Christ	2 MSS
5	Of the God in the Christ	2 MSS
6	of the God in the Christ Jesus	1 MS
7	of the God and Christ	1 MS
8	Of God the father Christ	4 MSS
9	Of God the father of Christ	5 MSS
10	Of God and Father of Christ	2 MSS
11	Of God father and of Christ	4 MSS
12	Of God father and of Christ Jesus	3 MSS
13	Of God father and of Lord of us Christ Jesus	2 MSS
14	Of God and father and of Christ	38 MSS
Total 14	**14 Variants in 79 MSS**	**79 MSS**

These variants are found in 79 MSS. Thus, we have 14 variants in 79 manuscripts, not 79 variants. We do not count manuscripts, as most textual scholars know. In trying to paint a picture about the trustworthiness of the text, this author does not think talking about variants is really helpful, and it can confuse the layperson. The churchgoer needs to know what a variant is and the general extent of the variants, but in the long run, it is the places in the text that are affected by variants that most matter and what we have as our text in the end.

The United Bible Society's "A" "B" "C" and "D" ratings are fine, and the definitions by UBS, i.e., [A] **certain**, [B] **almost certain**, [C] **difficulty in deciding**, and [D] **great difficulty in arriving at**, are helpful but should be

---

[122] Recall that NU is an acronym for two critical manuscripts: (1) Nestle-Aland Greek Text (28th ed.) and (2) United Bible Societies Greek Text (5th ed.)

[123] This is only a partial list of the manuscripts, as we are just offering an example, to see how we count the variants.

better qualified, with some numbers of what percentage of the text fall under each area.

All Variant Units (Places)

What we need to talk about is how many **places** there are where we find variants. What percentage is this of the entire New Testament text?

We can then discuss:

- What percentage of the text is untouched by variants?

- Of the percentage affected, how much can we say or surmise to be given an "A" rating, a "B" Rating, a "C," or "D" rating?

Variant Reading and Variation Unit

This section is based in large part on the work by Eldon Jay Epp and Gordon D. Fee, *Studies in the Theory and Method of New Testament Textual Criticism* (Grand Rapids, MI: Eerdmans, 1993), wherein Eldon J. Epp expands on the brief 1964 article of Ernest C. Colwell (1901–74) and Ernest W. Tune on "Variant Readings: Classification and Use."

Again, we need to discuss how many variation units (places) there are where we find variations. Before doing so, let us define some terms.

SIGNIFICANT AND INSIGNIFICANT READINGS AND OR VARIANTS: Below, we have what are commonly described as significant and insignificant variants. *Significant* would mean any reading that has an impact on the transmission history of a variant unit. For example, it would apply to how we determine the relationship of the manuscripts to one another, such as where a particular manuscript would fall in the history and transmission of the manuscripts. It would also be impactful if the reading could help the textual scholar establish the original. Therefore, *insignificant* would mean just the opposite, referring to a reading with very little to no impact in *many* aspects of a transmission history. We stop at "many" aspects here because all readings in a manuscript play a role in some aspects of the transmission history, such as the characteristics of the manuscript it is in and the scribal activity within that individual manuscript.

Insignificant—Nonsense Reading: As Epp points out, a nonsense reading is "a reading that fails to make sense because it cannot be construed grammatically, either in terms of grammatical/lexical form or in terms of grammatical structure, or because in some other way it lacks a recognizable meaning. Since authors and scribes do not produce nonsense intentionally, it is to be assumed (1) that nonsense readings resulted from errors in transmission, (2) that they, therefore, cannot represent either the original text or the intended text of any MS or alert scribe, and (3) that they do not aid in the process of discerning the relationships among MSS."[124] It should also be stated that the original did not contain any nonsense readings, as the Holy Spirit led the writers. Before publication, the inspired author would have corrected any error by a scribe such as Tertius or Silvanus.

Insignificant—Certainty of Scribal Errors: while these errors "can be construed grammatically and make sense," there is a certainty on the part of textual scholars that these are scribal errors. These are not nonsense readings but rather readings that make sense, which are scribal errors beyond all reasonable doubt. These would "be certain instances of haplography and dittography, cases of harmonization with similar contexts, hearing errors producing a similar-sounding word, and the transposition of letters or words with a resultant change in meaning."[125] The problem that we sometimes encounter here is that what may be listed as a *certainty* of the scribal error to one scholar may instead be an *almost certainty* to another, and even less so to another. The key element here in determining a reading that is understandable as insignificant is that it can be "demonstrated" so by the scholar making such a claim.

Insignificant—Incorrect Orthography (Greek for "correct writing"): this term is used loosely to refer to the spelling of words, which (for Greek) can include breathing and accent marks. Thus, one can refer to variations in the orthography of a word or even to incorrect orthography. When a variation in orthography is due merely to dialectical or historical changes in spelling for variant readings, the variations are often ignored in the decision process because the reading in question is identical to another reading, once the orthographical differences are factored in (*mutatis mutandis*). Epp writes, "Mere orthographic differences, particularly itacisms and nu-movables (as well as abbreviations) are 'insignificant' as here defined; they cannot be utilized in any decisive way for establishing manuscript relationships, and they are not substantive in the search for the original text. Again, the exception might be the work of a slavish scribe, whose scrupulousness might

---

[124] Eldon Jay Epp and Gordon D. Fee, *Studies in the Theory and Method of New Testament Textual Criticism* (Grand Rapids, MI: Eerdmans, 1993), 58.

[125] Ibid. 58.

be considered useful in tracing manuscript descent, but the pervasive character of itacism, for example, over wide areas and time-spans precludes the 'significance' of orthographic differences for this important text-critical task."[126]

Insignificant—Singular Readings: a singular reading is technically a variant reading that occurs only once in only one Greek manuscript and is therefore immediately suspect. There is some quibbling over this because critics who reject the Westcott and Hort position on the combination of 01 (Sinaiticus) and 03 (Vaticanus) might call a reading "nearly singular" if it has only the support of these two manuscripts. Moreover, it is understood that not all manuscripts are comparable. Thus, for example, one would comfortably reject a reading found only in a single late manuscript, while many critics would not find it so easy to reject a reading supported uniquely by 03. Some also give more credit to singular readings that have additional support from versions. Singular readings that are insignificant would be nonsense readings, transcriptional errors, meaningless transpositions, and itacisms.

Significant Variants: a *significant* reading/variant is any reading that has an impact on any major facet of the transmission history of a variant unit. One approach to identifying these is to remove the insignificant variants first: nonsense readings, determined (without doubt) scribal errors, incorrect orthography, and singular readings. Those readings that cannot be ruled out in this process are probably significant.

Number of Variants, Significant and Insignificant Variants vs. Level of Certainty

It would seem that some scholars have lost sight of the most important goal of textual criticism, namely, reconstructing the original. There is little doubt that agnostic Bible scholar Dr. Bart D. Ehrman has led the conversation on how many textual variants exist. The author of this publication is focusing their attention on the initial goal of textual criticism, returning to the original. We believe that even now, the Greek New Testament is entirely reliable. However, some 2,000 textual places within the New Testament need to be dealt with because the witnesses and internal evidence require consideration and deliberation.

---

[126] Ibid. 58.

Level of Certainty

The level of certainty charts below is generated from A TEXTUAL COMMENTARY ON THE GREEK NEW TESTAMENT (Second Edition), A Companion Volume to the UNITED BIBLE SOCIETIES' GREEK NEW TESTAMENT (Fourth Revised Edition) by Bruce M. Metzger.

The letter **{A}** signifies that the text is certain.

The letter **{B}** indicates that the text is almost certain.

The letter **{C}** indicates that the Committee had difficulty in deciding which variant to place in the text.

The letter **{D}**, which occurs only rarely, indicates that the Committee had great difficulty in arriving at a decision. In fact, among the **{D}** decisions sometimes none of the variant readings commended itself as original, and therefore the only recourse was to print the least unsatisfactory reading.

The Greek-English New Testament Interlinear (GENTI), Produced by Christian Publishing House, Cambridge, Ohio seeks to make a notable addition to the Greek-English Interlinear family by providing a text of the Greek New Testament that is based on the most recent research and is grounded in the earliest manuscript witnesses, to ascertain the original wording of the original texts.

TERMS AS TO HOW WE SHOULD OBJECTIVELY VIEW THE DEGREE OF CERTAINTY FOR THE READING ACCEPTED AS THE ORIGINAL by GENTI[127]

The modal verbs are *might* have been (30%), *may* have been (40%), *could* have been (55%), *would* have been (80%), *must* have been (95%), which are used to show that we believe the originality of a reading is certain, probable or possible.

The letter **[WP]** stands for **Weak Possibility (30%)**, which indicates that this is low-level proof that the reading *might have been* original in that it is enough evidence to accept that the variant *might have been possible*, but it is improbable. We can say the reading **might** have been original, as there is *some evidence* that is derived from manuscripts that carry very little weight, early versions, or patristic quotations.

---

[127] https://christianpublishinghouse.co/greek-english-interlinear/

The letter **[P]** stands for **Plausible (40%)**, which indicates that this is low-level proof that the reading *may have been* original in that it is enough to accept a variant to be original, and we have enough evidence for our belief. The reading **may have** been original but is probably not so.

The letter **[PE]** stands for **Preponderance of Evidence (55%)**, which indicates that this is a higher-level proof that the reading *could have been* original in that it is enough to accept as such *unless another reading emerges as more probable.*

The letter **[CE]** stands for **Convincing Evidence (80%)**, which indicates that the evidence is an even higher-level proof that the reading *surely* was the original in that the evidence is enough to accept it as substantially *certain* unless proven otherwise.

The letter **[BRD]** stands for **Beyond Reasonable Doubt (95%)**, which indicates that this is the highest level of proof: the reading **must have been** original in that *there is no reason to doubt it.* It must be understood that feeling as though we *have no reason to doubt* is not the same as one hundred percent absolute certainty.

NOTE: This system is borrowed from the criminal just legal terms of the United States of America, the level of certainty involved in the use of modal verbs, and Bruce Metzger in his A Textual Commentary on the Greek New Testament (London; New York: United Bible Societies, 1994), who borrowed his system from Johann Albrecht Bengel in his edition of the Greek New Testament (Tübingen, 1734). **In addition**, the percentages are in no way attempting to be explicit, but instead, they are nothing more than a tool to give the non-textual scholar a sense of the degree of certainty. However, this does not mean the percentages are not reflective of the certainty.

The word count below is taken from the Nestle-Aland Novum Testamentum Graece using Logos Bible Software.[128] While this author has compiled the numbers regarding the level of certainty of readings from Metzger's Textual Commentary, he has not gone to the point of counting the letters or words at each variant place. We will just offer the reader the general statement that almost all textual variants in the commentary were based on a letter or a few letters in a Greek word, to two-three words. Seldom was it an entire sentence or verse, very rarely several verses like the long ending of

---

[128] Word Counts for Every Book of the Bible ..., http://overviewbible.com/word-counts-books-of-bible/ (accessed April 20, 2017).

Mark. Therefore, we have chosen three words as the average to multiply the total number of variants so that the reader can see the truly small number of variants that are even worthy of consideration instead of the total number of words in the New Testament. For example, Matthew has 18,346 words with a mere 153 places where we find variants selected for the GNT, affecting about 459 words.

We need to add and emphasize that the GNT editors selected all of the variants counted as relevant for translation, and the total does not include other variant units that were not considered relevant for that purpose. A good number of these additional variants can be found in the NA apparatus, but only with considerable difficulty in many cases because the same variants are frequently handled differently in the GNT and NA apparatuses. The author of this book does consider all variant units relevant even if a good number of them are difficult or virtually impossible to represent in translation (depending on the target language). We recommend that the reader adjust the figures offered below by multiplying the numbers of variants by a factor of two, which should compensate for any variants that are not reported in the GNT text. We see no reason to assume a significantly different outcome in the ratings that might have been assigned to these variants if they had been included in the GNT, except possibly where no decisions might be possible in the cases of competing readings that were fully acceptable (rather than difficult).

For readers who have a working knowledge of NT Greek, it may be informative simply to select a few random pages of corresponding text from the GNT and NA and compare the apparatuses to see what is missing from the GNT relative to the NA apparatus. We believe that our suggestion of multiplying the variant figures below by a factor of two will appear more than reasonable; however, even using a factor of three or four will still leave a relatively minute percentage of "C" and "D" readings, as revealed below.

So then, if we look at Matthew and first multiply the GNT variant units by three for an average of three words a variant, we have 459 words. Of the 153 variant units found in Matthew, we are certain of about 32 of them, almost certain about 70, have a little difficulty deciding on 50, and great difficulty deciding on only one variant unit. When we say that we have difficulty deciding, this does not mean that we cannot decide as we can. Moreover, a good translation will list the alternative reading in a footnote. So, in the entirety of the Gospel of Matthew, there is only one variant place (Matt 23:26) which we would count as about three out of 18,346 words, where there was great difficulty in deciding the original. As it turns out, in this case, the

GNT apparatus handles it as a variant of eight words, while NA breaks it into two variants, thus illustrating our point about the difficulty of comparing the two apparatuses. Some translations have incorporated the variant (ESV, NASB, NIV, TNIV, NJB, and the NLT), viewing it as the original, while other translations (NRSV, NEB, REB, NAB, CSB, and the UASV) see the variant as an addition taken from the previous verse.

Matthew 23:26 Blind Pharisee, cleanse first the inside of the cup,[129] so that the outside of it may also become clean. (UASV)

NU has καθάρισον πρῶτον τὸ ἐντὸς τοῦ ποτηρίου, ἵνα γένηται καὶ τὸ ἐκτὸς αὐτοῦ καθαρόν "first cleanse the **inside of the cup, that the outside** of it may also become clean," which is supported by D Θ f¹ itᵃ,ᶜ syrˢ (bold mine).

Variant/Byz WH καθαρισον πρωτον το εντος του ποτηριου και της παροψιδος ινα γενηται και το εκτος αυτων καθαρον have "first cleanse the **inside of the cup [and the dish], that the outside** of them may also become clean," which is supported by א (B²) C L W 0102 0281 Maj.

Looking at the above support alone, it would seem that the witnesses for the longer reading ("and the dish") are weightier, making the longer reading the likely original. Then, when we consider the presence of a few manuscripts (B* f¹³ 28 al) that are not listed for the shorter reading because they have the longer reading ("and the dish"), the weight shifts over to the shorter reading's being the original. Why? Because these few manuscripts have the singular αυτου instead of αὐτῶν, even though they have the longer reading. This tells us that the archetype text was the shorter reading. Clearly, the copyist added ("and the dish") from the previous verse, Matthew 23:25, which reads, "Woe to you, scribes and Pharisees, hypocrites! because you cleanse **the outside of the cup and of the dish**, but inside they are full of greediness and self-indulgence."

Below, we will look at all of the numbers, the total words in the Greek New Testament, the number of A, B, C, and D variants in each book as they were selected by the GNT committee, followed by the total number of variants listed in Metzger's textual commentary.

---

[129] The NU (D Θ f¹ itᵃ,ᶜ syrˢ) has the above reading. A variant, WH and Byz (א (B²) C L W 0102 0281 Maj) add "and of the dish." The variant is an addition taken from the previous verse.

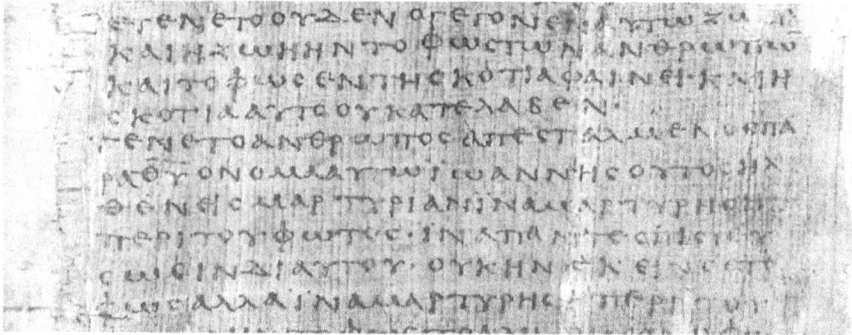

The Entire New Testament (138,020 Words)

{A-D}	New Testament
{A}	505
{B}	523
{C}	354
{D}	10
Total Var.	1,392
Words	138,020

The Gospels (64,767 Words)

{A-D}	Matt	Mark	Luke	John
{A}	32	45	44	44
{B}	70	49	73	62
{C}	50	45	44	41
{D}	1	1	0	2
Total Var.	153	140	161	149
Words	18,346	11,304	19,482	15,635

The Acts of the Apostles (18,450 Words)

{A-D}	Acts
{A}	74
{B}	82
{C}	40
{D}	1
Total Var.	197
Words	18,450

Paul's Fourteen Epistles (37,361 Words)

{A-D}	Rom	1 Cor	2 Cor	Gal.	Eph.	Php	Col.
{A}	39	21	12	16	16	10	8
{B}	19	22	17	3	11	7	12
{C}	20	15	10	8	7	3	8
{D}	1	1	0	0	0	0	0
Total Var.	79	59	39	27	34	20	28
WORDS	7,111	6,830	4,477	2,230	2,422	1,629	1,582

{A-D}	1 Th	2 Th	1 Tim	2 Tim	Tit	Phm.	Heb.
{A}	9	3	15	2	2	2	20
{B}	2	3	2	6	1	3	11
{C}	3	2	2	1	1	0	12
{D}	0	0	0	0	0	0	0
Total Var.	14	8	19	9	4	5	43
WORDS	1,481	823	1,591	1,238	659	335	4,953

The General Epistles (7,591 Words)

{A-D}	Jam	1 Pet	2 Pet	1 Jn	2 Jn	3 Jn	Jude
{A}	7	21	8	18	4	1	9
{B}	12	9	7	7	1	1	0
{C}	4	7	6	4	0	0	3
{D}	0	0	1	0	0	0	1

Total Var.	23	37	22	29	5	2	13
WORDS	1,742	1,684	1,099	2,141	245	219	461

The Book of Revelation (9,851 Words)

{A-D}	Revelation
{A}	23
{B}	31
{C}	18
{D}	1
Total Var.	73
Words	9,851

As noted above, the author of this publication maintains that all variation units or places where variations occur are significant because we are dealing with the Word of God, and reconstructing the original wording is of the utmost importance. Recall Lightfoot once more. "What about the significance of these variations? Are these variations immaterial, or are they important? What bearing do they have on the New Testament message and on faith? To respond to these questions, it will be helpful to introduce three types of textual variations, classified in relation to their significance for our present New Testament text. 1. Trivial variations which are of no consequence to the text. 2. Substantial variations which are of no consequence to the text. 3. Substantial variations that have a bearing on the text."[130]

Whether we are talking about the addition or omission of such words as "for," "and," and "the," or different forms of similar Greek words, differences in spelling, or the addition of a whole verse or even several verses, the importance lies **not with the significance of the impact** on the meaning of the text but rather **the certainty** of the wording in the original. What we want to focus on is the certainty level of reconstructing every single word that Matthew, Mark, Luke, John, Paul, Peter, James, and Jude penned.

We will use Lightfoot's example of Matthew 11:10-23, that is, fourteen verses of 231 words; we have eleven variants in verses 10, 15, 16, 17, 18, 19(2), 20, 21, and 23(2). This may seem worrisome to the churchgoer or

---

[130] *How We Got the Bibles*, by Neil R. Lightfoot (Grand Rapids: Baker, 1998; p. 95-103)

someone new to textual criticism. However, while all variants are found in the NA28 critical apparatus (2012), pp. 31–32,[131] the following sources below only covered seven of them because four are not even an issue. Why are they not an issue? We know what the original reading is with absolute certainty. The seven that have some uncertainty are mentioned in the textual commentaries below.

- Comfort *New Testament Text and Translation* covers verses 15 and 19

- Comfort *Commentary on the Manuscripts* and Text *of the New Testament* covers verses 12 and 19

- Metzger's *Textual Commentary on the Greek New Testament* covers 15, 17, 19, and 23.

Immediately we need to note that verse 12 is absolutely certain as to the original words as well. Verse 19a is mentioned in Comfort's textual commentary because he is drawing attention to the "Son of Man" being written as a nomen sacrum ("sacred name" that is abbreviated) in two early manuscripts (‭א‬ W), as well as in L. Therefore, verse 19a is absolutely certain as well. We are now down to five variants. The original readings of verses 15, 17, 19a and the two in verse 23 where variants occur are almost certain. The committee's textual scholars for four leading semi-literal and literal translations (ESV, LEB, CSB, and the NASB) agree on ten of the eleven variants. There is disagreement on **Matthew 11:15**. Even so, the reader has access to the original and alternatives in the footnote.

"He who has ears to hear, let him hear." (ESV, NASB, UASV)

The variant is ο εχων ωτα ακουειν ακουετω "the one having ears to hear let him hear," which is supported by ‭א‬ C L W Z Θ f[1,13] 33 Maj syr[c,h,p] cop

"The one who has ears to hear, let him hear!" (LEB, cf. CSB)

WH and NU have ὁ ἔχων ὦτα ἀκουέτω "the one having ears let him hear," which is supported by B D 700 it[k] syr[s]

As is usually the case in more difficult decisions, the variant readings are divided in their support between the leading Alexandrian manuscripts. One

---

[131] Eberhard Nestle and Erwin Nestle, *Nestle-Aland: NTG Apparatus Criticus*, ed. Barbara Aland et al., 28. revidierte Auflage. (Stuttgart: Deutsche Bibelgesellschaft, 2012), 31–32.

reading has 01 (Sinaiticus) on its side, the other has 03 (Vaticanus). This tends to cancel out the weight of documentary evidence.

Now, we return to the charts above. There are 138,020 words in the New Testament. Just 1,392 textual variants deemed relevant for translation have enough of an issue to even be considered in the textual commentary. Again, if we average three words per variant, this amounts only to about 3.026 percent of the 138,020 words, or about 6 percent when we compensate for variant units ignored by the GNT editors. We can also remove the 505 {A} ratings because they are certain. Then, we really have no concerns about the {B} ratings because they are almost certain as well. This means that out of 138,020 words in the Greek New Testament, we only have 364 variants (1,092 words by our average) with which we have difficulty, a mere 10 of which involve great difficulty in deciding which reading to put in the text. Our average would make these variants 0.791 percent of the text without accounting for any difficult variants not included because they were considered irrelevant for translation.

We need not be disturbed or distracted by worries of how many variants there are, or whether they are significant or insignificant. We need only to deal with the certainty of each variation unit, endeavoring to determine the original reading. We should also be concerned with the role textual criticism plays in apologetics. There is no possibility of apologetics if we do not have an authoritative and true Word of God. J. Harold Greenlee was correct when he wrote, "Textual criticism is the basic study for the accurate knowledge of any text. New Testament textual criticism, therefore, is the basic biblical study, a prerequisite to all other biblical and theological work. Interpretation, systemization, and application of the teachings of the NT cannot be done until textual criticism has done at least some of its work."[132] We would add apologetics to that list for which textual criticism is a prerequisite. How are we to defend the Word of God as inspired, inerrant, true, and authoritative if we do not know whether we even have the Word of God? Therefore, when Bible critics try to muddy the waters of truth with misinformation, it is up to the textual scholar to correct the Bible critic's misinformation.

Again, it is true that Lightfoot erred if he was counting the manuscripts instead of the variants. However, we need not count variants either but rather variation units, namely, the places where there are variations. The above Colossians 2:2 example of variations that are found in 79 manuscripts was

---

[132] *Introduction to New Testament Textual Criticism*, by J. Harold Greenlee (Peabody: Hendrickson Publishers, 1995; p. 7)

seen to have 14 variants in 79 manuscripts, not 79 variants. While this is true, it is also true that this is simply one variation unit, i.e., one place, where a variation occurs. This may sound as though we are trying to rationalize a major problem of hundreds of thousands of variants. However, it is actually the other way around. The Bible critic is misrepresenting the facts, trying to talk about an issue without giving the reader or listener all of the facts. We need to consider Benjamin Disraeli's words on statistics: "There are three types of lies: lies, damn lies, and statistics."

The Certainty of the Original Words of the Original Authors

Virgil (70-19 B.C.E.) wrote the *Aeneid* between 29 and 19 B.C.E. for which only five manuscripts are dating to the fourth and fifth centuries C.E.[133] Jewish historian Josephus (37-100 C.E.) wrote *The Jewish Wars* about 75 C.E., for which we have nine complete manuscripts, seven of major importance dating from the tenth to the twelfth centuries C.E.[134] Tacitus (59-129 C.E.) wrote *Annals of Imperial Rome* sometime before 116 C.E., a work considered vital to understanding the history of the Roman Empire during the first century, and we have only thirty-three manuscripts, two of the earliest that date 850 and 1050 C.E. Julius Caesar (100-44 B.C.E.) wrote his Gallic Wars between 51-46 B.C.E.,[135] which is a firsthand account in a third-person narrative of the war, of which we have 251 manuscripts dating between the ninth and fifteenth centuries.[136]

---

[133] Preface | Dickinson College Commentaries. (April 25, 2017) http://dcc.dickinson.edu/vergil-aeneid/manuscripts

[134] Honora Howell Chapman (Editor), Zuleika Rodgers (Editor), 2016, A *Companion to Josephus* (Blackwell Companions to the Ancient World), Wiley-Blackwell: p. 307.

[135] Carolyn Hammond, 1996, Introduction to *The Gallic War*, Oxford University Press: p. xxxii.

Max Radin, 1918, The date of composition of Caesar's Gallic War, *Classical Philology* XIII: 283–300.

[136] O. Seel, 1961, *Bellum Gallicum*. (Bibl. Teubneriana.) Teubner, Leipzig.

W. Hering, 1987, *C. Iulii Caesaris commentarii rerum gestarum, Vol. I: Bellum Gallicum.* (Bibl. Teubneriana.) Teubner, Leipzig.

Virginia Brown, 1972, *The Textual Transmission of Caesar's Civil War*, Brill.

Caesar's Gallic war - Tim Mitchell. (April 25, 2017) http://www.timmitchell.fr/blog/2012/04/12/gallic-war/

On the other hand, New Testament textual scholars have over 5,898 Greek manuscripts, not to mention ancient versions such as Latin, Coptic, Syriac, Armenian, Georgian, and Gothic, which number into the tens of thousands. We have many early and reliable manuscripts in Greek and the versions, a good number that cover almost the entire New Testament dating within 100 years of the originals. Therefore, reconstructing the original Greek New Testament is a realistic goal for Bible scholars. This belief and goal that we could anticipate a time when we would recover the original wording of the Greek New Testament had its greatest advocates in the nineteenth century, in Samuel Tregelles (1813-75), B. F. Westcott (1825-1901), and F. J. A. Hort (1828-92). While they acknowledged that we would never recover every word with absolute certainty, they knew that it was always the primary goal to come extremely close to the original. When we entered the twentieth century, there were two textual scholars who have since stood above all others, Kurt Aland and Bruce Metzger. These two men carried the same purpose with them, as they were instrumental in bringing us the Nestle-Aland and the United Bible Societies' critical editions, which are at the foundation of almost all modern translations.

From the days of Johann Jacob Griesbach (1745-1812) to Constantin Von Tischendorf (1815-1874), to Samuel Prideaux Tregelles (1813-1875), to Fenton John Anthony Hort (1828-1892), to Kurt Aland (1915-1994), to Bruce M. Metzger (1914-2007),[137] we have been blessed with extraordinary textual scholars. These scholars have devoted their entire lives to providing us with the transmission of the New Testament text and the methodologies by which we can recover the original words of the New Testament authors. They did not construct these histories and methodologies from textbooks or in university classrooms. No, they spent decades upon decades working with manuscripts and putting their methods of textual criticism into practice, as they provided us with one improved critical edition after another. As their knowledge grew, the number of manuscripts they had to work with fortunately grew.

---

[137] These textual scholars provided us with histories of the transmission of the New Testament text and methodologies. However, we have had dozens of textual scholars who have given their lives to the text of the New Testament. To mention just a few, we have Brian Walton (1600-1661), John Fell (1625-1686), John Mill (1645-1707), Edward Wells (1667-1727), Richard Bentley (1662-1742), Johann Albert Bengel (1687-1752), Johann Jacob Wettstein (1693-1754), Johann Salomo Semler (1725-1791), Johann Leonard Hug (1765-1846), Johann Martin Augustinus Scholz (1794-1852), Karl Lachmann (1793-1851), Erwin Nestle (1883-1972), Allen Wikgren (1906-1998), Matthew Black, (1908-1994), Barbara Aland (1937-present), and Carlo Maria Martini (1927-2012).

Samuel Tregelles stated that his purpose was to restore the Greek New Testament text "as nearly as can be done on existing evidence."[138] B. F. Westcott and F. J. A. Hort declared that their goal was "to present exactly the original words of the New Testament, so far as they can now be determined from surviving documents."[139] Metzger said that the goal of textual criticism is "to ascertain from the divergent copies which form of the text should be regarded as most nearly conforming to the original."[140] Sadly, after centuries, textual criticism is losing its way, as new textual scholars have begun to set aside the goal of recovering and establishing the original wording of the Greek New Testament. They have little concern for the certainty of a reading as to whether it is the original.

In speaking of the positions of agnostic Bart D. Ehrman (author of *The Orthodox Corruption of Scripture*) and David Parker (author of *The Living Text of the Gospels*), Elliott overserved, "Both emphasize the living and therefore changing text of the New Testament and the needlessness and inappropriateness of trying to establish one immutable original text. The changeable text in all its variety is what we textual critics should be displaying."[141] Elliott then reflects further on his goals within textual criticism: "Despite my own published work in trying to prove the originality of the text in selected areas of textual variation … I agree that the task of trying to establish the original words of the original authors with 100% certainty is impossible. More dominant in text critics' thinking now is the need to plot the changes in the history of the text. That certainly seemed to be the consensus at one of the sessions of the 1998 SBL conference in Orlando, where the question of whether the original text was an achievable goal received generally negative responses."[142]

We strongly disagree. The goal of textual criticism had been and still should be **to restore** the New Testament Greek text **in every word that the New Testament authors originally penned** in a critical edition. Suppose we are aiming only "to plot the changes in the history of the text," as Elliott put it. In that case, we are unable to do so precisely at the time when we have the greatest need to see what happened, i.e., soon after the NT books were first published, if we actually deny and rob ourselves of any chance to recover

---

[138] Tregelles, *An Account of the Printed Text of the Greek New Testament*, 174.

[139] Westcott and Hort, *Introduction to the New Testament in the Original Greek*, 1.

[140] Metzger, *The Text of the New Testament*, v.

[141] J. K. Elliott, *New Testament Textual Criticism: The Application of Thoroughgoing Principles: Essays on Manuscripts and Textual Variation*, 592.

[142] Ibid. 592.

the original. Then we must admit either that we can never have the complete word of God (the new position), or that any and potentially every quality Greek witness must be considered the word of God. The latter might even be said of a quality version, or at least of readings clearly inferred from such a version. In reality, however, any manuscript that departs from the original in its witness is more or less damaged goods.

We obviously do not think such pessimism is the necessary or inevitable response. In looking at the numbers above as to the certainty level of the restoration of the original Greek New Testament, we have come a long way since John Fell (1625-1686). A spot comparison of changes in ratings between GNT5 and previous GNT editions indicates that the level of certainty is increasing in most cases, and when it does not, the preference tends toward the earliest and most reliable manuscripts.[143] To set aside the primary goal of textual criticism now would be an insult to the lives of many textual scholars who preceded us, not to mention to the authors who penned the New Testament books and the Almighty God who inspired them.

---

[143] Sample comparisons of the General Epistles in GNT5 with previous GNT editions led to this conclusion. When the level of certainty decreased—which was infrequent compared to the reverse—the trend seemed to be that more weight was being given to 03 and/or 01 in opposition to internal factors. It is also expected that certainty levels will increase with the use of the CBGM.

CHAPTER 8 What Was the Early Christian's View of the Integrity of the Greek New Testament Books?

Paul was the author of fourteen letters within the Greek New Testament.[144] Paul's earliest letters were 1 Thessalonians (50 C.E.), 2 Thessalonians (51 C.E.), Galatians (50-52 C.E.), 1&2 Corinthians (55 C.E.), Romans (56 C.E.), Ephesians, Philippians, Colossians, Philemon (60-61 C.E.), Hebrews (61 C.E.), 1 Timothy, and Titus (61-64 C.E.). 2 Timothy was penned last, about 65 C.E. This means that the apostle Peter could have been aware of at least thirteen out of fourteen Pauline letters at the time of his penning 2 Peter in 64 C.E., in which he writes,

2 Peter 3:15-16 Updated American Standard Version (UASV)

[15] and regard the patience of our Lord as salvation; just as also **our beloved brother Paul**, according to the wisdom given him, wrote to you, [16] as also **in all his letters**, speaking in them of these things, in which are some things hard to understand, which the untaught and unstable distort, as they do also **the rest of the <u>Scriptures</u>**, to their own destruction. [bold is mine]

Notice that Peter speaks of Paul's letters, referring to them as a collection. Thus, Peter is our earliest reference to Paul's letters that were gathered together as a collection. Peter also states that the letters were viewed as being on equal footing with the Hebrew Scriptures when he says that "the untaught and unstable distort" Paul's letters as they do "the rest of the Scriptures." Günther Zuntz was certain that there was a full collection of Pauline letters by 100 C.E. (Zuntz 1953, 271-272) In 65 C.E.,[145] Peter could

---

[144] This author accepts that Paul is the author of the book of Hebrews. For further information see the CPH Blog article, Who Authored the Book of Hebrews: A Defense for Pauline Authorship

https://christianpublishinghouse.co/2016/11/02/who-authored-the-book-of-hebrews-a-defense-for-pauline-authorship/

[145] 2 Peter generally is wrongly dated to about 100-125 C.E. (e.g. **J. N. D. Kelly**, A *Commentary on the Epistles of Peter and of Jude: Introduction and Commentary*; **J. D. Mayor**, the *Epistle of St. Jude and the Epistle of Second Peter*; **D. J. Harrington**, Jude and 2 Peter). Other Bible scholars date 2 Peter to 80-90 C.E. (e.g., **R. Bauckham** *Jude, 2 Peter*; **B. Reicke**, *The Epistle of James,*

say of Paul, "in all his letters," and his readers would know who Paul was and of Paul's many letters. Also, his readers would have accepted the idea that Paul's letters were equal to the Hebrew Scriptures, which indicates that they were being collected among the churches.

1 Timothy 5:18 Updated American Standard Version (UASV)

[18] For **the Scripture says**, "You shall not muzzle the ox while he is threshing," and "The laborer is worthy of his wages." [bold is mine]

Notice that Paul says, "the Scripture says" (λέγει γὰρ ἡ γραφή), just before he quotes from two different Scriptures. The first half of the quote, "You shall not muzzle the ox while he is threshing," is from Deuteronomy 25:4. The Second half, "The laborer is worthy of his wages." seems to be from Luke 10:7. Here Paul is doing exactly what Peter did in the above at 2 Peter 3:16, placing the Gospel of Luke on par with the Hebrew Scriptures.

Some have tried to dismiss 1 Timothy 5:18 by saying that Paul was just quoting oral tradition, but that can hardly be the case when he says, "**the Scripture says**," which requires a written source, and it happens that we have such a source: The Gospel of Luke. Luke was written about 56-58 C.E. in Caesarea, and First Timothy was written about 61-64 C.E. in Macedonia. Then, there is the fact that Luke was a faithful traveling companion and co-worker of the apostle Paul. Luke was one of Paul's closest traveling companions from about 49 C.E. until Paul's martyrdom. The Gospel of Luke

---

Peter and Jude). We should begin with a date of about 64 C.E. for 2 Peter. Then, the Greek makes it apparent that the author is a contemporary of the apostle Paul because it suggests that Paul is speaking to the churches at the time of this writing. The Greek ἐν πάσαις ἐπιστολαῖς λαλῶν ("*in all letters [he] speaking*") strongly implies such. The author of the document says that he is "Simon Peter, a bond-servant and apostle of Jesus Christ" (2 Pet. 1:1, NASB). He refers to this as "the second letter I am writing to you" (2 Pet. 3:1, NASB). The author clearly states that he was an eyewitness to the transfiguration of Jesus Christ, at which only Peter, James, and John were present (Matt. 17:1-13; Mark 9:1-13; Lu 9:28–36; See 2 Pet. 1:16-21). The author mentions that Jesus foretold his death, "knowing that the laying aside of my *earthly* dwelling is imminent, as also our Lord Jesus Christ has made clear to me" (2 Pet. 1:14; John 21:18, 19.). The argument that the style is different from 1 Peter is moot because the subject and the purpose in writing were different. The implication of the phrases "in all *his* letters" and "the rest of the Scriptures" is that many of Paul's letters (thirteen of them) were viewed as "Scripture" by the first-century Christian congregation and should not be "twisted" or "distorted." In addition, Second Peter was regarded as canonical by a number of authorities prior to the Third Council of Carthage (i.e., Irenaeus of Asia Minor c. 180 C.E., Origen of Alexandria c. 230 C.E., Eusebius of Palestine c. 320 C.E., Cyril of Jerusalem c. 348 C.E., Athanasius of Alexandria c. 367 C.E., Epiphanius of Palestine c. 368 C.E., Gregory Nazianzus of Asia Minor c. 370 C.E., Philaster of Italy c. 383 C.E., Jerome of Italy c. 394 C.E., and Augustine of N. Africa c. 397 C.E.).

was written just after the two of them returned from Paul's third missionary journey. At the same time, Paul was imprisoned for two years at Caesarea, after which Paul was transferred to Rome in about 58 C.E. Other "scholars believe Luke wrote his Gospel and the book of Acts while in Rome with Paul during the apostle's first Roman imprisonment. Apparently, Luke remained nearby or with Paul also during the apostle's second Roman imprisonment. Shortly before his martyrdom, Paul wrote that 'only Luke is with me' (2 Tim. 4:11)."[146] Either way, Luke was a very close co-worker with Paul for almost twenty years. In fact, Luke's writing shows evidence of Paul's influence (Lu 22:19-20; 1 Cor. 11:23-25). We must remember that Luke was a first-rate historian, as well as being inspired. He says he "investigated everything carefully from the beginning, to write it out" (Lu 1:3). Regardless, the apostle Paul had access to Luke's Gospel for many years before penning 1 Timothy, where it appears that he made a direct quote from what we know now as Luke 10:7, referring to it as Scripture.

The use of the well-known phrase, "**it is written**," further confirms the authority of the New Testament books. We understand that when this phrase is used, it is a reference to the Scriptures of God, the inspired Word of God. It should be noted that the gospel writers themselves use the phrase "**it is written**" some forty times when referring to the inspired Hebrew Scriptures.

The *Epistle of Barnabas* dates after the destruction of the Second Temple in 70 C.E., but it dates before the Bar Kochba Revolt of 132 C.E. At Barn 4:14, we read, "let us be on guard lest we should be found to be, as **it is written**, 'many called, but few chosen.'"[147] Immediately after using the phrase "it is written," Barnabas quotes Jesus' words found in Matthew 22:14, "For many are called, but few are chosen."

The *Letter of Polycarp to the Philippians* dates to about 110 C.E. Poly 12:1 reads, "For I am convinced that you are all well trained in the sacred Scriptures and that nothing is hidden from you (something not granted to me). Only, as it is said in these Scriptures, 'be angry but do not sin,' and 'do not let the sun set on your anger.' Blessed is the one who remembers this, which I believe to be the case with you."[148] The first phrase, "be angry but do not sin," is a quotation from Ephesians 4:26, where Paul is quoting Psalm

---

[146] T. R. McNeal, "Luke," ed. Chad Brand et al., *Holman Illustrated Bible Dictionary* (Nashville, TN: Holman Bible Publishers, 2003), 1056–1057.

[147] Michael William Holmes, *The Apostolic Fathers: Greek Texts and English Translations*, Third ed. (Grand Rapids, MI: Baker Books, 2007), 373.

[148] Ibid., 294.

4:5. However, the latter part of the quote, "do not let the sun set on your anger" is Paul's words alone. It is clear here that Polycarp is referring to both the Psalm and the book of Ephesians when he writes, "it is said in these Scriptures."

Clement of Rome (c. 30-100 C.E.) penned two books: we focus on the second, *An Ancient Christian Sermon* (2 Clement), which dates to about 98-100 C.E. II Clement 2:4 reads, "And another Scripture says, 'I have not come to call the righteous, but sinners.'"[149] Here Clement is quoting Mark 2:17 or Matt. 9:13, which is likely the earliest quotation of a New Testament passage as Scripture. In the Gospel of Mark and Matthew, Jesus is quoted as saying, "I came not to call the righteous, but sinners." II Clement 14:2 reads, "But if we do not do the will of the Lord, we will belong to those of whom the Scripture says, 'My house has become a robbers' den'" which is a quote from Matthew 21:13, Mark 11:17, and Luke 19:46, where Jesus himself is quoting Jeremiah 7:11 after cleansing the temple of greedy merchants.

Indeed, we can garner from this brief look at early Christianity's view of Scriptures that the New Testament books were placed on the same footing as the Hebrew Scriptures quite early, starting with Peter's words about the apostle Paul's letters. Again, Justin Martyr tells us that at the early Christian meetings, "the memoirs of the apostles or the writings of the prophets are read, as long as time permits; then, when the reader has ceased, the president verbally instructs and exhorts to the imitation of these good things" (1 Apology 67).[150] Ignatius of Antioch (c. 35-108 C.E.), Theophilus of Antioch (d. 182 C.E.), and Tertullian (c. 155-240 C.E.) also spoke of the Prophets, the Law, and the Gospels as equally authoritative.

The Early Christian View of the Integrity of the Greek New Testament Originals

If the early Christians' view of the New Testament books were on the same footing as the Hebrew Scriptures, then we would see them guarding the New Testament's integrity in the same way the Old Testament authors and the scribes in ancient Israel guarded the Hebrew Old Testament.

---

[149] Ibid., 141.

[150] Justin Martyr, "The First Apology of Justin," in *The Apostolic Fathers with Justin Martyr and Irenaeus*, ed. Alexander Roberts, James Donaldson, and A. Cleveland Coxe, vol. 1, The Ante-Nicene Fathers (Buffalo, NY: Christian Literature Company, 1885), 186.

Deuteronomy 4:2 Updated American Standard Version (UASV) ² You shall **not add to** the word which I am commanding you, **nor take away** from it, that you may keep the commandments of Jehovah your God which I command you.	**Deuteronomy 12:32** Updated American Standard Version (UASV) ³² "Everything that I command you, you shall be careful to do; you shall **not add to** nor **take away from** it.

There indeed were severe consequences, even death to some, if scribes or copyists were to add to or take away from God's Word, disregarding these warnings. Eugene H. Merrill observes, "There is a principle of canonization here as well in that nothing is to be added to or subtracted from the word. This testifies to the fact that God himself is the originator of the covenant text and only he is capable of determining its content and extent."[151]

Proverbs 30:6 Updated American Standard Version (UASV)

⁶ **Do not add to** his words,
  lest he reprove you and you be found a liar.

This is an ongoing command about God's words that we had just seen above given to the Israelites in Deuteronomy 4:2 and 12:32. There is no need to add to or take away from God's Word, for it is sufficient. Bible commentator Duane A. Garrett, an expert on the book of Proverbs, tells us that "Verse 6 is an injunction against adding to God's words similar to the injunctions found in Deut. 12:32 and Rev 22:18. It is noteworthy that this text does not warn the reader not to reject or take away from divine revelation; it is more concerned that no one supplements it. This is, therefore, not a warning to the unbelieving interpreter but rather to the believer. The temptation is to improve on the text, if not by actually adding new material then by interpreting it in ways that make more of a passage's teaching than is really there. It is what Paul called "going beyond what is written" – 1 Corinthians 4:6.[152]

The Jewish people's attitude and their Hebrew Scriptures can be summed up in the words of Josephus, the first-century (37 – c.100 C.E.) Jewish historian wrote, "We have given practical proof of our reverence for our own Scriptures. Although such long ages have now passed, no one has ventured either to add, remove, or alter a syllable. It is an instinct with every

---

[151] Eugene H. Merrill, *Deuteronomy*, vol. 4, The New American Commentary (Nashville: Broadman & Holman Publishers, 1994), 229.

[152] Duane A. Garrett, *Proverbs, Ecclesiastes, Song of Songs*, vol. 14, The New American Commentary (Nashville: Broadman & Holman Publishers, 1993), 237.

Jew, from the day of his birth, to regard them as the decrees of God, to abide by them, and, if need be, cheerfully to die for them."[153] The longstanding view of the Jews toward the Hebrew Scriptures is fundamental, especially given what the apostle Paul wrote to the Roman Christian congregation. The apostle says, the Jews "were entrusted with the sayings[154] of God." – Romans 3:1-2.

Galatians 3:15 Updated American Standard Version (UASV)

[15] Brothers, I speak according to man:[155] even though it is only a man's covenant, yet when it has been ratified, **no one sets it aside or adds conditions to it**.

The letter from Paul to Galatians was penned about **50-52 C.E.** Here Paul's words in dealing with the covenant to Abraham and his descendants echo the words from the Law of Moses at Deuteronomy 4:2, when he says, "no one sets it aside or adds conditions to it," i.e., "not add to… nor take away." The covenant word of God was not to be altered.

Revelation 22:18-19 Updated American Standard Version (UASV)

[18] I testify to everyone who hears the words of the prophecy of this book: if anyone **adds to them**, God will add to him the plagues which are written in this book; [19] and if anyone **takes away from** the words of the book of this prophecy, God will take away his part from the tree of life and out of the holy city, which are written in this book.

Apostle John's letter to the seven congregations was penned about 95 C.E. Kistemaker, and Hendriksen wrote, "The solemn warning not to add to or detract from the words of this book is common in ancient literature. For instance, Moses warns the Israelites not to add to or subtract from the decrees and laws God gave them (Deut. 4:2; 12:32). This formula was attached to documents much the same as copyright laws protect modern manuscripts. In addition, curses were added in the form of a conditional sentence, 'If anyone adds or takes away anything from this book, a curse will rest upon him.' Paul wrote a similar condemnation when he told the Galatians that if anyone preached a gospel which was not the gospel of

---

[153] Josephus, *The Life/Against Apion*, vol. 1, LCL, ed. by H. St. J. Thackeray (Cambridge, MA: Harvard University Press, 1976), pp. 177–181.

[154] **Sayings**: (Gr. *logia, on* [only in the plural]) A saying or message, usually short, especially divine, gathered into a collection–Acts 7:38; Romans 3:2; Hebrews 5:12; 1 Peter 4:11.

[155] Or *in terms of human relations*; or *according to a human perspective*; or *using a human illustration*

Christ, 'let him be eternally condemned' (Gal. 1:6–8). Now Jesus pronounces a curse on anyone who distorts his message."[156]

The Didache (The Teaching of the Twelve Apostles) dates to about 100 C.E. At 4:13, it reads, "You must not forsake the Lord's commandments, but must guard what you have received, neither adding nor subtracting anything."[157] This author is drawing on the command in Deuteronomy 4:2 and 12:32.[158] The point here is that while the author uses "the Lord" (i.e., Jehovah, that is, the Father) in Deut. 4:2, 12:32, he is actually referring to Jesus' teaching found in the Gospels. Therefore, the Gospels and, more specifically, Jesus' teaching are equal to the Hebrew Scriptures.

Papias of Hierapolis, about 135 C.E., records what he had to tell about the details surrounding each apostles' personal life and ministry. Papias 3:3-4 says, "I will not hesitate to set down ... everything I carefully learned then from the elders and carefully remembered, guaranteeing their truth. For unlike most people, I did not enjoy those who have a great deal to say, but those who teach the truth. Nor did I enjoy those who recall someone else's commandments, but those who remember the commandments given by the Lord to the faith and proceeding from the truth itself. And if by chance someone who had been a follower of the elders should come my way, I inquired about the words of the elders—what Andrew or Peter said, or Philip, or Thomas or James, or John or Matthew or any other of the Lord's disciples."[159]

Papias says of Mark's Gospel: "Mark, having become Peter's interpreter, wrote down accurately everything he remembered." Further confirming the Gospel's accuracy, Papias continues: "Consequently Mark did nothing wrong in writing down some things as he remembered them, for he **made it his one concern not to omit anything** which he heard **or to make any false statement in them**."[160] This is an apparent reference to Deuteronomy 4:2 while referencing Mark's Gospel, again showing that Christians viewed the

---

[156] Simon J. Kistemaker and William Hendriksen, *Exposition of the Book of Revelation*, vol. 20, New Testament Commentary (Grand Rapids: Baker Book House, 1953–2001), 594.

[157] Michael William Holmes, *The Apostolic Fathers: Greek Texts and English Translations*, Third ed. (Grand Rapids, MI: Baker Books, 2007), 351.

[158] (LXX 13:1.)

[159] Michael William Holmes, *The Apostolic Fathers: Greek Texts and English Translations*, Third ed. (Grand Rapids, MI: Baker Books, 2007), 735.

[160] Ibid, 739-40.

New Testament books as being equal to the Hebrew Scriptures. Papias offers testimony that Matthew initially penned his Gospel in the Hebrew language. Papias says, "So Matthew composed the oracles in the Hebrew language, and each person interpreted them as best he could."[161] As the overseer of Hierapolis in Asia Minor, Papias was able to inquire and carefully learn from the elders throughout the church at the time, establishing the authenticity and divine inspiration of the New Testament. Sadly, though, only scanty fragments of the writings of Papias survived.

The *Epistle of Barnabas,* dated about 130 C.E., declares, "You shall guard what you have received, **neither adding nor subtracting** anything" (Barn 19:11).[162] Here again, Barnabas is drawing on Deuteronomy 4:2 as he expresses his concern about the Word of God, as he speaks about "the way of light" in chapter 19 of his letter, making multiple references to New Testament teachings and principles.

Dionysius of Corinth wrote in about 170 C.E. about those who had dared to alter his own writings. He writes, "For I wrote letters when the brethren requested me to write. And these letters the apostles of the devil have filled with tares [false information], **taking away some things and adding others**, for whom a woe is in store. It is not wonderful, then, if some have attempted to adulterate the Lord's writings when they have formed designs against those which are not such."[163] Here, Dionysius refers to Deuteronomy 4:2 and 12:32, noting the curse or woe that is in store for altering his own writings, and all the more so for daring to alter the Scriptures themselves. The reference to adulterating "the Lord's writings" is a reference to the New Testament writings – "A probable, though not exclusive, reference to Marcion, for he was by no means the only one of that age that interpolated and mutilated the works of the apostles to fit his theories. Apostolic works—true and false—circulated in great numbers and were

---

[161] Ibid, 741.

[162] Ibid, 437.

[163] Dionysius of Corinth, "Fragments from a Letter to the Roman Church," in *Fathers of the Third and Fourth Centuries: The Twelve Patriarchs, Excerpts and Epistles, the Clementina, Apocrypha, Decretals, Memoirs of Edessa and Syriac Documents, Remains of the First Ages,* ed. Alexander Roberts, James Donaldson, and A. Cleveland Coxe, trans. B. P. Pratten, vol. 8, The Ante-Nicene Fathers (Buffalo, NY: Christian Literature Company, 1886), 765.

made the basis for the speculations and moral requirements of many of the heretical schools of the second century."[164]

If there were no significant concerns over the New Testament originals' integrity, we would not see early church leaders showing such respect. The principle of not adding nor taking away found in Deuteronomy 4:2 and 12:32 can be applied to just one word or even a single number. We have the case of Irenaeus in about 180 C.E., who complained about the number 666 found in Revelation 13:18 that had been changed to 616. Irenaeus wrote, "Such, then, being the state of the case, and this number being found **in all the most approved and ancient copies** [of the Apocalypse], and those men who saw John face to face bearing their testimony [to it]; while reason also leads us to conclude that the number of the name of the beast, [if reckoned] according to the Greek mode of calculation by [the value of] the letters contained in it, will amount to six hundred and sixty and six."[165] The passage ἐν πᾶσι τοῖς σπουδαίοις καὶ ἀρχαίοις ἀντιγράφοις ("in all the most approved and ancient copies") shows that by then the autographs of the New Testament were not available, with various readings creeping into the manuscripts of the canonical books.

Irenaeus went on to let those guilty of willfully adding to or taking away from the Scriptures know that there will be severe punishment. He wrote, "Now, as regards those who have done this in simplicity, and without evil intent, we are at liberty to assume that pardon will be granted them by God. But as for those who, for the sake of vainglory, lay it down for certain that names containing the spurious number are to be accepted, and affirm that this name, hit upon by themselves, is that of him who is to come; such persons shall not come forth without loss, because they have led into error both themselves and those who confided in them. Now, in the first place, it is loss to wander from the truth, and to imagine that as being the case which is not; then again, as there shall be no light punishment [inflicted] **upon him**

---

[164] Philip Schaff and Henry Wace, eds., *Eusebius: Church History, Life of Constantine the Great, and Oration in Praise of Constantine*, vol. 1, A Select Library of the Nicene and Post-Nicene Fathers of the Christian Church, Second Series (New York: Christian Literature Company, 1890).

[165] Irenaeus of Lyons, "Irenæus Against Heresies," in *The Apostolic Fathers with Justin Martyr and Irenaeus*, ed. Alexander Roberts, James Donaldson, and A. Cleveland Coxe, vol. 1, The Ante-Nicene Fathers (Buffalo, NY: Christian Literature Company, 1885), 558.

who either <u>adds</u> or <u>subtracts</u> anything from the Scripture."[166] Here Irenaeus is referring to John's warning in Revelation 22:18.

Again, the *Letter of Polycarp to the Philippians,* dating to about 110 C.E., reads at 7:1, "For everyone who does not confess that Jesus Christ has come in the flesh is antichrist [cf. 1 John 4:2-3]; and whoever does not acknowledge the testimony of the cross is of the devil [cf. 1 John 3:8]; and **whoever twists the sayings of the Lord** to suit his own sinful desires and claims that there is neither resurrection nor judgment—well, that person is the first-born of Satan."[167] Of course, "the sayings of the Lord" come from the Gospels. Therefore, Polycarp was declaring a warning to anyone who would alter the Gospels. Some would argue that Polycarp was referring to oral traditions when he used the term "the sayings of the Lord" (τὰ λόγια τοῦ κυρίου), but this simply is not the case, since in the next verse he refers to these "sayings" (κυρίου) again and then quotes Matthew 6:13 and 26:41, where we find Matthew recording Jesus' sayings.

We could cite many more quotations from early church leaders about their concern for their integrity of the New Testament originals. However, we can see from our limited look at early Christianity's view of the Scriptures that the New Testament books were placed on the same footing as the Hebrew Scriptures from the very beginning. When we look at the first three centuries of Christianity, we find that the manuscripts were prepared for Christians' reading culture, who prioritized publishing and distributing a text that was accurate in content and reader-friendly. The Christian texts were prepared in such a way as to place the least demand on the reader to bring the Scriptures to a more diverse audience.

Clearly, Paul and Peter showed concern for their writings and equating NT books other than their own with the Hebrew Scriptures in authority. Early on, the church leaders were very concerned about preserving the integrity of the original, down to the individual words. The papyri of the first three centuries after Christ **provides evidence** that most scribes (copyists) also cared about preserving their exemplars' integrity and did not seek to change or alter the wording. On the other hand, we would be misleading others and ourselves if we were to deny that a small minority of the copyists

---

[166] Irenaeus of Lyons, "Irenæus Against Heresies," in *The Apostolic Fathers with Justin Martyr and Irenaeus,* ed. Alexander Roberts, James Donaldson, and A. Cleveland Coxe, vol. 1, The Ante-Nicene Fathers (Buffalo, NY: Christian Literature Company, 1885), 559.

[167] Michael William Holmes, *The Apostolic Fathers: Greek Texts and English Translations,* Third ed. (Grand Rapids, MI: Baker Books, 2007), 289.

did freely choose to make alterations–as Colwell said for example, that the scribe of **P⁴⁵** worked "without any intention of exactly reproducing his source. He writes with great freedom, harmonizing, smoothing out, substituting almost whimsically." However, the scribe who worked on **P⁷⁵** was a "disciplined scribe who writes with the intention of being careful and accurate." Then again, Colwell said that **P⁶⁶** reflects "a scribe working with the intention of making a good copy, falling into careless errors, … but also under the control of some other person, or second standard, … It shows the supervision of a foreman, or a scribe turned proofreader."[168]

Generally speaking, the early scribes were very concerned about the accuracy of their copying. Still, while some were more successful than others, every one of them–due to human imperfection–made some transcriptional errors at times, which were **unintentional** (Matt. 27:11; Mark 6:51; 10:40; Rom. 5:1; Eph. 1:15; 1 Thess. 2:7; Heb. 12:15). We can also attribute human imperfection to **intentional changes**, *purposeful* scribal alterations, such as *conflation* (Luke 24:53; John 1:34; Rom. 3:32), *interpolation* (Mark 9:29; Lu 23:19, 34; Rom. 8:1; 1 Cor. 15:51), and attempts to clarify the meaning of a text (1 Cor. 3:3) or to enhance a doctrinal position (1 John 5:7).

We can say that **on the whole**, the early church leaders valued the integrity of the original, and the scribes valued the integrity of the exemplars which they were copying. In fact, the high value placed on the integrity of the original ironically led to some erroneous changes because scribes were prone at times to correct what they believed to be mistakes within the sacred text. Many modern textual scholars will tell their readers that the early copying period was "'free,' 'wild,' 'in a state of flux,' 'chaotic,' 'a turbid textual morass.'" (Hill and Kruger 2012, 10) The truth was actually the opposite. The church leaders valued the originals above all else, and the scribes saw their exemplars as master copies of those originals and reverentially feared to make any mistakes.

The goal of textual scholarship since the days of Erasmus in the sixteenth century has been to get back to the original, preserving the exact wording of the original twenty-seven New Testament books penned by Matthew, Mark, Luke, John, James, Jude, Peter, and Paul. However, this has not always proved to be the case with recent scholarship. Philip W. Comfort has been one of the leading outspoken proponents of the traditional goal of

---

[168] Ernest Colwell, "Method in Evaluating Scribal Habits: A Study of P45, P66, P75," in *Studies in Methodology in Textual Criticism of the New Testament,* New Testament Tools and Studies 9 (Leiden: Brill, 1969), 114–21.

reconstructing the exact wording of the originals, and I quote the following observation by Comfort at length:

> The time gap between the autographs and the earliest extant copies is quite close—no more than 100 years for most of the books of the New Testament. Thus, we are in a good position to recover most of the original wording of the Greek New Testament. Such optimism was held by the well-known textual critics of the nineteenth century—most notably, Samuel Tregelles, B. F. Westcott, and F. J. A. Hort, who, although acknowledging that we may never recover all of the original text of the New Testament books with absolute certainty, believed that the careful work of textual criticism could bring us extremely close. In the twentieth century, two eminent textual critics, Bruce Metzger and Kurt Aland, affirmed this same purpose, and were instrumental in the production of the two critical editions of the Greek New Testament that are widely used today.
>
> Tregelles, Hort, Metzger, and Aland, as well as Constantine von Tischendorf, the nineteenth-century scholar who famously discovered Codex Sinaiticus, all provided histories of the transmission of the New Testament text and methodologies for recovering the original wording. Their views of textual criticism were derived from their actual experience of working with manuscripts and doing textual criticism in preparing critical editions of the Greek New Testament. Successive generations of scholars, working with ever-increasing quantities of manuscripts (especially earlier ones) and refining their methodologies, have continued with the task of recovering the original wording of the Greek New Testament.
>
> By contrast, a certain number of textual critics in recent years have abandoned the notion that the original wording of the Greek New Testament can ever be recovered. Let us take, for example, Bart Ehrman (author of *The Orthodox Corruption of Scripture*) and David Parker (author of *The Living Text of the Gospels*). Having analyzed their positions, J. K. Elliott writes, "Both [men] emphasize the living and therefore changing text of the New Testament and the needlessness and inappropriateness of trying to establish one immutable original text. The changeable text in all its variety is what we textual critics should be displaying" (1999, 17). Elliott then speaks for himself on the matter: "Despite my own published work in trying to prove the originality of the text in selected areas of textual variation, … I agree that the task of trying to establish the original words of the original authors with 100% certainty is impossible. More dominant

in text critics' thinking now is the need to plot the changes in the history of the text" (1999, 18).

Not one textual critic could or would ever say that any of the critical editions of the Greek New Testament replicates the original wording with 100 percent accuracy. But an accurate reconstruction has to be the goal of those who practice textual criticism as classically defined. To veer from this is to stray from the essential task of textual criticism. It is an illuminating exercise "to plot the changes in the history of the text," but this assumes a known starting point. And what can that starting point be if not the original text? In analyzing Ehrman's book, *The Orthodox Corruption of Scripture*, Silva notes this same paradox: "Although this book is appealed to in support of blurring the notion of an original text, there is hardly a page in that book that does not in fact mention such a text or assume its accessibility .... Ehrman's book is unimaginable unless he can identify an initial form of the text that can be differentiated from a later alteration" (2002, 149). In short, one cannot speak about the text being corrupted if there is not an original text to be corrupted.

I am not against reconstructing the history of the text. In fact, I devoted many years to studying all the early Greek New Testament manuscripts (those dated before A.D. 300) and compiling a fresh edition of them in The Text of the Earliest New Testament Greek Manuscripts (coedited with David Barrett). This work provides a representative sampling of New Testament books that were actually read by Christians in the earliest centuries of the church. But whatever historical insights we may gain by studying the varying manuscript traditions as texts unto themselves, this is no reason to abandon the goal of producing the best critical edition possible, one that most likely replicates the original wording. Thus, I echo Silva's comments entirely, when he says: "I would like to affirm—not only with Hort, but with practically all students of ancient documents—that the recovery of the original text (i.e., the text in its initial form, prior to the alterations produced in the copying process) remains the primary task of textual criticism" (2002, 149).[169]

The author of this work would echo the words of Silva and Comfort in that the primary task of a textual scholar is the process of attempting to

---

[169] Philip Comfort, NEW TESTAMENT TEXT AND TRANSLATUION COMMENTARY: Commentary on the variant readings of the ancient New Testament manuscripts and how they relate to the major English translations (Carol Stream, ILL: Tyndale House Publishers, Inc., 2008), Page xi.

ascertain the original wording of the original text that was published by Matthew, Mark, Luke, John, James, Jude, Peter, and Paul. Even if we acknowledge that we can never say with absolute **certainty** that we have established the original wording one hundred percent, this should always be the goal. Imagine any other field in life, the **certainty** of a successful heart transplant by a surgeon, the **certainty** of astronauts going to the moon and back, or just the certainty that our automobile will get us to our destination, and the like. Do we want a heart surgeon who aims for eighty-percent certainty in a successful operation on us? Most objective textual scholars would agree that between the 1881 Westcott and Hort text and the Nestle-Aland/United Bible Societies Greek text, we are in the very high nineties, if not ninety-nine percent mirror-like reflection of the original wording of the twenty-seven New Testament books. Of course, the ongoing objective is to reach one hundred percent even if it is not achievable.

CHAPTER 9 The Legacy of the Hebrew Scriptures: Divine Inspiration, Preservation, and Transmission

Imagine the inspired Word of God, the Hebrew Scriptures, as life-giving waters of truth gathered in a remarkable reservoir of sacred documents. As recipients of these divine messages, we are eternally grateful that Jehovah collected these "waters" to serve as a boundless source of truth. As with many ancient treasures, royal crowns and venerable monuments may have decayed over time, but the precious words of our God endure forever (Isa. 40:8, ASV). However, concerns may arise regarding the potential contamination of these truth-filled waters over time. Have they remained pure? Has their transmission from the original Hebrew and Aramaic texts been faithful, thus ensuring the reliability of today's Scriptures accessible to every language on earth? To answer these questions, let's explore the meticulously preserved Hebrew text's history, its transmission, and the extraordinary efforts to make it available to all humanity through various translations.

God's human secretaries, starting from Moses in 1556 B.C.E. and continuing until shortly after 440 B.C.E., recorded the original documents in Hebrew and Aramaic. As of today, none of these original writings are known to exist. Nonetheless, from the start, extraordinary care was taken to safeguard the inspired writings, including the authorized reproductions of them. Around 642 B.C.E., during King Josiah's reign, "the book of the law" attributed to Moses—likely the original copy—was found preserved in Jehovah's house, enduring faithfully for 871 years (2 Kings 22:8-10, ESV). Jeremiah, a scribe of the Bible, was so intrigued by this discovery that he documented it, and around 460 B.C.E., Ezra referenced the same event (2 Chron. 34:14-18, ASV).

Ezra, renowned for his expertise as a copyist of Moses's law, which Jehovah, the God of Israel, had bestowed, was deeply interested in these matters (Ezra 7:6, ASV). It's highly probable that Ezra had access to other Hebrew Scripture scrolls prepared up until his time, possibly even originals of some inspired writings. As a custodian of divine writings during his era, Ezra played an integral part in their preservation (Neh. 8:1,2, ESV).

The Evolution of the Hebrew Scriptures and Translation

In the era following the leadership of Ezra, the necessity for copies of the Hebrew Scriptures escalated. The Jewish community was dispersed post their restoration in 537 B.C.E, with a majority choosing to settle outside Jerusalem and Palestine. Many Jews undertook annual pilgrimages to Jerusalem for religious festivals, celebrating in the language of Biblical Hebrew. With Jews settling in distant lands, synagogues emerged as local assembly spots, necessitating the replication of the Hebrew Scriptures across numerous locales.

These synagogues usually featured a storage room called the genizah, where worn or damaged manuscripts were stored. With the passage of time, manuscripts with the sacred name of Jehovah were reverently interred in the earth to prevent any potential desecration. Consequently, thousands of ancient Hebrew Bible manuscripts faded from use. An exception to this practice was the genizah of the synagogue in Old Cairo, which was sealed and forgotten until rediscovered in the mid-19th century. After the synagogue underwent repairs in 1890, the genizah's contents were examined, leading to the discovery of invaluable manuscripts and fragments which now reside in libraries across Europe and America.

Today, the global library system houses over 6,000 manuscripts of the Hebrew Scriptures. Until recently, the oldest manuscripts were no earlier than the tenth century C.E. However, the discovery of the Dead Sea Scrolls in 1947 revolutionized biblical scholarship. These scrolls, which include a copy of the book of Isaiah and other biblical texts, date back to the last few centuries B.C.E. The analysis of these manuscripts provides a robust foundation for establishing the authenticity of the Hebrew text.

Hebrew, also known as man's language, is assumed to be the original language spoken by Adam in the Garden of Eden (Genesis 2:19-20, ASV). It was used during the time of Noah and survived the confusion of languages at the Tower of Babel (Genesis 11:1, 7-9, ASV). Moses, proficient in the wisdom of the Egyptians and the Hebrew language, was well positioned to read and interpret ancient documents that were later incorporated into the Book of Genesis. In the days of Jewish kings, this language came to be known as "the Jews' language" (2 Kings 18:26, 28, ASV). The Hebrew Scriptures encapsulate divine truths that are accessible only to those literate in Hebrew.

The Bible justifies translating its text into other languages to disseminate its divine guidance. Since the fourth or third century B.C.E., portions of the Bible have been translated into over 1,900 languages, quenching the spiritual thirst of multitudes worldwide. Ancient translations of the Bible, preserved in manuscript form, attest to the high degree of textual fidelity of the original Hebrew text (Deuteronomy 32:43, ASV; Matthew 24:14, ESV).

Early translations include the Samaritan Pentateuch and the Aramaic Targums. The most significant early version of the Hebrew Scriptures was the Greek Septuagint, a translation begun around 280 B.C.E. by 72 Jewish scholars. The Septuagint served as the Scripture for Greek-speaking Jews and was extensively used by Jesus and his apostles. Modern access to fragments of the Septuagint helps assess its text.

Another crucial version was the Latin Vulgate, translated by Jerome directly from Hebrew and Greek. Jerome's work, produced between 390 and 405 C.E., became the source text for numerous Catholic translations in Western Christendom. This brief overview of the evolution of Scripture replication and translation illuminates the diligent efforts of countless individuals to preserve and share the divine truths embedded in the Hebrew Scriptures.

The Evolution of Hebrew Scriptural Texts

The Sopherim Legacy

In the era of Ezra extending to the time of Jesus, the scribes, or Sopherim, took on the task of copying the Hebrew Scriptures. Over time, they started introducing textual alterations, a deviation that Jesus reproached for their usurpation of power they didn't possess (Matt. 23:2, 13, ESV).

Traces of Alteration: The Masora

The Sopherim's successors, known as the Masoretes, emerged in the centuries following Christ. These scholars recorded the changes implemented by the Sopherim in marginal notes or at the end of the Hebrew text, thereby forming the Masora. The Masora itemizes 15 "extraordinary points of the Sopherim," marked by dots or strokes in the Hebrew text. While some of these points don't significantly influence the English translation or interpretation, others do. The Sopherim's superstitious fear of pronouncing Jehovah's name led them to substitute it with 'Adonai' (Lord) at 134 locations and occasionally with 'Elohim' (God). The Masora records these alterations. The Sopherim are also believed to have conducted at least 18 corrections, as suggested by a Masora note, although the actual number might be higher. Despite their apparent good intentions, these alterations seemed to emerge from an irreverence for God or disrespect for His earthly representatives.

The Consonantal Text

The Hebrew alphabet consists of 22 consonants without vowels, requiring readers to incorporate vowel sounds from their linguistic understanding. This form of writing was akin to an abbreviated script, much like how modern English utilizes abbreviations that only feature consonants, such as "ltd" for "limited". Hence, the "consonantal text" refers to the Hebrew text devoid of any vowel markings. The consonantal text of Hebrew manuscripts was set in form between the first and second centuries C.E. Manuscripts with differing texts circulated for a while after that, but unlike the Sopherim period, no more alterations were introduced.

The Masoretic Text

In the latter half of the first millennium C.E., the Masoretes established a system of vowel points and accent marks to aid the reading and pronunciation of vowel sounds. Previously, pronunciation was conveyed orally. The Masoretes maintained the integrity of the texts they transmitted, recording marginal notes in the Masora as necessary, and refraining from taking textual liberties. Their Masora highlighted textual peculiarities and suggested corrected readings where needed. There were three schools of Masoretes - the Babylonian, Palestinian, and Tiberian. The printed editions of the Hebrew Bible now use the Tiberian system, developed by the Masoretes of Tiberias, a city by the Sea of Galilee. The Updated American Standard Version's footnotes often reference the Masoretic text (designated as M) and its marginal notes, the Masora (identified as MTmargin).

The Varied Vocalization Schools

The Palestinian school positioned vowel signs above the consonants, but only a few manuscripts following this system survived. The Babylonian system also had supralinear vowel pointing. The Petersburg Codex of the Prophets, from 916 C.E., preserved in the Leningrad Public Library, is an example of a manuscript with Babylonian pointing. A comparison of this codex with the Tiberian text revealed that despite its supralinear vocalization system, it largely aligns with the Tiberian text regarding its consonantal text, vowels, and Masora.

The Discovery of the Dead Sea Scrolls

The history of Hebrew manuscripts took a fascinating turn in 1947 with the discovery of the first Isaiah scroll, along with other biblical and non-biblical scrolls, in a cave at Wadi Qumran (Nahal Qumeran), near the Dead Sea. This well-preserved Isaiah scroll, thought to originate from the end of the second century B.C.E., is about a thousand years older than the oldest known manuscript of the recognized Masoretic text of Isaiah. The fragments of over 170 scrolls from these caves represent parts of all the books of the Hebrew Scriptures, except Esther.

Analyses of these scrolls reveal a high degree of agreement with the Masoretic text. The differences, primarily in spelling and grammatical construction, don't impact doctrinal points. The discovery and examination of these ancient texts, including the Samaritan Pentateuch, the Aramaic Targums, the Greek Septuagint, the Tiberian Hebrew text, the Palestinian Hebrew text, the Babylonian Hebrew text, and the Hebrew text of the Dead Sea Scrolls, assure us that the Hebrew Scriptures have been substantially preserved in the form originally recorded by God's inspired servants.

The Journey of Printed Critical Texts: From Jacob ben Chayyim to 2023

The development of printed critical texts of the Hebrew Bible, beginning with Jacob ben Chayyim's text in the 16th century to present day, is a rich narrative of evolving methodologies, technological advancements, and continuous scholarly effort.

The Beginnings: Jacob ben Chayyim (1524-25)

Jacob ben Chayyim Ibn Adonijah was a Jewish scholar whose monumental contribution was the Bomberg Rabbinic Bible, published in 1524-25. Daniel Bomberg, a Christian printer from Venice, commissioned the project. Jacob ben Chayyim gathered available Masoretic materials, compiled them into a comprehensive text, and systematized the Masorah (marginal and end notes). It became the first ever full edition of the Masoretic Bible and shaped Hebrew Bibles for centuries. Its organization, text, and accompanying Masorah served as the foundation for most future printed editions of the Hebrew Scriptures.

The Next Steps: 17th-19th Centuries

During the 17th century, Amsterdam-based Jewish publisher Joseph Athias improved upon Bomberg's text by rectifying typographical errors and meticulously revising its accuracy, even employing two proofreaders for verification. Athias' edition was notable for its aesthetics and precision, receiving acclaim from contemporary Christian Hebraists.

Further in the 18th century, German Hebraist Johann Buxtorf II worked to refine the Bomberg text. His edition, published posthumously in Basel (1712-13), aimed to enhance the clarity and consistency of the Masorah notes, even though it failed to significantly improve the text.

By the mid-19th century, progress in Semitic philology, manuscript discoveries, and printing technology led to a shift toward creating a critical text based on manuscript evidence. Prominent Orientalist S. D. Luzzatto argued against the infallibility of the Masoretic Text, critiquing the unexamined reliance on it. Meanwhile, pioneering textual criticism and comparative philology projects were underway in the realm of New Testament studies, which would soon cross over to Old Testament scholarship.

Into the 20th Century: Rudolf Kittel's Biblia Hebraica

The landmark Biblia Hebraica, published by German scholar Rudolf Kittel in 1906, was the first Old Testament edition employing a critical apparatus to compare different textual versions. Kittel used ben Chayyim's text as his base but consulted the Samaritan Pentateuch, Septuagint (Greek Old Testament), Syriac Peshitta, Latin Vulgate, and Aramaic Targums to notate probable errors and plausible corrections in the Masoretic Text. The first two editions of Biblia Hebraica (BHK) were pioneering but limited in their textual sources.

New manuscript discoveries in the 20th century, most notably the Dead Sea Scrolls, introduced rich, older, textual evidence, significantly impacting Hebrew Bible studies. This wealth of information prompted a revised Biblia Hebraica edition. Biblia Hebraica Stuttgartensia (BHS), completed in 1977, replaced Kittel's text with the oldest complete Masoretic manuscript, the Leningrad Codex (circa 1008). BHS maintained much of Kittel's approach and notations, enhancing its critical apparatus with data from the new manuscript findings.

21st Century: The Quinta Generation

In the 21st century, scholarly focus shifted towards a more comprehensive, evidence-based textual evaluation. The Biblia Hebraica Quinta (BHQ), the fifth edition under development since 2004, aims to use all available evidence from the Dead Sea Scrolls, Septuagint, and other ancient versions. It expands the critical apparatus, including detailed evaluations of each textual problem.

In Conclusion

Over the centuries, the production of critical Hebrew Bible texts has transformed from the solitary endeavor of Jacob ben Chayyim in the 16th century to a complex, international academic enterprise in the 21st. These texts' development mirrors the evolution of textual criticism and technological advancements, recording the journey from letterpress to digital databases, from an uncritical Masoretic text to a deeply researched critical apparatus.

Despite changes, the goal remains: to provide the most accurate, accessible Hebrew text possible, allowing for the continued study and appreciation of one of humanity's most significant religious and literary treasures—the Hebrew Bible. The work is far from finished; every new archaeological discovery, technological innovation, or scholarly insight brings us one step closer to understanding the original words and world of the Hebrew Scriptures.

CHAPTER 10 What Are the Dangers of Skepticism, Ambiguity, and Uncertainty Versus the Safety Ascertained Certainty and Faith?

Understanding Evidence and Historical Certainty through the Lens of Scriptures

In any exploration of ancient history, we're guided by evidence—facts or information that inform the validity of beliefs or propositions. The reliability of historical events, people, places, and even document readings can be gauged using such evidence, whether it comes from archival documents or physical objects. When looking into the Scriptures, both Old Testament (as per ASV) and New Testament (as per ESV), we apply similar principles of analysis.

Assessing Certainty in Historical Evidence

To determine the level of certainty for a historical event, place, person, or an original reading in a document, we use modal verbs that express varying degrees of certainty. These verbs are might have been (30% certainty), may have been (40%), could have been (55%), would have been (80%), and must have been (95%). Each level of certainty is denoted by a specific abbreviation—[WP] for Weak Possibility, [P] for Plausible, [PE] for Preponderance of Evidence, [CE] for Convincing Evidence, and [BRD] for Beyond Reasonable Doubt. This system was inspired by U.S. criminal justice legal terms and the works of scholars like Bruce Metzger and Johann Albrecht Bengel.

Edward D. Andrews

The Pursuit of Historical Truth

The quest for objectivity is central to historical research. Historians aim to separate personal biases from their investigations, approaching historical material with an open mind and striving to understand the context of the past without the influence of present-day preconceptions. This applies to the study of Scriptures as well, where the Holy Spirit guided the writers in the delivery of the divine message.

Exploring Reader-Response Criticism and Scientific Skepticism

In interpreting Scriptures, some adhere to the reader-response criticism approach, which validates all meanings derived from a text as correct. However, true skepticism involves questioning every claim for truth, clarity, consistency, and adequacy of evidence, as expressed by Paul Kurtz and Brian Dunning. A skeptic values reason and critical thinking to establish validity, as opposed to a pseudo-skeptic who defends preconceived ideological positions without investigating alternatives or trying to understand rational explanations.

Handling Skepticism Around Miracles and Selective Skepticism

Skepticism reaches its peak when faced with miracles, such as those reported in the Bible. David Hume, a philosopher, argued against miracles, stating they contradict common sense. However, is it reasonable to dismiss miracles outright? Genesis 1:1, "In the beginning, God created the heavens and the earth," points to an act far more miraculous than any reported in subsequent Scriptures.

Selective skepticism, another common occurrence, involves accepting some historical accounts readily while questioning others. For instance, the authenticity of manuscripts supporting Roman

176

historian Tacitus or philosopher Plato might not be scrutinized, whereas those of the New Testament often face rigorous skepticism, despite extensive supporting evidence.

Addressing Double Standards and Raising the Bar

The study of Scriptures sometimes falls victim to double standards in historical investigation. While substantial internal and external evidence supports the Bible, critics tend to raise the bar when it comes to validating its authenticity, often disregarding standard historical investigation practices. This includes creating higher standards or moving the goal post, which involves refusing to accept arguments even when the initial counterargument has been satisfied.

Feeding Faith, Not Skepticism

Feeding skepticism rather than faith can be a pitfall for many. An overreliance on works by skeptics, agnostics, or liberal Bible scholars can lead to spiritual derailment. Instead, one should also invest time in studying works by conservative Christian apologists.

Postmodern Culture and Skepticism

Postmodern philosophy argues that there's no objective entity called "history," only individuals' impressions captured in surviving sources. The belief in the relativity of truth and rejection of logic and rational arguments seem to characterize this viewpoint. However, the idea of postmodernism as an all-encompassing perspective is a myth. When it comes to matters of science, engineering, technology, and even daily life, people still rely on logic, rationality, and objective truth.

British Philosopher Bertrand Russell states that 'an easy and elegant skepticism is the attitude expected of an educated adult.' While skepticism can be a helpful tool in our quest for truth, we must approach it with balance and fairness, especially when investigating the historical veracity of Scriptures.

Daniel Wallace (born June 5, 1952) is an American professor of New Testament Studies at Dallas Theological Seminary. He is also the founder and executive director of the Center for the Study of New Testament Manuscripts. In the Foreword of *MYTHS AND MISTAKES In New Testament Textual Criticism,* **he writes in 2019,** "The **new generation of evangelical scholars is far more comfortable with ambiguity and uncertainty** than previous generations." – Elijah Hixon and Peter J. Gurry, *MYTHS AND MISTAKES In New Testament Textual Criticism* (Downer Groves, IL: InterVarsity Press, 2019), 14.

Samuel Tregelles (1813– 1875) an English Bible scholar, textual critic, and theologian, **writing in 1844** defines textual criticism as the means "by which we know, on grounds of **ascertained certainty,** the actual words and sentences of that charter [the Bible] in the true statement of its privileges, and in the terms in which the Holy Ghost gave it." – *An Account of the Printed Text of the Greek New Testament, with Remarks on Its Revision upon Critical Principles* (London: Samuel Bagster, 1854), viii.

Tregelles **writes in 1844** with no papyrus manuscripts, no catalog of manuscripts (5,898), no high definition images, no computer programs, no Wescott and Hort, no Nestle-Aland critical text, no textual commentaries, and having no insights from hundreds of world-renowned textual scholars from 1844 – 2020, and Wallace **writes in 2019,** having all of the above and more. Personally, I am adopting that phrase **ascertained certainty**. It is going to become my new textual studies motto.

Those who believe skepticism is needed in academia, those who have struggled with uncertainty, and doubts, ponder this, why have some Christians been martyred with horrible deaths throughout the last 2,000 years with only a basic Bible education by scholars like the happy Agnostic Dr. Bart D. Ehrman loses his faith having had access to mountains of evidence? **FAITH!** One ascertained certainty and maintained faith.

What Is Doubt

Below is a section taken from *The Baker Encyclopedia of Psychology and Counseling*, Second Edition, which will help the readers better understand what doubt is and when it has become a problem to the point of being concerned.

Doubt. A state of mind characterized by an absence of either assent or dissent to a certain proposition. It is a suspension of commitment to belief or disbelief, either because the evidence pro and con are evenly balanced (a positive doubt) or because the evidence is lacking for either side (negative doubt, exemplified by the apostle Thomas). Doubt is thus an integral part of each person's belief system since it is impossible for anyone to believe or disbelieve with complete certainty all propositions of which he or she is aware. Yet in spite of the natural occurrence of doubt in human cognition, many people view doubt as a negative mindset to be avoided if at all possible.

Doubt is a topic of interest to scholars from three academic disciplines. Philosophers study doubt because of its epistemological implications in relation to knowledge, truth, and awareness of existence. Theologians are concerned with doubt because it often occurs as a prelude to belief or as a precursor of disbelief. Psychologists investigate doubt because of the emotions that often accompany it (anxiety, depression, or fear) and because in certain pathologies doubt can become obsessional and debilitating.

Doubt, Unbelief, and Ambivalence. One can differentiate between doubt and unbelief. Unbelief is a positive conviction of falsity regarding an issue and hence is a form of belief. Doubt does not imply a belief in a contrary position; it is simply being unconvinced. If, however, doubt becomes pervasive and dominates the thinking of a person regarding all issues, it is more appropriately called skepticism or definitive doubt. The skeptic despairs of ever knowing truth with certainty.

One can also distinguish doubt from ambivalence. Ambivalence is a state of mind characterized by the concurrent presence of two or more differing feelings toward the same object. Indecisiveness and vacillation, although related to doubt, refer more to a lack of commitment to a proposition or to a frequent change of opinion. Ambivalence in massive quantities is classically seen as a primary indicator of schizophrenia, whereas massive doubt is more often a part of obsessional disorders.

One can differentiate between normal doubt and abnormal doubt chiefly by the degree to which the doubt impairs daily living. Doubt is normal when it does not dominate a person's thinking, when it is overshadowed by stable beliefs, and when the goal of the doubt is resolution into belief or disbelief. Doubt is also normal when employed, as René Descartes advocated, for the purpose of seeking truth. Normal doubt is a type of mental clarification and can help a person better organize his or her beliefs. Developmental theorists have noted several phases of life when doubts are characteristically found: in adolescence, when the teenager moves from childhood credulity toward a personalized belief system, and in the middle years, when issues of competence and direction predominate (Grant, 1974). Abnormal doubt, unlike normal doubt, focuses on issues having little consequence or issues without grave implications of error.

Religious Doubt. Religious doubt has been a concern of believers from biblical days to the present. In the garden of Eden the serpent used doubt as a tool to move Eve from a position of belief to one of disobedience. Abraham, Job, and David all had times of doubt that were painful yet growth-producing. The best-known example of doubt in the Bible is Thomas, who was absent when Jesus made a post resurrection appearance to the ten apostles. Jesus showed the ten his hands and his side (John 20), evidence that dispelled their doubt as to his identity. When told of Jesus' appearance, Thomas replied that he would not believe until he too had seen the evidence. Eight days later Jesus reappeared, showed Thomas his wounds, and made a gracious plea for faith.

By way of contrast, Jesus consistently condemned unbelief wherever he found it. Jesus presumably tolerated doubt because it was a transitory, nonpermanent state of mind, whereas he condemned unbelief because it was a fixed decision often accompanied by hardness of heart. Guinness (1976) cautions, however, that Scripture sometimes uses the word *unbelief* to refer to doubt (Mark 9:24). Hence exegetical care is needed when interpreting the Bible's teachings regarding doubt.

Doubt is a problem in theological systems committed to inscripturated truth. For example, evangelical Christians are generally not tolerant of doubt if it is prolonged, unyielding, and centered on cardinal truths. Doubt is not so much a problem in liberal theologies since truth in those systems is more relative and less certain. Thus the conservative Christian community sees doubt as risky and dangerous, whereas the liberal Christian community sees doubt as a sign of healthy intellectual inquiry. Some psychologists of religion even see doubt, particularly as envisioned within a questing religious orientation (see Batson, Schoenrade, & Ventis, 1993), as an indication of religious maturity.

Normal doubt tends to appear when a person's belief system "does not protect the individual in his life experiences and from its more painful states" (Halfaer, 1972, p. 216). Doubt is resolved into belief or disbelief in any of four ways: through conversion, through liberalization, through renewal, or through emotional growth. Individuals can construct rigid defenses designed to ensure belief and prevent doubt at all costs such as sometimes occurs in cults that discourage any reexamination of beliefs. (Benner and Hill 1985, 1999, P. 368)

Wrestling with Doubt: An In-depth Examination of Faith and Uncertainty

In the realm of spirituality and belief, doubt refers to a state of uncertainty or skepticism about aspects of God's Word or specific biblical teachings. This sentiment might manifest as a statement such as, "I think it's improbable that the Bible is entirely free of errors." Some individuals may grapple with uncertainty over the legitimacy of particular biblical teachings or question the overall accuracy and dependability of the Word of God. They might speculate on the likelihood of the Bible being entirely factual or its relevance to our contemporary world.

There are also those who encounter doubts, not because they dispute the precision of the Bible, but because their uncertainties are emotionally charged and require healing on an emotional level. Perhaps you've recently lost a loved one—a child, spouse, or parent—and the grief has left you questioning. Or maybe you've been dealing with a significant life challenge. You've turned to God in prayer, seeking His guidance to handle or conquer this problem. But without a clear answer, you might feel as though the Holy Spirit is silent, leading you to question God's existence.

Sometimes, a grave sin committed might leave you feeling abandoned by God, leading to a creeping doubt about His existence. Observing the suffering and injustice in the world—children starving and dying, the prevalence of violence, the existence of radical ideologies, the use of chemical weapons against innocent people, the universal human experience of aging, illness, and death—might lead you to question how a loving, omnipotent, righteous, and fair God could allow such pain. Doubts may also arise from personal struggles, such as grappling with same-sex attraction.

We must recognize that doubt—a feeling of uncertainty or being unconvinced—is not an anomaly, even in the most mature and knowledgeable Christian. Experiencing doubt is part of our human condition. Why? Even though we can hold certain knowledge with absolute certainty, we cannot claim to know everything, leading us to question certain doctrines. However, after enough research and contemplation, we can believe beyond a reasonable doubt (borrowing from legal terminology) that we have arrived at the truth on a particular matter.

So, if you're struggling with a specific doctrine, a particular Bible difficulty, or a personal issue, it doesn't have to overwhelm you emotionally. That being said, excessive doubts should be addressed before they lead to spiritual distress or a crisis of faith. It is important to remember that doubt and faith are not mutually exclusive. Doubt

CHAPTER 11 How Can We Respond to Selective Skepticism When It Comes to God and the Bible?

Selective Skepticism: A Faithful Response to Doubts about God and the Bible

Selective skepticism is an attitude that characterizes a certain segment of people in our society. While they are highly critical and skeptical about God, the Bible, and religious phenomena, they often do not extend the same level of scrutiny to other areas of life or other belief systems. This selective skepticism is a challenge that those of us with faith in God and the Bible frequently face in conversations and debates. So, how do we respond to such skepticism?

First, we must understand and appreciate the root of skepticism. Skepticism is not inherently bad; it is a tool for discerning truth from falsehood. The capacity for skepticism is part of our God-given ability to reason and discern. We see examples of healthy skepticism even in the Bible itself. The Bereans, mentioned in Acts 17:11 (ESV), were commended because they received the Word with all eagerness but examined the Scriptures daily to see if what Paul and Silas were teaching was true. The Bible invites us to "test everything; hold fast what is good." (1 Thessalonians 5:21, ESV).

However, skepticism becomes problematic when it is selectively applied. Selective skepticism is biased and unbalanced. It subjects certain areas or ideas to extreme scrutiny while unquestioningly accepting others. In conversations about faith, selective skeptics often dismiss or doubt the Bible's validity, miracles, and the existence of God without applying the same level of skepticism to their own worldviews or the presuppositions of other belief systems.

When responding to selective skepticism, we must do so with grace, respect, and sound reasoning. As 1 Peter 3:15 (ESV) instructs, we are to make a defense to anyone who asks for a reason for the hope that is in us; yet do it with gentleness and respect. This response is not merely about winning an argument but about demonstrating the love of Christ in our interactions.

We can begin by pointing out the bias inherent in selective skepticism. Encourage skeptics to apply the same level of critical thinking and scrutiny to all areas of their belief system. Why is it that they doubt the existence of God, yet readily accept the assumptions underlying naturalism, humanism, or relativism?

One of the ways we can address selective skepticism is by presenting the consistent internal coherence of the Bible. Unlike other religious texts, the Bible was written over a span of approximately 1600 years, by over 40 different authors from various walks of life, yet it presents a consistent narrative and message. This extraordinary consistency is a compelling argument for the divine inspiration and trustworthiness of the Bible.

Next, we can highlight the wealth of historical and archaeological evidence supporting the biblical narrative. From the discovery of ancient cities mentioned in the Old Testament to the numerous historical documents validating New Testament accounts, the Bible's historical credibility is well-established. The selective skeptic often overlooks or diminishes these pieces of evidence.

We can also address the skepticism about God's existence by discussing the philosophical and moral arguments for God. The argument from design, the moral argument, the cosmological argument, and others provide reasonable grounds for belief in God. These arguments challenge the presuppositions of atheism and naturalism and invite the skeptic to reconsider their bias against the possibility of God's existence.

The issue of miracles is another area where selective skeptics often exhibit bias. They dismiss miracles a priori based on a naturalistic worldview. However, if God exists and created the natural laws, is it not reasonable to believe that He can intervene and supersede those laws? Miracles are not a violation of natural laws but a manifestation of a higher, divine law.

When we address selective skepticism, we must remember to do so lovingly, with the intent of encouraging thoughtful reflection rather than provoking defensive reactions. Our aim is not to coerce belief, but to foster an open and honest examination of the evidence.

Finally, it's important to remember that ultimately, it's the Holy Spirit that convicts and convinces. Our role is to present the truth faithfully, but we must rely on the Holy Spirit to work in people's hearts. As Jesus Himself said in John 16:8 (ESV), "And when He [the Holy Spirit] comes, He will convict the world concerning sin and righteousness and judgment."

In conclusion, the response to selective skepticism about God and the Bible is a balanced combination of grace and truth, challenging biases, presenting evidence, and above all, relying on the Holy Spirit. It's not merely a battle of wits and arguments, but a matter of the heart that calls for divine intervention.

Overcoming Doubt: A Christian's Path to Certainty

Doubts can creep into the minds of even the most devoted Christians. Whether these doubts are about the existence of God, the validity of the Bible, or questions about our personal faith journey, they can be unsettling. Yet, it is essential to remember that doubts can also serve as catalysts for deeper faith and understanding. The following are some ways that Christians can navigate and overcome their doubts.

Seek Knowledge and Understanding

The Bible reminds us in Hosea 4:6 (ASV) that "My people are destroyed for lack of knowledge". Knowledge plays a crucial role in overcoming doubts. Often, our doubts arise from misunderstandings or lack of information. This is why it's vital for every Christian to study the Bible diligently, for the Word of God is the bedrock of our faith.

Ask Questions and Seek Answers

Many people feel guilty for harboring doubts, but questioning is an essential part of faith formation. We see examples in the Bible, such as the father who cried out to Jesus, "I believe; help my unbelief!" (Mark 9:24, ESV) and Thomas, who wanted proof of Jesus' resurrection. Engage with your questions, explore them, and seek answers. This can involve reading theological works, listening to sermons, attending Bible study groups, or consulting with mentors and leaders in your faith community.

Engage in Prayer and Meditation

Prayer is not merely a routine or ritual, but a profound communion with God. When doubts arise, bring them before God in prayer. Remember, the Holy Spirit is our Helper and Teacher (John 14:26, ESV). Ask for wisdom and guidance, and trust that the Holy Spirit will provide. Additionally, meditating on the scriptures can help quiet our restless thoughts and draw us closer to God's truth.

Experience the Christian Community

The Church is not just a group of individuals but a body (1 Corinthians 12:27, ESV). When faced with doubts, it can be comforting and enlightening to engage with fellow believers. Others may have experienced similar doubts and can provide insight, encouragement, and testimonies of their own faith journey.

Live Out Your Faith

Faith is not merely a cognitive belief but a lived experience. James reminds us that "faith by itself, if it does not have works, is dead" (James 2:17, ESV). Living out our faith allows us to experience God's grace, love, and power in tangible ways, reinforcing our belief and dispelling doubts.

Remember the Role of the Holy Spirit

In our pursuit of certainty, it's crucial to remember the role of the Holy Spirit in overcoming doubts. As Christians, we believe that the Holy Spirit guides us into all truth (John 16:13, ESV). Hence, lean on the Holy Spirit's guidance, knowing that He can illuminate the Word of God and clarify its truths to your heart.

Embrace Doubt as a Pathway to Deeper Faith

Finally, remember that doubt is not the opposite of faith; rather, it is a part of the journey of faith. As theologian Frederick Buechner said, "Doubts are the ants in the pants of faith. They keep it awake and moving." Doubts can spur us to dig deeper into God's Word, seek His face in prayer, and lean more heavily on His promises.

CHAPTER 12 Why Do We Need to Beware of Most Skeptics Who Are Seeking to Feed Our Doubts?

Beware the Skeptic: A Christian's Guide to Safeguarding Faith

In the Christian faith, doubts are natural and, to a certain extent, unavoidable. However, it's imperative to discern between healthy, self-directed doubts that lead to spiritual growth and those that are fuelled by external skepticism, particularly by skeptics who have a vested interest in undermining faith. Paul warns in 1 Timothy 4:1 (ESV), "The Spirit explicitly says that in later times some will fall away from the faith." Why does this happen, and how can we guard against it?

The Allure of Skepticism

In our modern era, skepticism has been lauded as an intellectual virtue. Prominent philosophers like Bertrand Russell have encouraged an attitude of systematic doubt, positing that "an easy and elegant skepticism is the attitude expected of an educated adult." While skepticism can be a healthy tool to scrutinize unverified claims, it becomes a problem when applied inconsistently or with bias. This is particularly apparent when skeptics apply a harsher level of scrutiny to the Bible compared to other historical documents.

When examining secular history, historians tend to be balanced, fair, and reasonable. However, when approaching the Bible, many apply a double standard. The bar is raised when it comes to the level of evidence required to accept Biblical accounts as credible, while secular history is often taken at face value with far less supporting evidence.

191

The Skeptic's Game

One needs to understand that skeptics have a different goal compared to believers seeking to resolve doubts. While the believer seeks truth and reassurance, many skeptics aren't interested in answers, but rather in feeding their doubt and undermining the Christian faith. They may challenge the Bible's validity by presenting alleged contradictions, errors, or historical inaccuracies. When believers provide reasonable, logical, rational answers to their claims, they often dismiss these out of hand, moving on to their next objection.

Engaging in such debates can be like trying to plug holes in a sinking ship: every resolved issue is replaced with a new challenge. The skeptic is rarely satisfied because the goal isn't resolution, but rather the perpetuation of doubt and skepticism.

The Power of Faith

Despite the skepticism and doubt that can abound in scholarly discourse and society, Christians should strive to be like the man described in Jeremiah 17:7 (ASV), who is blessed because he trusts in Jehovah. Christians need not fall into the trap of perpetual skepticism. We have joyful confidence in the truth of God's Word and the assurance that our faith is not unfounded.

Paul expresses this confidence in 2 Timothy 1:12 (ESV), writing, "For this reason I also suffer these things, but I am not ashamed; for I know whom I have believed and I am convinced that he is able to guard what I have entrusted to him until that day." Such conviction is the antithesis of skepticism.

Guarding Against the Influence of Skeptics

Christians should be aware of skeptics who aim to dismantle faith, especially those who employ selective skepticism, applying rigorous doubt to religious belief while accepting secular claims without the same level of scrutiny. To guard against such influence, Christians need to build a firm foundation of Biblical knowledge and understanding, rooted in diligent study of the Scriptures.

In addition, Christians should also cultivate their relationship with the Holy Spirit, our Helper and Teacher, who guides us into all truth (John 16:13, ESV). The Holy Spirit can provide clarity, discernment, and wisdom, helping us to navigate the challenges presented by skeptics.

Finally, while Christians should not shy away from honest questions about their faith, they should also discern when it's fruitful to engage in debate with skeptics. At times, it may be wiser to disengage and instead focus on growing in knowledge and faith.

In conclusion, skepticism isn't inherently detrimental to faith. It can, in fact, spur believers to gain a deeper understanding of their faith. However, Christians need to beware of skeptics who wield skepticism not as a tool for discovery, but as a weapon to sow doubt. With knowledge, faith, and the guidance of the Holy Spirit, Christians can stand firm in their beliefs, despite the challenges presented by skepticism.

The Sacred Boundary: Understanding the Unreceptive Heart in Christian Evangelism

The essence of Christianity entails spreading the Gospel, an act known as evangelism. However, this effort can sometimes hit a wall, particularly when the intended recipients of the Good News appear to be skeptics with seemingly unreceptive hearts. To navigate this delicate balance, Christians can turn to scriptural guidance, such as Matthew 7:6, which suggests an important limitation on evangelism.

The Figurative Dogs and Swine: Unreceptive Hearts

When Jesus said, "Do not give what is holy to dogs, and do not throw your pearls before swine," He was not degrading anyone by comparing them to animals. Instead, He used these metaphors to describe individuals who are unappreciative or hostile towards the spiritual truths of God's Word.

It is crucial to note that this passage does not categorize all non-believers as "dogs" or "swine." There are many individuals who are genuinely searching for spiritual answers, and these seekers should not be mistaken for those who scorn and reject the message of the Gospel.

However, we do encounter individuals who show no interest in genuine dialogue but instead seek to mock, ridicule, or find fault with the Christian faith. In these cases, the act of evangelism can become an exercise in futility. To discern between seekers and scoffers, one can refer to the teachings in Proverbs 9:7-9.

The Scoffer's Response to Correction

The wisdom literature in Proverbs offers profound insights into the character of those who scoff at wisdom and instruction. According to these scriptures, those who scoff—those unreceptive to wisdom and correction—respond to reproof with hostility and contempt. Instead of taking to heart the corrective counsel offered, they dismiss it, ridicule it, or react with anger.

Contrastingly, the wise and the righteous respond positively to reproof. They appreciate the correction and see it as an opportunity to grow in wisdom and understanding. This difference in response serves as a yardstick to differentiate between those with receptive hearts and those with unreceptive ones.

Setting the Boundaries of Evangelism

While evangelism is a core mandate for Christians, it is neither a mandate to convert every individual nor an invitation to enter into fruitless debates. There are times when the best course of action is to withdraw from an unproductive conversation, especially with individuals who show signs of a hard, unreceptive heart.

The Apostle Paul sets an excellent precedent in Acts 13:45-46. When he encountered Jews who merely sought to contradict and argue, he recognized the futility of his efforts and turned his focus towards those who were receptive—the Gentiles. Similarly, when we face opposition and hostility from individuals who dismiss the message of Christ, it might be wise to disengage and focus on those who are open to receiving the Gospel.

The Wise Approach to Evangelism

Discernment is crucial in the process of evangelism. While Christians should not shy away from defending their faith and presenting the hope they carry, they must be mindful of the context and the receptivity of their audience.

In public settings, it might be appropriate to provide a reasoned response to challenges or objections to the faith. However, Christians should also know when to exit such exchanges graciously, especially when they devolve into arguments and heated debates.

Moreover, Christians are called to stand apart from the world. As disciples of Christ, they should cultivate a love for discipline and correction. Each time a Christian engages with God's Word, it provides an opportunity for correction and growth. No Christian, regardless of their age or experience, can outgrow the need for counsel from God's Word.

Satan Has Blinded the Minds of the Unbeliever

Let us take a look at our primary text: 2 Corinthians 4:3-4 (ESV), "And even if our gospel is veiled, it is veiled to those who are perishing. In their case the god of this world has blinded the minds of the unbelievers, to keep them from seeing the light of the gospel of the glory of Christ, who is the image of God."

A crucial question arises: how does Satan blind the minds of unbelievers? The text doesn't specify the mechanics of this process, but it suggests a metaphorical 'veiling', comparable to a cover placed over something to obstruct its view. The veil symbolizes the barriers that hinder spiritual understanding, such as prejudices, misconceptions, stubbornness, and sinfulness, all which are, in a way, propagated by Satan.

To get a more profound understanding of this spiritual blindness, we should consider the parallel scripture in 2 Corinthians 3:12-18 (UASV). Here, Paul references Moses who used to put a veil over his face to prevent the Israelites from seeing the fading glory. The 'veil' is used metaphorically to represent spiritual blindness. In the context of our primary text, the veil isn't just physical, but it's a spiritual barrier that prevents people from understanding the gospel. This veil remains unlifted because it can be taken away only by Christ. This suggests that it's not mere intellectual understanding that's required, but spiritual transformation and revelation that comes from turning to Christ.

The role of Satan as the 'god of this world' plays out in various ways in perpetuating spiritual blindness. He promotes a system of values, beliefs, and behaviors that are contrary to God's Word. He manipulates people's understanding through deception, distraction, and the promotion of sinful desires. He lures people away from the light of the gospel and into the darkness of disbelief. Unbelievers, under the sway of Satan, become so engrossed in the ways of this world that they fail to recognize the glory of Christ and the truth of the gospel.

Yet, this spiritual blindness isn't permanent. The same passage assures us that the veil can be taken away by turning to the Lord, affirming the redemptive and restorative power of Christ. As we submit ourselves to Christ and invite the Holy Spirit into our lives, we're gradually transformed and begin to see the glory of God clearly.

Even so, the hardened heart plays a significant role in this spiritual blindness. As Jesus illustrated in the Parable of the Sower (Matthew 13:3-23), the gospel message doesn't penetrate hardened hearts, comparable to the seeds falling on the path where birds (symbolizing the evil one) come and snatch them away. Similarly, the unbelievers' hearts are hardened by the deceitfulness of sin and the seduction of worldly pleasures, preventing the gospel message from taking root.

Understanding this concept of spiritual blindness highlights the urgency of proclaiming the gospel. The antidote to this blindness is the illuminating power of the gospel that brings light and life to those living in spiritual darkness. As we share the good news, we do so with the awareness that only Christ can lift the veil of spiritual blindness and open people's minds to the truth. Therefore, our role isn't to argue or convince, but to faithfully share the gospel message, praying that the Holy Spirit will awaken spiritual sight and understanding.

It's important to note, however, that this process doesn't negate human responsibility. While Satan works to blind minds and harden hearts, individuals still have a personal responsibility to respond to the gospel message. The gospel remains veiled to those who choose to reject it, those who, despite hearing the truth, dismiss it as folly.

In conclusion, the spiritual blindness that Paul speaks of is a complex phenomenon caused by a combination of Satan's deceptive influence and personal hard-heartedness, creating a veil that hinders understanding and acceptance of the gospel. But hope remains in the power of Christ to lift this veil, as we turn to Him and allow the Holy Spirit to transform us, revealing the glory of God that was once hidden.

The Risk of Grieving the Holy Spirit in a Christian Life

As followers of Christ, we recognize the importance of being in tune with the Holy Spirit. The Holy Spirit, granted to us as believers, guides, empowers, and convicts us in our Christian walk. Ephesians 4:30 warns us against grieving the Holy Spirit. The scripture states, "And do not grieve the Holy Spirit of God, by whom you were sealed for the day of redemption." The question is, how do Christians grieve the Holy Spirit, and what can we do to avoid such a grievous act?

Understanding the Holy Spirit's Role

To answer this question, we first need to comprehend the role of the Holy Spirit in a believer's life. In Ephesians 1:18, Paul prays that the Ephesians would have the "eyes of your heart enlightened, that you may know what is the hope to which he has called you, what are the riches of the glory of his inheritance in the holy ones." This phrase, "eyes of your heart," is a metaphorical expression, denoting spiritual insight or understanding.

The Holy Spirit guides us into this spiritual understanding, enlightening the eyes of our heart to comprehend and apply God's Word. We pray for the Holy Spirit's guidance, and our spirit, or mental disposition, needs to align with God and His Spirit through study and application. If our disposition is not harmonious with the Spirit, we risk misinterpreting the Word, thereby grieving the Spirit.

Grieving the Holy Spirit: A Process of Misalignment

Grieving the Holy Spirit occurs when our actions contradict its leading. This could be due to deception, human frailties, or setting our heart on something other than God's leading. In essence, grieving the Holy Spirit manifests when we allow human imperfection and bias to overshadow the Spirit's guidance, resulting in incorrect understanding and application of God's Word.

Consider a scenario where an individual embarks on a Bible study session. He prays earnestly for the Holy Spirit's guidance and sets out to study a chapter. However, during the study, he allows his biases, preconceptions, or erroneous worldview to influence his interpretation of the scripture. Instead of seeking the simple, essential, or obvious meaning of the text (the fundamental of grammatical-historical interpretation), he rationalizes the scripture to align with his presuppositions. This act grieves the Holy Spirit because he has prioritized his personal biases above the Spirit's guidance.

Grieving the Holy Spirit: Uncovering Bias and Dishonesty

Another scenario that illustrates grieving the Holy Spirit is when an individual uses a translation that is tainted with theological bias. This bias, whether deliberate or unintentional, can distort the original meaning of the scripture. The individual might uncover that the scripture could be interpreted differently in light of its context. However, he might choose to suppress this evidence, adhering to the biased interpretation that aligns with his preconceived ideas. This act of dishonesty and preference for bias grieves the Holy Spirit.

Grieving the Holy Spirit: Ignoring Spiritual Awareness

Nonbelievers can understand the Bible's text, hence our mandate to witness to them. They can study the setting, words, and sentences of Scripture in their normal, plain sense. However, they lack the spiritual awareness to see the significance of the Scripture, leading to the rejection of its truth. As stated in 1 Corinthians 2:14, "The natural person does not accept the things of the Spirit of God." The word "accept" (dechomai in Greek) means to welcome or receive. Therefore, a nonbeliever might comprehend a text but not accept, receive, or welcome it as truth. This denial grieves the Holy Spirit.

In contrast, the Bereans in Acts 17:10-11 were lauded as noble-minded because they received the Word of God eagerly, examining the Scriptures daily to verify Paul's teachings. They did not grieve the Holy Spirit but were receptive to its guidance.

Avoiding Grieving the Holy Spirit

It's evident that grieving the Holy Spirit stems from dishonesty, bias, preconceived notions, and lack of spiritual awareness. These factors can dilute the Spirit's guidance and impact our understanding and application of God's Word. As believers, we should strive to avoid grieving the Holy Spirit by adhering to God's Word honestly and without bias.

We should strive to live free of sin, approach scripture with humility, and openness, always seeking the simple and obvious meaning of the text. We must remember that no interpreter is infallible and that the Holy Spirit's guidance is contingent on our willingness to cooperate with it.

The Holy Spirit guides us in our understanding as we invest time in personal study and Christian meetings. It helps us make sense of God's Word as we set aside our biases, imperfections, and open our hearts to the Spirit's leading. We must always remember the importance of not grieving the Holy Spirit as we strive to live a life that pleases God.

The Holy Spirit's Influence: Transformative Power through the Word of God

A prominent pillar in the Christian faith is the work of the Holy Spirit. It is a significant theological tenet, intimately tied to God's inspired and inerrant Word, essential in shaping believers' spiritual lives. This understanding is not in alignment with the ecstatic and irrational interpretation often associated with charismatic groups but is rooted in a calm and rational context. The Holy Spirit operates through the words and ideas expressed in Scripture, offering spiritual strength and enlightenment to those who receive them. It initiates the path to salvation and persuades individuals towards this ultimate goal. However, this persuasive power is neither abstract nor separate from the Word of God.

The Holy Spirit and the Word of God

The Apostles did not separate the Spirit and the Word of God in their teachings, attributing specific influence to one over the other. Instead, they affirmed the synergistic interplay between them in the process of conversion. The Spirit works through the Word, ensuring believers are led to salvation. It is not an abstract Spirit or Word that we believe in and teach, but the Word and Spirit combined, working together seamlessly. Importantly, the Holy Spirit's promise is exclusive to those within the fold of Christ, specifically those who believe in Him and obey His teachings.

The Holy Spirit's Role in Conversion

The Holy Spirit plays a significant role in the conversion of sinners, operating exclusively through the Word of God. In other words, the Spirit, acting through the Word of God, can bring about the transformation attributed to a personal indwelling of the Spirit. Zachary Taylor Sweeney, a long-time preacher and author of "The Spirit and the Word: A Treatise on the Holy Spirit in the Light of a Rational Interpretation of the Word of God," explored this concept extensively. He evaluated every Scripture advocating a literal personal indwelling of the Holy Spirit and concluded that all possible actions of a direct indwelling Spirit are achievable through the Word of God.

Sweeney reasoned that a direct indwelling Spirit does not provide new revelations, offer new motives, or add any new reasons not already present in the Word of God. Consequently, he questioned the necessity of a direct indwelling Spirit. He argued that God creates nothing in vain and suggested that God's interaction with His children is psychologically similar to His engagement with individuals he seeks to convert into His children.

The Holy Spirit and the Transformation of the Believer

Our interpretation, aligned with the philosophy of Christian Publishing House, contradicts Holiness and Pentecostal understandings of the Holy Spirit. We acknowledge the transformative power of the Holy Spirit through the Word of God in empowering believers to embrace the "new person" that defines the Christian life. The verse from Colossians 3:12 reads, "So, as those who have been chosen of God, holy and beloved, put on a heart of compassion, kindness, humility, gentleness, and patience."

The Holy Spirit, through the Word of God, helps us to "put off" our former way of life, as instructed in Ephesians 4:20-24, and to "put

201

on the new man who is being renewed through accurate knowledge according to the image of the one who created him," as highlighted in Colossians 3:9-10. These Scriptures underscore the transformative work of the Holy Spirit as it works through the Word of God to shape believers into the image of Christ, encouraging a lifestyle that is righteous and true.

In conclusion, the work of the Holy Spirit is integrally connected to the Word of God, driving believers towards salvation and spiritual transformation. It operates through the Word of God, aiding believers to discard their former way of life and embrace the new one, molded in the image of God. This understanding encourages a calm, rational appreciation of the Holy Spirit's work, contrary to ecstatic and irrational interpretations.

CHAPTER 13 How Were the Bible Authors Inspired by God, Moved Along by the Holy Spirit, and How Did Jesus Bring Remembrance to the Apostles?

The Divine Inspiration of Biblical Authors: The Interplay of God, the Holy Spirit, and Remembrance

The concept of divine inspiration plays a vital role in understanding the composition of the Bible. It refers to the state of being moved, guided, or directed by the Holy Spirit, under the authority of God. This inspiration and direction lead to the writing of the scriptures, considered both sacred and authoritative within Christianity. This process of divine inspiration has multiple layers, involving the Greek terms "inspired by God" (θεόπνευστος - theopneustos), "carried along" (φερόμενοι - pheromenoi), and "bring to remembrance" (ὑπομνήσει - hupomnēsei).

Theopneustos: Inspiration by God

The term "inspired by God" (θεόπνευστος - theopneustos), literally translates as "God-breathed" or "breathed by God." This implies a divine influence that guided the biblical authors without dictating their writing. Although God directed the authors, they were allowed to express His message using their individual writing styles. Yet, the influence was strong enough to prevent the miscommunication of the intended message.

203

Christians can experience a similar, albeit lesser, form of this divine guidance through their understanding and application of God's Word. Yet, this inspiration can only be experienced if the word of God is interpreted correctly and applied appropriately in life.

Pheromenoi: Being Carried Along by the Holy Spirit

The term "carried along" (φερόμενοι - pheromenoi) refers to the idea of being moved or guided by the Holy Spirit. It suggests a form of divine direction leading the biblical authors during their composition of the scriptures.

This carrying along by the Holy Spirit was not limited to the inspirational stage but continued during the writing process. The Spirit's guidance ensured the accurate transcription of God's message, making the Bible a reliable source of God's word for all generations.

Hupomnēsei: God Bringing Remembrance

The term "bring to remembrance" (ὑπομνήσει - hupomnēsei) implies that God enabled the Gospel authors to recall in detail the events they had experienced. This divine act of bringing to remembrance served a significant role, especially in the creation of the Gospels.

The authors of the Gospels (Matthew and John directly, Mark through Peter, and Luke through Peter, extensive research, and other sources) were divinely reminded of the events they witnessed. God brought to their remembrance the teachings and actions of Jesus Christ, allowing them to record the Gospel with a level of detail and accuracy that would have been impossible to achieve through human memory alone.

Divine Inspiration in Various Forms

These three Greek terms illustrate the complexity and depth of the divine inspiration behind the composition of the Bible. The Bible authors were inspired by God, moved by the Holy Spirit, and reminded by God of the events they witnessed.

In addition to this, God communicated with His servants in several ways throughout the Old Testament times. This communication ranged from direct dictation, like the Ten Commandments and specific messages to prophets, to dreams and visions. Angelic messengers also played a role in delivering God's Word.

Regardless of the method, all of these forms of divine inspiration share the common trait of being "God-breathed" or inspired by God. This divine inspiration and guidance, whether through direct dictation, visions, dreams, or angelic messages, ensured the accurate transcription of God's message in the Bible.

The process of divine inspiration, as outlined in 2 Timothy 3:16, 2 Peter 1:21, and John 14:26, is complex yet beautifully orchestrated. It signifies the careful guidance of God and the Holy Spirit over the biblical authors to ensure the delivery of God's word to humanity. This divine inspiration underpins the authority and authenticity of the scriptures, forming the foundation of Christian belief and practice.

The Interplay of Human Individuality and Divine Inspiration in the Composition of the Bible

The compilation of the Bible is a remarkable interweaving of human individuality and divine inspiration. It represents the harmonious cooperation between the human authors' unique personalities, backgrounds, and writing styles, and the overarching direction of God through the Holy Spirit. It is a delicate balance that manifests itself in the sacred text's diversity and uniformity.

The Bible is a divinely inspired text, but it is not a book of rote dictation from God. The individuals who penned the scriptures were not mechanical transcribers, but they were active participants in the process of conveying God's message. This is vividly illustrated in

Revelation 1:1-2, where the "God-breathed" revelation was delivered to John through an angel, and he expressed it using his words and literary style. This implies that God, in His wisdom, allowed the authors to utilize their God-given faculties, their intellect, their understanding of language, and their personal styles while ensuring that they wrote in complete alignment with His intentions (Proverbs 30:5-6).

The individuality of the biblical authors is seen in their distinctive styles and perspectives, shaped by their experiences and backgrounds. For instance, Matthew, a former tax collector, exhibits a particular inclination towards numbers and financial terms (Matthew 17:27; 26:15; 27:3). Luke, a physician, frequently uses medical terminology and shows a keen interest in people's physical conditions (Luke 4:38; 5:12; 16:20). These subtle stylistic differences do not detract from the Bible's divine inspiration; instead, they add richness to its narrative, making it relatable to a wide range of readers.

In some instances, biblical authors were given an image or concept from God, which they then articulated in their own words. Passages in Isaiah, Micah, and Habakkuk, among others, often speak of the author 'seeing' visions rather than 'hearing' explicit words from God (Isaiah 13:1; Micah 1:1; Habakkuk 1:1; 2:1-2). This method of inspiration permitted the authors to communicate divine truths through their unique perspectives and linguistic styles.

The biblical authors were individuals whose hearts were in tune with God's will. Isaiah expressed an eager longing for God's guidance (Isaiah 26:9), and Paul wrote to address specific needs within the early Christian communities (1 Corinthians 1:10-11; 5:1; 7:1). Their personal experiences and perceptions, coupled with divine inspiration, led to the creation of texts that were both relatable and authoritative.

The process of divine inspiration also involved different methods and degrees of divine intervention. In some cases, the authors used pre-existing records, such as genealogies and historical accounts (Luke 1:3; 3:23-38; Numbers 21:14,15; 1 Kings 14:19,29; 2 Kings 15:31; 24:5), under the Holy Spirit's guidance, ensuring the accuracy of their accounts. In other instances, they were granted knowledge beyond human acquisition, such as insights into the spiritual realm (Job 1:6-12) or future events prophesied centuries or millennia in advance.

Paul's writings provide an excellent example of the harmonious interplay between personal insights and divine inspiration. There were instances when Paul spoke from his experience and understanding, yet, it was always under the guidance of the Holy Spirit (1 Corinthians 7:12-15; 25; 40). His teachings, though borne out of personal conviction, were considered "God-breathed" and carried the same weight and authority as other Scripture (2 Peter 3:15-16).

In conclusion, the Bible is the product of a complex interaction between human authors and divine inspiration. Each author brought their unique perspective and style to their writings, while the Holy Spirit ensured that the resulting text was aligned with God's intentions. This harmonious blend of human individuality and divine inspiration gives the Bible its depth, diversity, and enduring relevance. It is a testament to the wisdom of God, who employed human individuality as an instrument to achieve His divine purposes.

CHAPTER 14 Bible Difficulties Explain

IT SEEMS THAT the charge that the Bible contradicts itself has been made more and more in the last 20 years. Generally, those making such claims are merely repeating what they have heard because most have not even read the Bible, let alone done an in-depth study of it. I do not wish, however, to set aside all concerns as though they have no merit. There are many who raise legitimate questions that seem, on the surface anyway, to be about well-founded contradiction. Sadly, these issues have caused many to lose their faith in God's Word, the Bible. The purpose of this chapter is, to help its readers to be able to defend the Bible against Bible critics (1 Pet. 3:15), to contend for the faith (Jude 1:3), and help those, who have begun to doubt. – Jude 1:22-23.

Before we begin explaining things, let us jump right in, getting our feet wet, and deal with two major Bible difficulties, so we can see that there are reasonable, logical answers. After that, we will delve deeper into explaining Bible difficulties.

Is God permitting Human Sacrifice?

Judges 11:29-34, 37-40? Updated American Standard Version (UASV)

²⁹ Then the Spirit of the Lord was upon Jephthah, and he passed through Gilead and Manasseh; and passed on to Mizpah of Gilead, and from Mizpah of Gilead he passed on to the sons of Ammon. ³⁰ And Jephthah **made a vow** to Jehovah and said, "If You will indeed give the sons of Ammon into my hand, ³¹ then it shall be that **whatever** comes out of the doors of my house to meet me when I return in peace from the sons of Ammon, it shall be Jehovah's, and I will offer it up as a burnt offering." ³² So Jephthah crossed over to the sons of Ammon to fight against them; and Jehovah gave them into his hand. ³³ He struck them with a very great slaughter from Aroer as far as Minnith, twenty cities, and as far as Abel-keramim. So the sons of Ammon were subdued before the sons of Israel.

[34] When Jephthah came to his house at Mizpah, behold, **his daughter was coming out to meet him** with tambourines and with dancing. Now she was his one and only child; besides her he had no son or daughter.

[37] And she said to her father, "Let this thing be done for me: leave me alone two months, that I may go up and down on the mountains and weep because of my virginity, I and my companions." [38] And he said, "Go." So he sent her away for two months; and **she left with her companions, and wept on the mountains because of her virginity.** [39] At the end of two months she returned to her father, who **did to her according to the vow that he had made**; and she never known a man.[171] Thus it became a custom in Israel, [40] that the daughters of Israel went year by year **to commemorate**[172] **the daughter** of Jephthah the Gileadite four days in the year.

It is true; to infer that having the idea of an animal sacrifice would really have not been an impressive vow, which the context requires. Human sacrifice will be repugnant if we are talking about taking a life. Jephthah had no sons, so he likely knew it was the daughter, who would come to greet him.

First, the text does not say he killed his daughter. The idea of some that he did kill her is concluded only by inference. While it is not good policy to interpret backward, using Paul on Judges, he does say humans are to be **"as a living sacrifice."** Therefore, Jephthah could have offered his daughter at the temple, "as a living sacrifice" in service, like Samuel.

This is not to be taken dismissively, because, under Jewish backgrounds, it is no small thing to offer a **perpetual virginity** as a sacrifice. This would mean Jephthah's lineage would not be carried on, the family name, was no more.

Second, the context says she went out to weep for two months, not mourn her death. It says, "she left with her companions, and **wept on the mountains because of her virginity."**

---

[171] I.e., *never had relations with a man*
[172] Or *lament*

If she was facing imminent death, she could have married, and spent that last two months as a married woman. There would be absolutely no reason for her to mourn her virginity if she were not facing perpetual virginity. – Exodus 38:8; 1 Samuel 2:22

Third, it was completely forbidden to offer a human sacrifice. – Leviticus 18:21; 20:2-5; Deuteronomy 12:31; 18:10

Imagine an Israelite believing that he could please God with a human sacrifice that was intended to offer up a human life. To do so would have been a rejection of Jehovah's Sovereignty (the very person you are asking for help), and a rejection of the Law that made them a special people. Worse still, this interpretation would have us believe that Jehovah knew this was coming, allowed the vow, and then aided this type of man to succeed over his enemies.

The last point is simple enough. If such a man as one who would make such a vow, in gross violation of the law, and then carry it out; there is no way he would be mentioned by Paul in Hebrews chapter 11 among the most faithful men and women in Israelite history.

In review, there is no way God would have granted and helped in Jephthah's initial success knowing the vow that was coming because both Jehovah and Jephthah would be as bad as the Canaanites. There is no way that God would accept such a vow and then go on to help Jephthah with his enemies yet again. Then, to allow such a vow to be carried out, to then put Jephthah on the wall of star witnesses for God in Hebrews chapter 11.

Does Isaiah 45:7 mean that God Is the Author of Evil?

Isaiah 45:7 King James Version (KJV)	Isaiah 45:7 English Standard Version (ESV)
[7] I form the light, and create darkness: I make peace, and **create evil**: I the Lord do all these things.	[7] I form light and create darkness, I make well-being and **create calamity**, I am the Lord, who does all these things.[173]

---

[173] See Jeremiah 18:11, Lamentations 3:18, and Amos 3:6

Encarta Dictionary: (Evil) (1) morally bad: profoundly immoral or wrong (2) deliberately causing great harm, pain, or upset

QUESTION: Is this view of evil always the case? No, as you will see below.

Some apologetic authors try to say, 'we do not understand Isaiah 45:7 correctly, because there are other verses that say God is not evil (1 John 1:5), cannot look approvingly on evil (Hab. 1:13), and cannot be tempted by evil. (James 1:13)' Well, while all of these things are Scripturally true, the question at hand is not: Is God evil, can God approvingly look on evil, or can God be tempted with evil? Those questions are not relevant to the one at hand, as God cannot be those things, and at the same time, he can be the yes to our question. The question is, is God the author, the creator of evil?

We would hardly argue that God was **not just** in his bringing "calamity" or "evil" down on Adam and Eve. Thus, we have Isaiah 45:7 saying that God is the creator of "calamity" or "evil."

Let us begin simple, without trying to be philosophical. When God removed Adam and Eve from the Garden of Eden, he sentenced them and humanity to sickness, old age, and death. (Rom. 5:8; i.e., enforce penalty for sin), which was to bring "calamity" or "evil" upon humankind. Therefore, as we can see "evil" does not always mean wrongdoing. Other examples of God bringing "calamity" or "evil" are Noah and the flood, the Ten Plagues of Egypt, and the destruction of the Canaanites. These acts of evil were not acts of wrongdoing. Rather, they were righteous and just, because God, the Creator of all things, was administering justice to wrongdoers, to sinners. He warned the perfect first couple what the penalty was for sin. He warned the people for a hundred years by Noah's preaching. He warned the Canaanites centuries before.

Nevertheless, there are times, when God extends mercy, refraining from the execution of his righteous judgment to one worthy of calamity. For example, he warned Nineveh, the city of blood, and they repented, so he pardoned them. (Jonah 3:10) God has made it a practice to warn persons of the results of sin, giving them undeservedly many opportunities to change their ways. – Ezekiel 33:11.

God cannot sin; it is impossible for him to do so. So, when did he create evil? Without getting into the eternity of his knowing what he was going to do, and when, let us just say, evil did not exist when he was the only person in existence. We might say the idea of evil existed because he knew what he was going to do. However, the moment he created creatures (spirit and human), the potential for evil came into existence because both have free will to sin (fall short of perfection). Evil became a reality the moment Satan entertained the idea of causing Adam to sin, to get humanity for himself, and then acted on it.

God has the right and is just to bring the *calamity of* or *evil* down on anyone that is an unrepentant sinner. God did not even have to give us the underserved kindness of offering us his Son. God is the author or agent of evil regardless of the source books that claim otherwise. If he had never created free will beings, evil would have never gone from the idea of evil to the potential of evil, to the existence of evil. However, God felt that it was better to get the sinful state out of angel and human existence, recover, and then any who would sin thereafter; he would be justified in handing out evil or calamity to only that person or angel alone.

Who among us would argue that he should have created humans and angels like robots, automatons with no free will? The moment he chose the free will, he moved evil from an idea to a potential, and Satan moved it to reality. God has a moral nature that does not bring about evil and sin when he is the only person in existence. However, the moment he created beings in his image, which had the potential to sin, he brought about evil. The moment we have a moral code of good and evil that is placed upon one's with free will; then, we have evil as a potential.

In English, the very comprehensive Hebrew word ra' is variously translated as "bad," "downcast (sad, NASB)," "ugly," "evil," "grievous (distressing, NASB)," "sore," "selfish (stingy, HCSB)," and "envious," depending upon the context. (Gen 2:9; 40:7; 41:3; Ex 33:4; Deut. 6:22; 28:35; Pro 23:6; 28:22)

Evil as an adjective **describes** the **quality of** a class of people, places, or things, or of a specific person, place, or thing

Evil as a noun, **defines** the **nature** of a class of people, places, or things, or of a specific person, place, or thing (e.g., the evil one, evil eye).

We can agree that "evil" is a thing. Create means to bring something into existence, be it people, places, or things, as well something abstract, for lack of a better word at the moment. We would agree that when God was alone evil was not a reality; it did not exist? We would agree that the moment that God created free will creatures (angels and humans), creating humans in his image, with his moral nature, he also brought the potential for evil into existence, and it was realized by Satan?

Inerrancy: Can the Bible Be trusted?

If the Bible is the Word of God, it should be in complete agreement throughout; there should be no contradictions. Yet, the rational mind must ask, why is it that some passages appear to be contradictions when compared with others? For example, Numbers 25:9 tells us that 24,000 died from the scourge, whereas at 1 Corinthians 10:8, the apostle Paul says it was 23,000. This would seem to be a clear error. Before addressing such matters, let us first look at some background information.

Full inerrancy in this book means that the original writings are fully without error in all that they state, as are the words. The words were not dictated (automaton), but the intended meaning is inspired, as are the words that convey that meaning. The Author allowed the writer to use his style of writing, yet controlled the meaning to the extent of not allowing the writer to choose a wrong word, which would not convey the intended meaning. Other more liberal-minded persons hold with *partial inerrancy*, which claims that as far as faith is concerned, this portion of God's Word is without error, but that there are historical, geographical, and scientific errors.

There are several different levels of inerrancy. *Absolute Inerrancy* is the belief that the Bible is fully true and exact in every way; including not only relationships and doctrine, but also science and history. In other words, all information is completely exact. *Full Inerrancy* is the belief that the Bible was not written as a science or historical textbook, but is phenomenological, in that it is written from the human perspective. In other words, speaking of such things as the sun rising, the four corners of the earth or the rounding off of number approximations are all from a human perspective. *Limited Inerrancy* is the belief that the Bible is meant only as a reflection of God's purposes and will, so the science and history is the understanding of the author's day, and is limited. Thus, the Bible is susceptible to errors in these areas. *Inerrancy of Purpose* is the belief that it is only inerrant in the purpose of bringing its readers to a saving faith. The Bible is not about facts, but about persons and relationships, thus, it is subject to error. *Inspired: Not Inerrant* is the belief that its authors are human and thus subject to human error. It should be noted that this author holds the position of full inerrancy.

For many today, the Bible is nothing more than a book written by men. The Bible critic believes the Bible to be full of myths and legends, contradictions, and geographical, historical, and scientific errors. University professor Gerald A. Larue had this to say, "The views of the writers as expressed in the Bible reflect the ideas, beliefs, and concepts current in their own times and are limited by the extent of knowledge in those times."[174] On the other hand, the Bible's authors claim that their writings were inspired of God, as Holy Spirit moved them along. We will discover shortly that the Bible critics have much to say, but it is inflated or empty.

2 Timothy 3:16-17 Updated American Standard Version (UASV)

[16] All Scripture is inspired by God and profitable for teaching, for reproof, for correction, for training in righteousness; [17] so that the man of God may be fully competent, equipped for every good work.

2 Peter 1:21 Updated American Standard Version (UASV)

[21] for no prophecy was ever produced by the will of man, but men carried along by the Holy Spirit spoke from God.

The question remains as to whether the Bible is a book written by imperfect men and full of errors, or is written by imperfect men, but

---

[174] Gerald Larue, "The Bible as a Political Weapon," *Free Inquiry* (Summer 1983): 39.

inspired by God. If the Bible is just another book by imperfect man, there is no hope for humankind. If it is inspired by God and without error, although penned by imperfect men, we have the hope of everything that it offers: a rich, happy life now by applying counsel that lies within and the real life that is to come, everlasting life. This author contends that the Bible is inspired of God and free of human error, although written by imperfect humans.

Before we take on the critics who seem to sift the Scriptures looking for problematic verses, let us take a moment to reflect on how we should approach these alleged problem texts. The critic's argument goes something like this: 'If God does not err and the Bible is the Word of God, then the Bible should not have one single error or contradiction, yet it is full of errors and contradictions.' If the Bible is riddled with nothing but contradictions and errors as the critics would have us believe, why, out of 31,173 verses in the Bible, should there be only 2-3 thousand Bible difficulties that are called into question, this being less than ten percent of the whole?

First, let it be said that it is every Christian's obligation to get a deeper understanding of God's Word, just as the apostle Paul told Timothy:

1 Timothy 4:15-16 Updated American Standard Version (UASV)

[15] Practice these things, be absorbed in them, so that your progress will be evident to all. [16] Pay close attention to yourself and to your teaching; persevere in these things, for as you do this you will ensure salvation both for yourself and for those who hear you.

Paul also told the Corinthians:

2 Corinthians 10:4-5 Updated American Standard Version (UASV)

[4] For the weapons of our warfare are not of the flesh[175] but powerful to God for destroying strongholds.[176] [5] We are destroying speculations and every lofty thing raised up against the knowledge of

---

[175] That is *merely human*
[176] That is *tearing down false arguments*

God, and we are taking every thought captive to the obedience of Christ,

Paul also told the Philippians:

Philippians 1:7 Updated American Standard Version (UASV)

[7] It is right for me to feel thus about you all, because I hold you in my heart, for you are all partakers with me of grace, both in my imprisonment and in the defense and confirmation of the gospel.

In being able to defend against the modern-day critic, one has to be able to reason from the Scriptures and overturn the critic's argument(s) with mildness. If someone were to approach us about an alleged error or contradiction, what should we do? We should be frank and honest. If we do not have an answer, we should admit such. If the text in question gives the appearance of difficulty, we should admit this as well. If we are unsure as to how we should answer, we can simply say that we will look into it and get back to them, returning with a reasonable answer.

However, we do not want to express disbelief and doubt to our critics, because they will be emboldened in their disbelief. It will put them on the offense and us on the defense. With great confidence, we can express that there is an answer. The Bible has withstood the test of 2,000 years of persecution and interrogation and yet it is the most printed book of all time, currently being translated into 2,287 languages. If these critical questions were so threatening, the Bible would not be the book that it is.

When we are pursuing the text in question, be unwavering in purpose, or resolved to find an answer. In some cases, it may take hours of digging to find the solution. Consider this: as we resolve these difficulties, we are also building our faith that God's Word is inerrant. Moreover, we will want to do preventative maintenance in our personal study. As we are doing our Bible reading, take note of these surface discrepancies and resolve them as we work our way through the Bible. We need to make this part of our prayers as well. I recommend the following program. Below are several books that deal with difficult passages. As we daily read and study our Bible from

Genesis to Revelation, do not attempt it in one year; make it a four-year program. Use a good exegetical commentary like *The Holman Old/New Testament Commentary* (HOTC/HNTC) or *The New American Commentary* set, and *The Big Book of Bible Difficulties* by Norman L. Geisler, as well as *The Encyclopedia of Bible Difficulties* by Gleason Archer.

We should be aware that men under inspiration penned the originally written books. In fact, we do not have those originals, what textual scholars call autographs, but we do have thousands of copies. The copyists, however, were not inspired; therefore, as one might expect, throughout the first 1,400 years of copying, thousands of errors were transmitted into the texts that were being copied by imperfect hands that were not under inspiration when copying. Yet, the next 450 years saw a restoration of the text by textual scholars from around the world. Therefore, while many of our best literal translations today may not be inspired, they are a mirror-like reflection of the autographs by way of textual criticism.[177] Therefore, the fallacy could be with the copyist error that has simply not been weeded out. In addition, we must keep in mind that God's Word is without error, but our interpretation and understanding of that Word is not.

It should be noted that the Bible is made up of 66 smaller books that were hand-written over a period of 1,600 years, having some 40 writers of various trades such as shepherd, king, priest, tax collector, governor, physician, copyist, fisherman, and a tentmaker. Therefore, it should not surprise us that some difficulties are encountered as we casually read the Bible. Yet, if one were to take a deeper look, one would find that these difficulties are easily explained. Let us take a few pages to examine some passages that have been under attack.

This chapter's objective is not to be exhaustive, not even close. What we are looking to do is cover a few alleged contradictions and a couple of alleged mistakes. This is to give us a small sampling of the reasonable answers that we will find in the above recommended books. Remember, our Bible is a sword that we must use both offensively and

---

[177] Textual criticism is the study of copies of any written work of which the autograph (original) is unknown, with the purpose of ascertaining the original text. Harold J. Green, Introduction to New Testament Textual Criticism (Peabody, MA: Hendrickson, 1995), 1.

defensively. One must wonder how long a warrior of ancient times would last who was not expertly trained in the use of his weapon. Let us look at a few scriptures that support our need to learn our Bible well so will be able to defend what we believe to be true.

When "false apostles, deceitful workmen, disguising themselves as apostles of Christ" were causing trouble in the congregation in Corinth, the apostle Paul wrote that under such circumstances, we are to *tear down their arguments* and *take every thought captive*. (2 Corinthians 10:4, 5; 11:13–15) All who present critical arguments against God's Word, or contrary to it, can have their arguments overturned by the Christian, who is able and ready to defend that Word in mildness. – 2 Timothy 2:24–26.

1 Peter 3:15 Updated American Standard Version (UASV)

[15] but sanctify Christ as Lord in your hearts, always being prepared to make a defense[178] to anyone who asks you for a reason for the hope that is in you; yet do it with gentleness and respect;

Peter says that we need to be prepared to make a *defense*. The Greek word behind the English 'defense' is *apologia*, which is actually a legal term that refers to the defense of a defendant in court. Our English apologetics is just what Peter spoke of, having the ability to give a reason to any who may challenge us, or to answer those who are not challenging us but who have honest questions that deserve to be answered.

2 Timothy 2:24-25 Updated American Standard Version (UASV)

[24] For a slave of the Lord does not need to fight, but needs to be kind to all, qualified to teach, showing restraint when wronged [25] with gentleness correcting those who are in opposition, if perhaps God may grant them repentance leading to accurate knowledge[179] of the truth,

Look at the Greek word (*epignosis*) behind the English "knowledge" in the above. "It is more intensive than *gnosis* (1108),

---

[178] Or *argument*, or *explanation*

[179] *Epignosis* is a strengthened or intensified form of *gnosis* (*epi,* meaning "additional"), meaning, "true," "real," "full," "complete" or "accurate," depending upon the context. Paul and Peter alone use *epignosis*.

knowledge because it expresses a more thorough participation in the acquiring of knowledge on the part of the learner."[180] The requirement of all of the Lord's servants is that they be able to teach, but not in a quarrelsome way, and in a way to correct his opponents with mildness. Why? Because the purpose of it all is that by God, and through the Christian teacher, one may come to repentance and begin taking in an accurate knowledge of the truth.

Inerrancy: Practical Principles to Overcoming Bible Difficulties

Below are several ways of looking at the Bible that enable the reader to see he is not dealing with an error or contradiction, but rather a Bible difficulty.

Different Points of View

At times, you may have two different writers who are writing from two different points of view.

Numbers 35:14 Updated American Standard Version (UASV)

[14] You shall give three cities across the Jordan and three cities you shall give in the land of Canaan; they will be cities of refuge.

Joshua 22:4 Updated American Standard Version (UASV)

[4] And now Jehovah your God has given rest to your brothers, as he spoke to them; therefore turn now and go to your tents, to the land of your possession, which Moses the servant of Jehovah gave you beyond the Jordan. [on the other side of the Jordan, ESV]

Here we see that Moses is speaking about the east side of the Jordan when he says "on this side of the Jordan." Joshua, on the other hand, is also speaking about the east side of the Jordan when he says "on the other side of the Jordan." So, who is correct? Both are. When Moses was penning Numbers the Israelites had not yet crossed the

---

[180] Spiros Zodhiates, *The Complete Word Study Dictionary: New Testament,* Electronic ed. (Chattanooga, TN: AMG Publishers, 2000, c1992, c1993), S. G1922.

Jordan River, so the east side was "this side," the side he was on. On the other hand, when Joshua penned his book, the Israelites had crossed the Jordan, so the east side was just as he had said, "on the other side of the Jordan." Thus, we should not assume that two different writers are writing from the same perspective.

A Careful Reading

At times, it may simply be a case of needing to slow down and carefully read the account, considering exactly what is being said.

Joshua 18:28 Updated American Standard Version (UASV)

[28] and Zelah, Haeleph and the Jebusite (that is, Jerusalem), Gibeah, Kiriath; fourteen cities with their villages. This is the inheritance of the sons of Benjamin according to their families.

Judges 1:21 Updated American Standard Version (UASV)

[21] But the sons of Benjamin did not drive out the Jebusites who lived in Jerusalem; so the Jebusites have lived with the sons of Benjamin in Jerusalem to this day.

Joshua 15:63 Updated American Standard Version (UASV)

[63] But as for the Jebusites, the inhabitants of Jerusalem, the sons of Judah could not drive them out; so the Jebusites live with the sons of Judah at Jerusalem until this day.

Judges 1:8-9 Updated American Standard Version (UASV)

[8] And then the sons of Judah fought against Jerusalem and captured it and struck it with the edge of the sword and set the city on fire. [9] And afterward the sons of Judah went down to fight against the Canaanites living in the hill country and in the Negev[181] and in the Shephelah.[182]

2 Samuel 5:5-9 Updated American Standard Version (UASV)

---

[181] I.e. *South*
[182] I.e., lowland

⁵At Hebron he reigned over Judah seven years and six months, and in Jerusalem he reigned thirty-three years over all Israel and Judah.

⁶And the king and his men went to Jerusalem against the Jebusites, the inhabitants of the land, and they said to David, "You shall not come in here, but the blind and lame will turn you away"; thinking, "David cannot come in here." ⁷Nevertheless, David captured the stronghold of Zion, that is the city of David. ⁸And David said on that day, "Whoever would strike the Jebusites, let him get up the water shaft to attack 'the lame and the blind,' who are hated by David's soul." Therefore it is said, "The blind and the lame shall not come into the house." ⁹And David lived in the stronghold and called it the city of David. And David built all around from the Millo and inward.

There is no doubt that even the advanced Bible reader of many years can come away confused because the above accounts seem to be contradictory. In Joshua 18:28 and Judges 1:21, we see that Jerusalem was an inheritance of the tribe of Benjamin, yet the Benjamites were unable to conquer Jerusalem. However, in Joshua 15:63 we see that the tribe of Judah could not conquer them either, with the reading giving the impression that it was a part of their inheritance. In Judges 1:8, however, Judah was eventually able to conquer Jerusalem and burn it with fire. Yet, to add even more to the confusion, we find at 2 Samuel 5:5–8 that David is said to have conquered Jerusalem hundreds of years later.

Now that we have the particulars let us look at it more clearly. The boundary between Benjamin's inheritances ran right through the middle of Jerusalem. Joshua 8:28 is correct, in that what would later be called the "city of David" was in the territory of Benjamin, but it also in part crossed over the line into the territory of Judah, causing both tribes to go to war against this Jebusite city. It is also true that the tribe of Benjamin was unable to conquer the city and that the tribe of Judah eventually did. However, if you look at Judges 1:9 again, you will see that Judah did not finish the job entirely and moved on to conquer other areas. This allowed the remaining ones to regroup and form a resistance that neither Benjamin nor Judah could overcome, so these Jebusites remained until the time of David, hundreds of years later.

Intended Meaning of Writer

First, the Bible student needs to understand the level that the Bible intends to be exact in what is written. If Jim told a friend that 650 graduated with him from high school in 1984, it is not challenged, because it is all too clear that he is using rounded numbers and is not meaning to be exactly precise. This is how God's Word operates as well. Sometimes it means to be exact, at other times, it is simply rounding numbers, in other cases, the intention of the writer is a general reference, to give readers of that time and succeeding generations some perspective. Did Samuel, the author of judges, intend to pen a book on the chronology of Judges, or was his focus on the falling away, oppression, and the rescue by a judge, repeatedly. Now, it would seem that Jeremiah, the author of 1 Kings was more interested in giving his readers an exact number of years.

Acts 2:41 Updated American Standard Version (UASV)

[41] So those who received his word were baptized, and there were added that day about three thousand souls.

As you can see here, numbers within the Bible are often used with approximations. This is a frequent practice even today, in both written works and verbal conversation.

Acts 7:2-3 Updated American Standard Version (UASV)

[2] And Stephen said:

"Brothers and fathers, hear me. The God of glory appeared to our father Abraham when he was in Mesopotamia, before he lived in Haran, [3] and said to him, 'Go out from your land and from your kindred and go into the land that I will show you.'

If you were to check the Hebrew Scriptures at Genesis 12:1, you would find that what is claimed to have been said by God to Abraham is not quoted word-for-word; it is simply a paraphrase. This is a normal practice within Scripture and in writing in general.

Numbers 34:15 Updated American Standard Version (UASV)

[15] The two and a half tribes have received their inheritance beyond the Jordan opposite Jericho, eastward toward the sunrising."

Just as you would read in today's local newspaper, the Bible writer has written from the human standpoint, how it appeared to him. The Bible also speaks of "to the end of the earth" (Psalm 46:9), "from the four corners of the earth" (Isa 11:12), and "the four winds of the earth" (Revelation 7:1). These phrases are still used today.

Unexplained Does Not Mean Unexplainable

Considering that there are 31,173 verses in the Bible, encompassing 66 books written by about 40 writers, ranging from shepherds to kings, an army general, fishermen, tax collector, a physician and on and on, and being penned over a 1,600 year period, one does find a few hundred Bible difficulties (about one percent). However, 99 percent of those are explainable. Yet no one wants to be so arrogant to say that he can explain them all. It has nothing to do with the inadequacy of God's Word but is based on human understanding. In many cases, science or archaeology and the field of custom and culture of ancient peoples has helped explain difficulties in hundreds of passages. Therefore, there may be less than one percent left to be answered, yet our knowledge of God's Word continues to grow.

Guilty Until Proven Innocent

This is exactly the perception that the critic has of God's Word. The legal principle of being "innocent until proven guilty" afforded mankind in courts of justice is withheld from the very Word of God. What is ironic here is that this policy has contributed to these Bible critics looking foolish over and over again when something comes to light that vindicates the portion of Scripture they are challenging.

Daniel 5:1 Updated American Standard Version (UASV)

[1] Belshazzar the king made[183] a great feast for a thousand of his nobles, and he was drinking wine in the presence of the thousand.

---

[183] I.e., held

Bible critics had long claimed that Belshazzar was not known outside of the book Daniel; therefore, they argue that Daniel was mistaken. Yet it hardly seems prudent to argue error from absence of outside evidence. Just because archaeology had not discovered such a person did not mean that Daniel was wrong, or that such a person did not exist. In 1854, some small clay cylinders were discovered in modern-day southern Iraq, which would have been the city of Ur in ancient Babylonia. The cuneiform documents were a prayer of King Nabonidus for "Bel-sar-ussur, my eldest son." These tablets also showed that this "Bel-sar-ussur" had secretaries as well as a household staff. Other tablets were discovered a short time later that showed that the kingship was entrusted to this eldest son as a coregent while his father was away.

He entrusted the 'Camp' to his oldest (son), the firstborn [Belshazzar], the troops everywhere in the country he ordered under his (command). He let (everything) go, entrusted the kingship to him and, himself, he [Nabonidus] started out for a long journey, the (military) forces of Akkad marching with him; he turned towards Tema (deep) in the west."[184]

Ignoring Literary Styles

The Bible is a diverse book when it comes to literary styles: narrative, poetic, prophetic, and apocalyptic; also containing parables, metaphors, similes, hyperbole, and other figures of speech. Too often, these alleged errors are the result of a reader taking a figure of speech as literal, or reading a parable as though it is a narrative.

Matthew 24:35 Updated American Standard Version (UASV)

[35] Heaven and earth will pass away, but my words will not pass away.

If some do not recognize that they are dealing with a figure of speech, they are bound to come away with the wrong meaning. Some have concluded from Matthew 24:35 that Jesus was speaking of an

---

[184] J. Pritchard, ed., *Ancient Near Eastern Texts* (1974), 313.

eventual destruction of the earth. This is hardly the case, as his listeners would not have understood it that way based on their understanding of the Old Testament. They would have understood that he was simply being emphatic about the words he spoke, using hyperbole. What he was conveying is that his words are more enduring than heaven and earth, and with heaven and earth being understood as eternal, this merely conveyed even more so that Jesus' words could be trusted.

Two Accounts of the Same Incident

If you were to speak to officers that take accident reports for their police department, you would find that there is cohesion in the accounts, but each person has merely witnessed aspects that have stood out to them. We will see that this is the case as well with the examples below, which is the same account in two different gospels:

Matthew 8:5 Updated American Standard Version (UASV)

[5] When he[185] had entered Capernaum, a centurion came forward to him, imploring him,

Luke 7:2-3 Updated American Standard Version (UASV)

[2] And a centurion's[186] slave, who was highly regarded[187] by him, was sick and about to die. [3] When he heard about Jesus, he sent some older men of the Jews[188] asking him to come and bring his slave safely through.[189]

Immediately we see the problem of whether the centurion or the elders of the Jews spoke with Jesus. The solution is not really hidden from us. Which of the two accounts is the most detailed account? You are correct if you said, Luke. The centurion sent the elders of the Jews to represent him to Jesus, so; that whatever response Jesus might give, it would be as though he were addressing the centurion; therefore,

---

[185] That is *Jesus*

[186] I.e., army officer over a hundred solderiers

[187] Lit *to whom he was honorable*

[188] Or *Jewish elders*

[189] I.e., *save the life of his slave*

Matthew gave his readers the basic thought, not seeing the need of mentioning the elders of the Jews aspect. This is how a representative was viewed in the first century, just as some countries see ambassadors today as being the very person they represent. Therefore, both Matthew and Luke are correct.

Man's Fallible Interpretations

Inspiration by God is infallible, without error. Imperfect man and his interpretations over the centuries, as bad as many of them have been, should not cast a shadow over God's inspired Word. The entire Word of God has one meaning and one meaning only for every penned word, which is what God willed to be conveyed by the human writer he chose to use.

The Autograph Alone Is Inspired and Inerrant

It has been argued by conservative scholars that only the autograph manuscripts were inspired and inerrant, not the copying of those manuscripts over the next 3,000 years for the Old Testament and 1,500 years for the New Testament. While I would agree with this position as well, it should be noted that we do not possess the autographs, so to argue that they are inerrant is to speak of nonexistent documents. However, it should be further understood that through the science of textual criticism, we can establish a mirror reflection of the autograph manuscripts. B. F. Westcott, F. J. A. Hort, F. F. Bruce, and many other textual scholars would agree with Norman L Geisler's assessment: "The New Testament, then, has not only survived in more manuscripts than any other book from antiquity, but it has survived in a purer form than any other great book—*a form that is 99.5 percent pure.*"[190]

An example of a copyist error can be found in Luke's genealogy of Jesus at Luke 3:35–37. In verse 37 you will find a Cainan, and in verse 36 you will find a second Cainan between Arphaxad

---

[190] Norman L. Geisler and William E. Nix: *A General Introduction to the Bible* (Chicago, Moody Press, 1980), 367. (Emphasis is mine.)

(Arpachshad) and Shelah. As one can see from most footnotes in different study Bibles, the Cainan in verse 36 is seen as a scribal error, and is not found in the Hebrew Old Testament, the Samaritan Pentateuch, or the Aramaic Targums, but is found in the Greek Septuagint. (Genesis 10:24; 11:12, 13; 1 Chronicles 1:18, but not 1 Chronicles 1:24) It seems quite unlikely that it was in the earlier copies of the Septuagint, because the first-century Jewish historian Josephus lists Shelah next as the son of Arphaxad, and Josephus normally followed the Septuagint.[191] So one might ask why this second Cainan is found in the translations at all if this is the case? The manuscripts that do contain this second Cainan are some of the best manuscripts that are used in establishing the original text: 01 B L A¹ 33 (Kainam); A 038 044 0102 A¹³ (Kainan).

The Bible Was Miraculously Restored, not Miraculously Preserved

The Hebrew text was like the Greek NT; it had accumulated copyist errors, a few intentional, a good number accidental, between the Malachi days of 440 BCE and Rabbi Judah ha-Nasi (135 to 217 CE). The same thing happened to the Greek New Testament from about 400 CE to 1550 CE, a period of copyist errors. The good news is for the NT is fourfold: (1) the 144 NT papyri discovered in the early part of the 20th century, (2) a number of them dated within decades of the originals, and the great Codex Vaticanus (300-330 CE) and Codex Sinaiticus (330-360 CE), (3) that we have 5,898 Greek NT MSS; (4) then, there was the era of many dozens of textual scholars, from 1550 to the present who restored the text to its original words.

So, the Hebrew OT corruption ran in earnest between 440 BCE to 220 CE. At that time, the Greek Septuagint, a translation of the Hebrew Scriptures, was produced between 280 – 150 BCE, which became favored by the Jews to the point that they claimed it was inspired. However, the fact that the lingua franca of the Roman Empire ran from 330 BCE to 330 CE, the Christians in the first

---

[191] *Jewish Antiquities*, I, 146 [vi, 4].

century CE wisely used the Greek Septuagint to evangelize, to show that Jesus Christ was the long-awaited Messiah. Then, Jerusalem was destroyed by General Titus and the Roman army in 70 CE, killing one million one hundred thousand Jews and carrying another seventy thousand back to Rome as slaves. No temple led to the creation of the Mishnah, an authoritative collection of exegetical material embodying the oral tradition of Jewish law and forming the first part of the Talmud. During the 150 years in the wake of the temple's destruction in Jerusalem in 70 CE, rabbinic sages throughout Israel at once were quick to seek out a new source for preserving Jewish practice. They debated and combined various traditions of their oral law. Growing this foundation, they set new constraints, boundaries, and requirements for Judaism. This gave the Jewish people direction for their day-to-day life of holiness, even though they lacked a temple. This new spiritual structure was summarized in the Mishnah, which Judah ha-Nasi compiled by about 200-217 CE.

In addition, the Jewish scholars set about creating a corrected text of the Hebrew Old Testament because they realized it had some textual variants from the sopherim (scribes). But it was the greatest textual scholars who have ever lived, the Masoretes, who made corrected copies from 500 to 900 CE. Below is an article about them. The beauty is that they did not erase the manuscripts with the errors; they kept them, then simply put the corrections in the margin, called the Masorah. So, the Hebrew text was corrected just as the Greek text was. And then, in 1947, we found the Dead Sea Scrolls, which dated as early as the 3rd century BCE and validated the Masoretic text. And ironically at this same time, many of the **best** NT papyri were coming to light that validated the work of Johann Jakob Wettstein [1693-1754 A.D.], Karl Lachmann [1793-1851], Samuel Prideaux Tregelles [1813-1875], Friedrich Constantin von Tischendorf [1815-1874], and especially Westcott and Hort of 1881.

MIRACULOUS RESTORATION, NOT MIRACULOUS PRESERVATION

OLD TESTAMENT
Transmission: 1500 BCE – 440 BCE
Corruption: 440 BCE – 220 CE

Restoration: 500 – 900 CE – Present
Corroboration MSS (Dead Sea Scrolls): 1947

NEW TESTAMENT
Transmission: 45 CE – 98 CE
Corruption: 440 CE -1550 CE
Restoration: 1550 CE – Present
Corroboration MSS (NT Papyri): 1900s-1960s-Present

A Lack of **Preservation** Does Not Mean a Lack of **Inspiration**

- The Bible **was miraculously inspired** as men were moved along by the Holy Spirit (*Absolute Inerrancy*)

- The Bible **was not miraculously preserved** as men's human imperfection gave us corruption (*Limited Inerrancy*)

- The Bible **was restored** through tens of millions of hours by many hundreds of (men) textual scholars from the 16th to the 21st centuries. (*Absolute Inerrancy Restored*)

The **men who restored the text** are no more perfect than the **men who** intentionally and unintentionally **corrupted the text**. However, even hundreds of **imperfect men**, through dozens of lifetimes of sweat and toil, arrived at **a perfect text** that was lost but now is found. With the copyists, you have tens of thousands of men **focusing on their work as an individual** in reproducing a copy; with the textual scholars, it is teams of hundreds of men focusing on all of the manuscripts to ascertain the original words of the original texts.

Many of the above scholars gave their entire lives to God and the Hebrew and Greek text.[192] Each of these could have an entire book devoted to them and their work alone. The amount of work they accomplished before the era of computers is nothing short of astonishing. Rightly, the preceding history should serve to strengthen our faith in the authenticity and general integrity of the Hebrew

---

[192] **The Climax of the Restored Text**

Scriptures and the Greek New Testament. Unlike Bart D. Ehrman, men like Sir Frederic Kenyon have been moved to say that the books of the Greek New Testament have "come down to us substantially as they were written." And all this is especially true of the critical scholarship of the almost two hundred years since the days of Karl Lachmann. All today can feel confident that what they hold in their hands is a mirror reflection of the Word of God that was penned in twenty-seven books, some two thousand years ago.

It is true that the Jewish copyists and the later Christian copyists were not led along by the Holy Spirit, and therefore their manuscripts were not inerrant, infallible. Errors (textual variants) crept into the manuscripts unintentionally and intentionally. However, the vast majority of the Hebrew Old Testament and Greek New Testament has not been infected with textual errors. For the portions impacted with textual errors, it is the many tens of thousands of copies that we have to help us to weed out the errors. How? Well, not every copyist made the same textual errors. Hence, by comparing the work of different copyists and different manuscripts, textual scholars can identify the textual variants (errors) and remove those, leaving us with the original content.

Yes, it would be the greatest discovery of all time if we found the actual original five books that were penned by Moses himself, Genesis through Deuteronomy. However, there would be no way of establishing that they were the originals. The fact is, we do not need the originals. We do not need those original documents. What is so important about the documents? The documents are not important; it is the content on the original documents that we are after. And truly, miraculously, we have more copies than needed to do just that. We do not need miraculous preservation because we have miraculous restoration. We now know beyond a reasonable doubt that the Hebrew Old Testament and the Greek New Testament critical texts are a 99.99% reflection of the content that was in those ancient original manuscripts. Some textual scholars might say that I am exaggerating with the 99.99%. An example of how that is not so can be found in the 1881 Westcott and Hort critical Greek NT, which is 99.5% the same as the 2012 28th edition of the critical Greek NT. The discovery of the NT papyri from the 1900s to the 1960s and up to the present has validated Westcott and Hort's Greek NT and let us know that the 2012 Nestle-Aland Greek NT is a mirror-like reflection of the original. To be frank, there are about 100+ textual variants where Westcott and Hort were correct, and the Nestle-Aland text is likely not correct. This is because they took the textual eclecticism method of determining the original, which was to focus on both external and internal evidence. Still, they leaned heavily on internal evidence, which is a bit more subjective. Regardless, we have the apparatus in the 28th edition of the Nestle-Aland that gives the translator the variants, allowing him to make an objective determination. Therefore, the 100+ textual variants can be decided on a case-by-case basis. So, yes, what we have is 99.99% reflective of the original.

The critical text of Westcott and Hort of 1881 [(FENTON JOHN ANTHONY HORT (1828 – 1892) and BROOKE FOSS WESTCOTT (1825 – 1901)] has been commended by leading textual scholars over the last one hundred and forty years, and still stands as the standard. Numerous additional critical editions of the Greek text came after Westcott and Hort: Richard F. Weymouth (1886), Bernhard Weiss (1894–1900); the British and Foreign Bible Society (1904, 1958), Alexander Souter (1910), Hermann von Soden (1911–1913); and Eberhard Nestle's Greek text, *Novum Testamentum Graece*, published in 1898 by the Württemberg Bible Society, Stuttgart, Germany. The Nestle in twelve editions (1898–1923) to subsequently be taken over by his son, Erwin Nestle (13th–20th editions, 1927–1950), followed by Kurt Aland (21st–25th editions, 1952–1963), and lastly, it was coedited by Kurt Aland and Barbara Aland (26th–28th editions, 1979, 1993, 2012).

Look at the Context

Many alleged inconsistencies disappear by simply looking at the context. Taking words out of context can distort their meaning. *Merriam-Webster's Collegiate Dictionary* defines context as "the parts of a discourse that surround a word or passage and can throw light on its meaning."[193] Context can also be "the circumstances or events that form the environment within which something exists or takes place." If we were to look in a thesaurus for a synonym, we would find "background" for this second meaning. At 2 Timothy 2:15, the apostle Paul brings home the point of why context is so important: "Do your best to present yourself to God as one approved, a worker who has no need to be ashamed, rightly handling the word of truth."

Ephesians 2:8-9 Updated American Standard Version (UASV)

[8] For by grace you have been saved through faith; and that not of yourselves, it is the gift of God; [9] not from works, so that no man may boast.

James 2:26 Updated American Standard Version (UASV)

[26] For as the body apart from the spirit[194] is dead, so also faith apart from works is dead.

So, which is it? Is salvation possible by faith alone as Paul wrote to the Ephesians, or is faith dead without works as James wrote to his readers? As our subtitle brings out, let us look at the context. In the letter to the Ephesians, the apostle Paul is speaking to the Jewish Christians who were looking to the works of the Mosaic Law as a means to salvation, a righteous standing before God. Paul was telling these legalistic Jewish Christians that this is not so. In fact, this would invalidate Christ's ransom because there would have been no need for it if one could achieve salvation by meticulously keeping the Mosaic Law. (Rom. 5:18) But James was writing to those in a congregation who were concerned with their status before other men, who were looking for prominent positions within the congregation, and not taking care of those that were in need. (Jam. 2:14–17) So, James is merely addressing those who call themselves Christian, but in name only. No person could truly be a Christian and not possess some good works, such as feeding the poor, helping the elderly. This type of work was an evident demonstration of one's Christian personality. Paul was

---

[193] Merriam-Webster, Inc: *Merriam-Webster's Collegiate Dictionary.* Eleventh ed. (Springfield, Mass.: Merriam-Webster, Inc. 2003).

[194] Or *breath*

in perfect harmony with James on this. – Romans 10:10; 1 Corinthians 15:58; Ephesians 5:15, 21–33; 6:15; 1 Timothy 4:16; 2 Timothy 4:5; Hebrews 10:23-25.

Inerrancy: Are There Contradictions?

Below I will follow this pattern. I will list the critic's argument first, followed by the text of difficulty, and conclude with an answer to the critic. What should be kept at the forefront of our mind is this: one is simply looking for the best answer, not absoluteness. If there is a reasonable answer to a Bible difficulty, why are the critics able to set them aside with ease? Because they start with the premise that this is not the Word of God, but only a book by imperfect men and full of contradictions; thus, the bias toward errors has blinded their judgment.

Critic: The critic would argue that there was an Adam and Eve, and an Abel who was now dead, so, where did Cain get his wife? This is one of the most common questions by Bible critics.

Genesis 4:17 Updated American Standard Version (UASV)

[17] Cain had sexual relations[195] with his wife and she conceived, and gave birth to Enoch; and he built a city, and called the name of the city Enoch, after the name of his son, Enoch.

Answer: If one were to read a little further along, they would come to the realization that Adam had a son named Seth; it further adds that Adam "became father to sons *and daughters.*" (Genesis 5:4) Adam lived for a total of 800 years after fathering Seth, giving him ample opportunity to father many more sons and daughters. So it could be that Cain married one of his sisters. If he waited until one of his brothers and sisters had a daughter, he could have married one of his nieces once she was old enough. In the beginning, humans were closer to perfection; this explains why they lived longer and why at that time there was little health risk of genetic defects in the case of children born to closely related parents, in contrast to how it is today. As time passed, genetic defects increased and life spans decreased. Adam lived

---

[195] Lit *knew*

to see 930 years. Yet Shem, who lived after the Flood, died at 600 years, while Shem's son Arpachshad only lived 438 years, dying before his father died. Abraham saw an even greater decrease in that he only lived 175 years while his grandson Jacob was 147 years when he died. Thus, due to increasing imperfection, God prohibited the marriage of closely related people under the Mosaic Law because of the likelihood of genetic defects.—Leviticus 18:9.

Critic: If God is here hardening Pharaoh's heart, what exactly makes Pharaoh responsible for the decisions he makes?

Exodus 4:21 Updated American Standard Version (UASV)

²¹ Jehovah said to Moses, "When you go and return to Egypt see that you perform before Pharaoh all the wonders which I have put in your hand; but I will harden his heart so that he will not let the people go.

Answer: This is actually a prophecy. God knew that what he was about to do would contribute to a stubborn and obstinate Pharaoh, who was going to be unwilling to change or give up the Israelites so they could go off to worship their God. Therefore, this is not stating what God is going to do; it is prophesying that Pharaoh's heart will harden because of the actions of God. The fact is, Pharaoh allowed his own heart to harden because he was determined not to agree with Moses' wishes or accept Jehovah's request to let the people go. Moses tells us at Exodus 7:13 (ESV) that "Pharaoh's heart was hardened, and he would not listen to them, as the Lord had said." Again, at 8:15 we read, "When Pharaoh saw that there was a respite, he hardened his heart and would not listen to them, as the Lord had said."

Critic: The Israelites had just received the Ten Commandments, with one commandment being: "You shall not make for yourself a carved image or any likeness of anything that is in heaven above, or that is in the earth beneath, or that is in the water under the earth." Therefore, how is the bronze serpent not a violation of this commandment?

Numbers 21:9 Updated American Standard Version (UASV)

⁹ And Moses made a bronze serpent and set it on the standard;[196] and it came about, that if a serpent bit any man, when he looked to the bronze serpent, he lived.

Answer: First, an idol is "a representation or symbol of an object of worship; *broadly:* a false god."[197] Second, it should be noted that not all images are idols. The bronze serpent was not made for the purpose of worship, or for some passionate devotion or veneration. There were times, however, when images were created with absolutely no intention of it receiving devotion, veneration, or worship, yet were later made into objects of veneration. That is exactly what happened with the copper serpent that Moses had formed in the wilderness. Many centuries later, "in the third year of Hoshea son of Elah, king of Israel, Hezekiah the son of Ahaz, king of Judah, began to reign. He removed the high places and broke the pillars and cut down the Asherah. And he broke in pieces the bronze serpent that Moses had made; for until those days the people of Israel had made offerings to it (it was called Nehushtan)."—2 Kings 18:1, 4.

Critic: Deuteronomy 15:11 (NET) says: "*There will never cease to be some poor people in the land;* therefore, I am commanding you to make sure you open your hand to your fellow Israelites who are needy and poor in your land." Is this not a contradiction of Deuteronomy 15:4? Will there be no poor among the Israelites, or will there be poor among them? Which is it?

Deuteronomy 15:4 Updated American Standard Version (UASV)

⁴ However, there will be no poor among you, since Jehovah will surely bless you in the land which Jehovah your God is giving you as an inheritance to possess,

Answer: If you look at the context, Deuteronomy 15:4 is stating that if the Israelites obey Jehovah's command to take care of the poor,

---

196 I.e., *pole*

197 Merriam-Webster, Inc: *Merriam-Webster's Collegiate Dictionary.* Eleventh ed. (Springfield, Mass.: Merriam-Webster, Inc., 2003).

"there should not be any poor among" them. Thus, for every poor person, there will be one to take care of that need. If an Israelite fell on hard times, there was to be a fellow Israelite ready to step in to help him through those hard times. Verse 11 stresses the truth of the imperfect world since the rebellion of Adam and inherited sin: there will always be poor among mankind, the Israelites being no different. However, the difference with God's people is that those who were well off financially were to offset conditions for those who fell on difficult times. This is not to be confused with the socialistic welfare systems in the world today. Those Jews were hard-working men, who labored from sunup to sundown to take care of their families. But if disease overtook their herd or unseasonal weather brought about failed crops, an Israelite could sell himself into the service of a fellow Israelite for a period of time; thereafter, he would be back on his feet. And many years down the road, he may very well do the same for another Israelite, who fell on difficult times.

Critic: Joshua 11:23 says that Joshua took the land according to what God had spoken to Moses and handed it on to the nation of Israel as planned. However, in Joshua 13:1, God is telling Joshua that he has grown old and much of the Promised Land has yet to be taken possession of. How can both be true? Is this not a contradiction?

Joshua 11:23 Updated American Standard Version (UASV)

²³ So Joshua took the whole land, according to all that Jehovah had spoken to Moses, and Joshua gave it for an inheritance to Israel according to their divisions by their tribes, and the land had rest from war.

Joshua 13:1 Updated American Standard Version (UASV)

13 Now Joshua was old and advanced in years, and Jehovah said to him, "You are old and advanced in years, and there remains yet very much land to possess.

Answer: No, it is not a contradiction. When the Israelites were to take the land, it was to take place in two different stages: the nation as a whole was to go to war and defeat the 31 kings of this land; thereafter, each Israelite tribe was to take their part of the land based on their individual actions. (Joshua 17:14–18; 18:3) Joshua fulfilled his role, which is expressed in 11:23 while the individual tribes did not complete their campaigns, which is expressed in 13:1. Even though the individual tribes failed to live up to taking their portion, the remaining Canaanites posed no real threat. Joshua 21:44, *ASV,* reads: "Jehovah gave them rest round about."

Critic: The critic would point out that John 1:18 clearly says that *"no one has ever seen God,"* while Exodus 24:10 explicitly states that Moses and Aaron, Nadab and Abihu, and seventy of the elders of Israel *"saw the God of Israel."* Worse still, God informs them in Exodus 33:20: "You cannot see my face, for man shall not see me and live." The critic with his knowing smile says, 'This is a blatant contradiction.'

John 1:18 Updated American Standard Version (UASV)

[18] No one has seen God at any time; the only begotten god[198] who is in the bosom of the Father,[199] that one has made him fully known.

Exodus 24:10 Updated American Standard Version (UASV)

[10] and they saw the God of Israel; and under his feet was what seemed like a sapphire pavement, as clear as the sky itself.

Exodus 33:20 Updated American Standard Version (UASV)

[20] But he [God] said, "You cannot see my face, for no man can see me and live!"

Answer: Exodus 33:20 is one-hundred percent correct: No human could see Jehovah God and live. The apostle Paul at Colossians 1:15 tell us that Christ is the image of the invisible God, and the writer informs us at Hebrews 1:3 that Jesus is the "exact representation of His nature." Yet if you were to read the account of Saul of Tarsus (the apostle Paul), you would see that a mere partial manifestation of Christ's glory blinded Saul – Acts 9:1–18.

---

[198] Jn 1:18: "only-begotten god", P66א*BC*Lsyrhmg,p; **[V1]** "the only-begotten god," P7513אcopbo; **[V2]** "the only-begotten Son." AC3(Ws)QYf1,13 MajVgSyrc

[199] Or *at the Father's side*

When the Bible says that Moses and others have seen God, it is not speaking of *literally* seeing him, because first of all He is an invisible spirit person. It is a *manifestation* of his glory, which is an act of showing or demonstrating his presence, making himself perceptible to the human mind. In fact, it is generally an angelic representative that stands in his place and not him personally. Exodus 24:16 informs us that "the glory of the Lord dwelt on Mount Sinai," not the Lord himself personally. When texts such as Exodus 24:10 explicitly state that Moses and Aaron, Nadab and Abihu, and seventy of the elders of Israel "*saw the God of Israel*," it is this "glory of the Lord," an angelic representative. This is shown to be the case at Luke 2:9, which reads: "And *an angel of the Lord* appeared to them, and *the glory of the Lord shone around them* [the shepherds], and they were filled with fear."

Many Bible difficulties are cleared up elsewhere in Scripture; for example, in the New Testament, you will find a text clarifying a difficulty from the Old Testament, such as Acts 7:53, which refers to those "who received the law *as delivered by angels* and did not keep it." Support comes from Paul at Galatians 3:19: "Why then the law? It was added because of transgressions until the offspring should come to whom the promise had been made, and it was put in place through angels by an intermediary." The writer of Hebrews chimes in at 2:2 with "For since the message *declared by angels* proved to be reliable, and every transgression or disobedience received a just retribution. . . ." As we travel back to Exodus again, to 19:19 specifically, we find support that it was not God's own voice, which Moses heard; no, it was an angelic representative, for it reads: "Moses was speaking, and God was answering him with a voice." Exodus 33:22–23 also helps us to appreciate that it was the back of these angelic representatives of Jehovah that Moses saw: "While my glory passes by . . . Then I will take away my hand, and you shall see my back, but my face shall not be seen."

Exodus 3:4 states: "God called to him out of the bush, 'Moses, Moses!' And he said, 'Here I am.'" Verse 6 informs us: "I am the God of your father, the God of Abraham, the God of Isaac, and the God of Jacob." Yet, in verse 2 we read: "And the angel of the Lord appeared to him in a flame of fire out of the midst of a bush." Here is another example of using God's Word to clear up what seems to be unclear or difficult to understand at first glance. Thus, while it speaks of the Lord making a direct appearance, it is really an angelic representative. Even today, we hear such comments, as 'the president of the United States is to visit the Middle East later this week.' However, later in the article it is made clear that he is not going personally, but it is one of his high-ranking representatives. Let us close with two examples, starting with,

Genesis 32:24-30 Updated American Standard Version (UASV)

[24] And Jacob was left alone, and a man wrestled with him until daybreak. [25] When he saw that he had not prevailed against him, he touched the socket of his thigh; so the socket of Jacob's thigh was dislocated as he wrestled with him. [26] Then he said, "Let me go, for the dawn is breaking." But he said, "I will not let you go unless you bless me." [27] And he said to him, "What is your name?" And he said, "Jacob." [28] And he said, "Your name shall no longer be called Jacob, but Israel,[200] for you have struggled with God and with men and have prevailed." [29] Then Jacob asked him and said, "Please tell me your name." But he said, "Why is it that you ask my name?" And he blessed him there. [30] So Jacob named the place Peniel,[201] for he said, "I have seen God face to face, yet my soul has been preserved."

It is all too obvious here that this man is simply a materialized angel in the form of a man, another angelic representative of Jehovah God. Moreover, the reader of this book should have taken in that the Israelites as a whole saw these angelic representatives and spoke of them as though they were dealing directly with Jehovah God himself.

This proved to be the case in the second example found in the book of Judges where an angelic representative visited Manoah and his wife. Like the above mentioned account, Manoah and his wife treated this angelic representative as if he were Jehovah God himself: "And Manoah said to the angel of the Lord, 'What is your name, so that, when your words come true, we may honor you?' And the angel of the Lord said to him, 'Why do you ask my name, seeing it is wonderful?'

---

[200] Meaning *he contends with God*
[201] Meaning *face of God*

Then Manoah knew that he was the angel of the Lord. And Manoah said to his wife, "We shall surely die, *for we have seen God.*" – Judges 13:3–22.

Inerrancy: Are There Mistakes?

I have addressed the alleged contradictions, so it would seem that our job is done here, right? Not hardly. Yes, there are just as many who claim that the Bible is full of mistakes.

Critic: Matthew 27:5 states that Judas hanged himself, whereas Acts 1:18 says, "Falling headlong, he burst open in the middle and all his intestines gushed out."

Matthew 27:5 Updated American Standard Version (UASV)

⁵ And he threw the pieces of silver into the temple and departed; and he went away and hanged himself.

Acts 1:18 Updated American Standard Version (UASV)

¹⁸ (Now this man acquired a field with the price of his wickedness, and falling headlong, he burst open in the middle and all his intestines gushed out.

Answer: Neither Matthew nor Luke made a mistake. What you have is Matthew giving the reader the manner in which Judas committed suicide. On the other hand, Luke is giving the reader of Acts, the result of that suicide. Therefore, instead of a mistake, we have two texts that complement each other, really giving the reader the full picture. Judas came to a tree alongside a cliff that had rocks below. He tied the rope to a branch and the other end around his neck and jumped over the edge of the cliff in an attempt at hanging himself. One of two things could have happened: (1) the limb broke plunging him to the rocks below, or (2) the rope broke with the same result, and he burst open onto the rocks below.

Critic: The apostle Paul made a mistake when he quotes how many people died.

Numbers 25:9 Updated American Standard Version (UASV)

⁹The ones who died in the plague were twenty-four thousand.

1 Corinthians 10:8 Updated American Standard Version (UASV)

⁸Neither let us commit sexual immorality, as some of them committed sexual immorality, only to fall, twenty-three thousand of them in one day.

Answer: We must keep in mind the above principle that we spoke of, the *Intended Meaning of the Writer*. We live in a far more precise age today, where specificity is highly important. However, we round large numbers off (even estimate) all the time: "there were 237,000 people in Time Square last night." The simplest answer is that the number of people slain was in between 23,000 and 24,000, and both writers rounded the number off. However, there is even another possibility, because the book of Numbers specifically speaks of "all the chiefs of the people" (25:4-5), which could account for the extra 1,000, which is mentioned in Numbers 24,000. Thus, you have the people killing the chiefs of the people and the plague killing the people. Therefore, both books are correct.

Critic: After 215 years in Egypt, the descendants of Jacob arrived at the Promised Land. As you recall they sinned against God and were sentenced to forty years in the wilderness. But once they entered the Promised Land, they buried Joseph's bones "at Shechem, in the piece of land that *Jacob bought* from the sons of Hamor the father of Shechem," as stated at Joshua 24:32. Yet, when Stephen had to defend himself before the Jewish religious leaders, he said that Joseph was buried "in the tomb that *Abraham had bought* for a sum of silver from the sons of Hamor." Therefore, at once it appears that we have a mistake on the part of Stephen.

Acts 7:15-16 Updated American Standard Version (UASV)

¹⁵And Jacob went down to Egypt and died, he and our fathers. ¹⁶And they were brought back to Shechem and buried in the tomb that Abraham had bought for a sum of silver from the sons of Hamor in Shechem.

Genesis 23:17-18 Updated American Standard Version (UASV)

[17] So Ephron's field, which was in Machpelah, which faced Mamre, the field and cave which was in it, and all the trees which were in the field, that were in all its border around, were made over [18] to Abraham for a possession in the presence of the sons of Heth, before all who went in at the gate of his city.

Genesis 33:19 Updated American Standard Version (UASV)

[19] And he bought the piece of land where he had pitched his tent from the hand of the sons of Hamor, Shechem's father, for one hundred qesitahs.[202]

Joshua 24:32 Updated American Standard Version (UASV)

[32] As for the bones of Joseph, which the sons of Israel brought up from Egypt, they buried them at Shechem, in the piece of land that Jacob bought from the sons of Hamor the father of Shechem for one hundred qesitahs.[203] It became an inheritance of the sons of Joseph.

Answer: If we look back to Genesis 12:6-7, we will find that Abraham's first stop after entering Canaan from Haran was Shechem. It is here that Jehovah told Abraham: "To your offspring I will give this land." At this point Abraham built an altar to Jehovah. It seems reasonable that Abraham would need to purchase this land that had not yet been given to his offspring. While it is true that the Old Testament does not mention this purchase, it is likely that Stephen would be aware of such by way of oral tradition. As Acts chapter seven demonstrates, Stephen had a wide-ranging knowledge of Old Testament history.

Later, Jacob would have had difficulty laying claim to the tract of land that his grandfather Abraham had purchased, because there would have been a new generation of inhabitants of Shechem. This would have been many years after Abraham moved further south and Isaac moved to Beersheba, and including Jacob's twenty years in Paddan-aram (Gen 28:6, 7). The simplest answer is that this land was not in

---

202 Or *pieces of money*; money of unknown value
203 Or *pieces of money*; money of unknown value

use for about 120 years because of Abraham's extensive travels and Isaac's having moved away, leaving it unused; likely it was put to use by others. So, Jacob simply repurchased what Abraham had bought over a hundred years earlier. This is very similar to the time Isaac had to repurchase the well at Beersheba that Abraham had already purchased earlier. – Genesis 21:27–30; 26:26–32.

Genesis 33:18–20 tells us that 'Jacob bought this land for a hundred pieces of money, from the sons of Hamor.' This same transaction is also mentioned at Joshua 24:32, in reference to transporting Joseph's bones from Egypt, to be buried in Shechem.

We should also address the cave of Machpelah that Abraham had purchased in Hebron from Ephron the Hittite. The word "tomb" is not mentioned until Joshua 24:32, and is in reference to the tract of land in Shechem. Nowhere in the Old Testament does it say that Abraham bought a "tomb." The cave of Machpelah obtained by Abraham would eventually become a family tomb, receiving Sarah's body and, eventually, his own, and those of Isaac, Rebekah, Jacob, and Leah. (Genesis 23:14–19; 25:9; 49:30, 31; 50:13) Gleason L. Archer, Jr., concludes this Bible difficulty, saying:

> The reference to a *mnema* ("tomb") in connection with Shechem must either have been proleptic [to anticipate] for the later use of that shechemite tract for Joseph's tomb (i.e., 'the tomb that Abraham bought' was intended to imply 'the tomb location that Abraham bought"); or else conceivably the dative relative pronoun *ho* was intended elliptically [omission] for *en to topo ho onesato Abraam* ("in the place that Abraham bought") as describing the location of the *mnema* near the Oak of Moreh right outside Shechem. Normally Greek would have used the relative-locative adverb *hou* to express 'in which' or 'where'; but this would have left o*nesato* ("bought") without an object in its own clause, and so *ho* was much more suitable in this context. (Archer 1982, 379–81)

Another solution could be that Jacob is being viewed as a representative of Abraham, for he is the grandson of Abraham. This was quite appropriate in Biblical times, to attribute the purchase to Abraham as the Patriarchal family head.

Critic: 2 Samuel 24:1 says that God moved David to count the Israelites, while 1 Chronicles 21:1 Satan, or a resister did. This would seem to be a clear mistake on the part of one of these authors.

2 Samuel 24:1 Updated American Standard Version (UASV)

[1] Now again the anger of Jehovah burned against Israel, and it incited David against them to say, "Go, number Israel and Judah."

1 Chronicles 21:1 Updated American Standard Version (UASV)

[1] Then Satan stood up against Israel and moved David to number Israel.

Answer: In this period of David's reign, Jehovah was very displeased with Israel, and therefore he did not prevent Satan from bringing this sin on them. Often in Scripture, it is spoken of as though God did something when he allowed an event to take place. For example, it is said that God 'hardened Pharaoh's heart' (Exodus 4:21), when he actually allowed the Pharaoh's heart to harden.

Inerrancy: Are There Scientific Errors?

Many truths about God are beyond the scope of science. Science and the Bible are not at odds. In fact, we can thank modern day science as it has helped us to better under the creation of God, from our solar system to the universes, to the human body and mind. What we find is a level of order, precision, design, and sophistication, which points to a Designer, the eyes of many Christians, to an Almighty God, with infinite intelligence and power. The apostle Paul makes this all too clear, when he writes, "For his invisible attributes, namely, his eternal power and divine nature, have been clearly perceived, ever since the creation of the world, in the things that have been made. So they are without excuse." – Romans 1:20.

Back in the seventeenth century, the world-renowned scientist Galileo proved beyond any doubt that the earth was not the center of the universe, nor did the sun orbit the earth. In fact, he proved it to be the other way around (no pun intended), with the earth revolving around the sun. However, he was brought up on charges of heresy by the Catholic Church and ordered to recant his position. Why? From the viewpoint of the Catholic Church, Galileo was contradicting God's Word, the Bible. As it turned out, Galileo and science were correct, and the Church was wrong, for which it issued a formal apology in 1992. However, the point we wish to make here is that in all the controversy, the Bible was never in the wrong. It was a misinterpretation on the part of the Catholic Church and not a fault with the Bible. One will find no place in the Bible that claims the sun orbits the earth. So where would the Church get such an idea? The Church got such an idea from Ptolemy (b. about 85 C.E.), an ancient astronomer, who argued for such an idea.

As it usually turns out, the so-called contradiction between science and God's Word lies at the feet of those who are interpreting Scripture incorrectly. To repeat the sentiments of Galileo when writing to a pupil–Galileo expressed the same sentiments: "Even though Scripture cannot err, its interpreters and expositors can, in various ways. One of these, very serious and very frequent, would be when they always want to stop at the purely literal sense."[204] I believe that today's scholars, in hindsight, would have no problem agreeing.

While the Bible is not a science textbook, it is scientifically accurate when it touches on matters of science.

The Circle of the Earth Hangs on Nothing

Isaiah 40:22 Updated American Standard Version (UASV)

[22] It is he who sits above **the circle of the earth,**
    and its inhabitants are like grasshoppers;
who stretches out the heavens like a curtain,
    and spreads them like a tent to dwell in.

More than 2,500 years ago, the prophet Isaiah wrote that the earth is a circle or sphere. First, how would it be possible for Isaiah to know the earth is a circle or sphere, if not from inspiration? Scientific

---

[204] Letter from Galileo to Benedetto Castelli, December 21, 1613.

America writes, "As countless photos from space can attest, Earth is round–the "Blue Marble," as astronauts have affectionately dubbed it. Appearances, however, can be deceiving. Planet Earth is not, in fact, perfectly round."[205] Scientifically speaking, the sun is not perfectly, absolutely 100 percent round but in everyday speech, this verse is both acceptable and accurate, when we keep in mind it is written from a human perspective, not from a scientific perspective. Moreover, Isaiah was not discussing astronomy; he was simply making an inspired observation that man came to realize once he was in space, looking back at the earth, it is round. See the section about title, "Intended Meaning of Writer."

Job 26:7 Updated American Standard Version (UASV)

[7] "He stretches out the north over empty space
and hangs the earth on nothing.

Here the author describes the earth as hanging upon nothing. Many have never heard of the Greek mathematician and astronomer Eratosthenes. He was born in about 276 B.C.E. and received some of his education in Athens, Greece. In 240 B.C., the "Greek astronomer, geographer, mathematician and librarian Eratosthenes calculates the Earth's circumference. His data was rough, but he wasn't far off."[206] While man very early on used their God given intelligence to arrive at some outstanding conclusion that was actually very accurate, we learn two points here. Eratosthenes was a very astute scientist, while Isaiah, who wrote some 500 years earlier, was no scientist at all. Moreover, Moses, who wrote the book of Job over 1,230 years before Eratosthenes, knew that the earth hung upon nothing.

---

[205] Charles Q. Choi (April 12, 2007). Scientific America. Strange but True: Earth Is Not Round. Retrieved Monday, August 03, 2015.

http://www.scientificamerican.com/article/earth-is-not-round/

[206] Alfred, Randy (June 19, 2008). "June 19, 240 B.C.E: The Earth Is Round, and It's This Big". Wired. Retrieved Monday, August 03, 2015.

How Is the Sun Standing Still Possible?

Joshua 10:13 Updated American Standard Version (UASV)

[13] And the sun stood still, and the moon stopped,
until the nation avenged themselves of their enemies.

Is this not written in the Book of Jashar? The sun stopped in the midst of heaven and did not hurry to set for about a whole day.

The Canaanites had besieged the Gibeonites, a group of people that gained Jehovah God's backing because they had faith in Him. In this battle, Jehovah helped the Israelites continue their attack by causing "the sun [to stand] still, and the moon stopped, until the nation took vengeance on their enemies." (Jos 10:1-14) Those who accept God as the creator of the universe and life can accept that he would know a way of stopping the earth from rotating. However, there are other ways of understanding this account. We must keep in mind that the Bible speaks from an earthly observer point of view, so it need not be that he stopped the rotation. It could have been a refraction of solar and lunar light rays, which would have produced the same effect.

Psalm 136:6 Updated American Standard Version (UASV)

[6] to him who spread out the earth above the waters,
for his lovingkindness is everlasting;

Hebrews 3:4 Updated American Standard Version (UASV)

[4] For every house is built by someone, but the builder of all things is God.

2 Kings 20:8-11 Updated American Standard Version (UASV)

[8] And Hezekiah said to Isaiah, "What shall be the sign that Jehovah will heal me, and that I shall go up to the house of Jehovah on the third day?" [9] And Isaiah said, "This shall be the sign to you from Jehovah, that Jehovah will do the thing that he has spoken: shall the shadow go forward ten steps or go back ten steps?" [10] And Hezekiah answered, "It is an easy thing for the shadow to decline ten steps; no, but let the shadow turn backward ten steps." [11] And Isaiah the prophet cried to Jehovah, and he brought the shadow on the steps back ten steps, by which it had gone down on the steps of Ahaz.

How is it that the stars fought on behalf of Barak?

Judges 5:20 Updated American Standard Version (UASV)

[20] From heaven the stars fought, from their courses they fought against Sisera.

Judges 4:15 Updated American Standard Version (UASV)

[15] And Jehovah routed Sisera and all his chariots and all his army with the edge of the sword before Barak; and Sisera alighted from his chariot and fled away on foot.

In the Bible, you have Biblical prose, and Biblical poetry.

Prose: language that is not poetry: (1) writing or speech in its normal continuous form, without the rhythmic or visual line structure of poetry **(2)** ordinary style of expression: writing or speech that is ordinary or matter-of-fact, without embellishment.

Poetry: literature in verse: (1) literary works written in verse, in particular verse writing of high quality, great beauty, emotional sincerity or intensity, or profound insight **(2) beauty or grace:** something that resembles poetry in its beauty, rhythmic grace, or imaginative, elevated, or decorative style.

We have a beautiful example of both of these forms of writing communication in chapters four and five of the book of Judges. Judges, Chapter 4 is a prose account of Deborah and Barak, while Judges Chapter 5 is a poetic account. As we have learned from the above, poetry is less concerned with accuracy than evoking emotions. Poetry has a license to say things like what we find in of 5:20, which is in the poetry chapter: "from heaven the stars fought." This can be said, and the reader is expected not to take the language literally. What we can surmise from it though, is that God was acting against Sisera in some way, there was divine intervention.

Procedures for Handling Biblical Difficulties

1. You need to be completely convinced a reason or understanding exists.

2. You need to have total trust and conviction in the inerrancy of the Scripture as originally written down.

3. You need to study the context and framework of the verse carefully, to establish what the author meant by the words he used. In other words, find the beginning and the end of the context that your passage falls within.

4. You need to understand exegesis: find the historical setting, determine author intent, study key words, and note parallel passages. You need to slow down and carefully read the account, considering exactly what is being said

5. You need to find a reasonable harmonization of parallel passages.

6. You need to consider a variety of trusted Bible commentaries, dictionaries, lexical sources, encyclopedias, as well as books on Bible difficulties.

7. You should investigate as to whether the difficulty is a transmission error in the original text.

8. You must always keep in mind that the historical accuracy of the biblical text is unmatched; that thousands of extant manuscripts some of which date back to the second century B.C. support the transmitted text of Scripture.

9. We must keep in mind that the Bible is a diverse book when it comes to literary styles: narrative, poetic, prophetic, and apocalyptic; also containing parables, metaphors, similes, hyperbole, and other figures of speech. Too often, these alleged errors are the result of a reader taking a figure of speech as literal or reading a parable as though it is a narrative.

10. The Bible student needs to understand what level that the Bible intends to be exact in what is written. If Jim told a friend that 650 graduated with him from high school in 1984, it is not challenged, because it is all too clear that he is using rounded numbers and is not meaning to be precise.

CHAPTER 15 The Bible— Authentic and True

The Divine Genesis of the Bible: A Discourse on Its Authenticity and Accuracy

The Bible, apart from its artistic excellence, stands as an astonishing compilation of life-guiding wisdom and knowledge, tracing its roots back to Jehovah, the omnipotent deity. Its literary beauty and the profound worth it holds as a book of life-giving wisdom can be attributed to its divine origins. Jesus, the Son of God, confirmed the spiritual and life-giving nature of His words and frequently referenced the ancient Hebrew Scriptures. The apostle Paul upheld the sanctity and divine inspiration of the scriptures, referring to them as the "sacred utterances of God" (2 Timothy 3:16; Romans 3:1,2).

The Holy Spirit's active influence over God's prophets is further evidenced by the apostle Peter's testimony, and King David's assertion: "The Spirit of the Lord speaks by me; His word is on my tongue" (2 Samuel 23:2 ASV). These prophecies are repeatedly attributed to Jehovah. A stern warning against any modifications to the sacred words was conveyed by Moses, underlining the Holy Scriptures' inviolability. Both Peter and Jude acknowledged Paul's writings as inspired, and the former even referenced Jude's assertion as an authoritative divine commandment. John, the author of Revelation, relayed his words under the Holy Spirit's influence and cautioned against any alterations to the prophetic revelation, stressing the ultimate accountability to God (1 Peter 1:10-12; 2 Peter 1:19-21; Deuteronomy 4:2; 2 Peter 3:15,16; Jude 17,18; Revelation 1:1,10; 21:5; 22:18,19).

These devout servants of God collectively vouch for the Bible's divine inspiration and authenticity. Further evidences backing the Holy Scriptures' authenticity will be discussed in the ensuing sections under twelve distinct themes.

251

(1) **Historical Accuracy:** The canonical books of the Hebrew Scriptures, accepted by the Jewish community since ancient times, are considered inspired and completely trustworthy. These accounts, spanning from Genesis to First Samuel, were universally recognized as the true history of the Jewish nation and their relationship with God during David's era, as reflected in Psalm 78, which references over 35 specific details.

The Pentateuch has been the subject of intense scrutiny by Bible critics, particularly regarding its authenticity and authorship. However, along with the Jewish acceptance of Moses as the Pentateuch's author, multiple ancient writers - even those hostile to Jews - confirm Moses as the lawgiver who distinguished Jews from other nations. These writers include Hecataeus of Abdera, the Egyptian historian Manetho, Lysimachus of Alexandria, Eupolemus, Tacitus, and Juvenal. Most of these authors explicitly state that Moses documented these laws. Numenius, the Pythagorean philosopher, even identifies Jannes and Jambres as the Egyptian priests who resisted Moses (2 Timothy 3:8). These writers' accounts span from Alexander's era (4th century B.C.E.) to the reign of Emperor Aurelian (3rd century C.E.). Numerous other ancient writers acknowledge Moses as a leader, ruler, or lawgiver. The historical accuracy of the events documented in the Bible involving God's people with neighboring nations is often corroborated by archaeological findings.

The Greek New Testament not only validate the Hebrew Scripture narratives but are also established as historically precise, authentic, and divinely inspired, equal in standing with the Hebrew Scriptures. The authors, often eyewitnesses or participants in the events they recorded, received acceptance from thousands of their contemporaries. Their testimonies gain further support from numerous ancient writers, such as Juvenal, Tacitus, Seneca, Suetonius, Pliny the Younger, Lucian, Celsus, and the Jewish historian Josephus.

The New Testament is seen as more authentic than any secular history, according to the esteemed scholar Sir Isaac Newton. Dr. Johnson further establishes the Gospels' truthfulness by asserting that there is more evidence for Jesus Christ's crucifixion at Calvary than Julius Caesar's death in the Capitol. The ample evidence supporting the

Holy Scriptures' authenticity is deemed compelling enough to convince anyone but the most stubborn or ignorant.

Christianity, which includes the Old Testament dispensation, is distinguished from other religions by its objective and historical character, as highlighted by George Rawlinson. Unlike speculative systems, the religion of the Bible is deeply intertwined with historical facts. The doctrines propounded in the Old and New Testaments are rooted in these facts and are rendered null without them. The acceptance of these facts practically establishes the validity of the doctrines espoused in the Bible.

Scripture-Informed Geographic and Scientific Accuracy: A Scholarly Examination

(2) The Biblical account's **geographical and geological accuracy** has garnered praise for its precise representation of the Promised Land and neighboring territories. Dr. A. P. Stanley, an Oriental traveler, noted the alignment of geographic features with those recorded in the Biblical accounts of the Israelites' wilderness journey. Such details include the sporadic springs, brooks, and wells, mirroring the 'waters' of Marah, the 'springs' of Elim, and the 'brook' of Horeb, among others. The Bible's depiction of Egypt, characterized by lush grain fields, reed-bordered Nile River (Genesis 41:47-49; Exodus 2:3), and the naming of cities is also commendable.

Modern scientists have been guided by these Biblical geographic and geological records, reaping benefits. For instance, Dr. Ben Tor, a noted geologist, pursued the scriptural direction that "The Lord your God is bringing you into a good land... a land the stones of which are iron" (Deuteronomy 8:7, 9 ASV). He discovered immense cliffs filled with red-black ore near Beer-sheba. Such is the trustworthiness of the Bible's geologic records.

(3) In terms of humanity's **races and languages**, the Bible asserts that man was created in a unified manner rather than as divided racial groups (Genesis 1:27, 28; 2:7, 20-23; 3:20; Acts 17:26 ESV; and Romans 5:12 ESV). According to this account, all racial diversities we

see today have descended naturally from the first human pair, Adam and Eve.

The Bible's recounting of the dispersion of ancient languages from a central location aligns with archeological findings. Renowned archaeologist Sir Henry Rawlinson affirms that even without considering the Biblical record, linguistic trails would lead us back to the plains of Shinar (Genesis 11:1-9 ESV).

(4) The Bible's **practicality** for everyday living stands as a testament to its authenticity. Its principles provide guidelines for every aspect of life, ranging from understanding the origin of all things and the purpose of creation (Genesis 1; Isaiah 45:18 ESV) to standards of justice (Exodus 23:1, 2, 6, 7; Deuteronomy 19:15-21 ESV), proper business dealings, morality, familial relationships, and many more. The Bible even offers insights on physical and mental health (Proverbs 15:17; 17:22 ESV).

(5) In terms of **scientific accuracy**, the Bible aligns with proven scientific facts, despite not being a scientific manuscript. For instance, the sequence of creation, the earth's spherical shape (Isaiah 40:22 ESV), and its suspension in space on 'nothing' (Job 26:7 ESV) have been affirmed by modern scientific discoveries. The Bible's anatomical and zoological accuracy, as seen in the differentiation of 'flesh' (1 Corinthians 15:39 ESV) and the classification of the hare as a cud-chewing animal (Leviticus 11:6 ESV), is also supported by science.

(6) In terms of **culture and customs**, the Bible reflects the socio-political structures and experiences of its time. For instance, A. Rendle Short, in Modern Discovery and the Bible, extols the accuracy of the book of Acts in terms of cultural and political nuances. Similarly, the apostle Paul's letters reflect the distinct customs and situations of the locations he wrote to, validating his firsthand knowledge of these places. This attests to the Bible's credibility.

Additionally, the Bible correctly depicts various customs, laws, and traditions of different periods, such as the code of Hammurabi in the patriarchal narratives (Genesis 23:3-20), Levirate marriage among the Israelites (Deuteronomy 25:5-6), and Roman citizenship laws as seen in the book of Acts (Acts 22:25-29).

(7) In terms of **historical accuracy**, the Bible provides a faithful record of ancient history that aligns with archaeological findings. Prominent archaeologists such as William F. Albright and Sir Flinders Petrie have verified the Bible's historical accounts. For instance, the Hittite civilization, once thought to be a Biblical invention, was discovered and recognized as a significant empire in the late 19th and early 20th century, corroborating the Bible's historical validity.

(8) The Bible's **prophetic accuracy** is another striking testament to its authenticity. For instance, the prophecy of the destruction of Jerusalem (Matthew 24:1-2; Luke 21:20-24) was fulfilled in A.D. 70. Another example is the prophecy about Cyrus the Persian, named approximately 150 years before his birth, who played a crucial role in rebuilding Jerusalem and the temple (Isaiah 44:28; 45:1; Ezra 1:1-4).

(9) **The Honesty of Biblical Authors**. One of the key attributes that underscores the trustworthiness of the Bible is the unvarnished honesty of its authors. Take Moses as an example, who explicitly confessed his own transgressions and acknowledged the decree of God that barred both him and his brother Aaron from entering the Promised Land (Numbers 20:7-13; Deuteronomy 3:23-27).

Similarly, the missteps of David, including his transgressions that are recounted in the second book of Samuel (Chapters 11, 12, 24), and the apostasy of his son Solomon, which is detailed in 1 Kings 11:1-13, are presented without sugarcoating. Jonah's personal account of his disobedience and the ensuing consequences also adds to the forthrightness of the biblical narratives.

Interestingly, almost all the authors of the Hebrew Scriptures, themselves being Jews, do not shy away from chastising the entire nation of Israel for its disobedience to God. This reproach is found in the very record that the Jews revered as the declarations of God and the authentic history of their nation.

The candor extends to the writers of The Greek New Testament as well. The denial of Christ by Peter, a prominent apostle, is revealed by all four Gospel writers (Matthew 26:69-75; Mark 14:66-72; Luke 22:54-62; John 18:15-27). In addition, Paul pointedly draws attention to Peter's major mistake regarding the segregation between Jews and Gentiles in the Christian congregation in Antioch (Galatians 2:11-14).

The reality that the Bible's authors did not spare anyone, including themselves, in the pursuit of recording the truth inspires trust in the Bible as the embodiment of truth (John 17:17).

(10) **The Consistency among Bible Writers**. The Bible, composed over a span of more than 1,600 years by roughly 40 writers, exhibits an extraordinary unity and harmony. Despite the considerable time frame, diverse cultural backgrounds, and varying writing styles, there is a remarkable coherence in the overarching message and theological concepts.

Moreover, the Bible has been disseminated in vast quantities even amidst the most vehement opposition and rigorous efforts to annihilate it. This not only speaks volumes about its resilience and the devotion of its followers but also testifies to its claim of being the Word of the Almighty God.

This uniformity and tenacity of the Bible, along with its influential teachings and moral instructions, establish its role as a valuable tool "for teaching, for reproof, for correction, and for training in righteousness," as mentioned in 2 Timothy 3:16.

Taken together, the honesty of its writers and the consistency of its teachings across centuries strongly affirm the authenticity and reliability of the Bible.

CHAPTER 16 Why Has God Allowed So Many Different Religions, 41,000 Christian Denominations, and Hundreds of Thousands of Textual Variants In Books He Inspired?

Here are some of the issues God's people face based on the questions in the title of our chapter.

- "Why Are There So Many Different Religions? A Look at God's Plan and Purpose"

- "The Diversity of Christianity: Exploring the Origins and Implications of 41,000 Denominations"

- "The Bible and Its Variants: Understanding God's Role in the Preservation of Sacred Texts"

- "God, Humans, and the Transmission of Scripture: Examining the Controversies and Complexities of Biblical Copying and Editing"

- "The Mystery of Divine Providence: Wrestling with the Complexities of Religious Diversity and Unity"

This actually needs to be biblically understood. We need to look at the Problem of Evil doctrine to get at why God has allowed so many different religions, why he has allowed 41,000 different varieties of the "Christian" denominations, and why he inspired the Bible writers but allowed the copyist to intentionally and unintentionally add variants into the text.

GOD IS SOVEREIGN: As indicated in the Bible (Psalm 47:9), God is the Sovereign of the universe, affirmed in his Creatorship,

Godship, and supremacy as the Almighty (Genesis 17:1; Exodus 6:3; Revelation 16:14). He is the owner of all things and the source of all authority and power, serving as the supreme ruler in government (Psalm 24:1; Isaiah 40:21-23; Revelation 4:11; 11:15).

God's Sovereignty Challenged

The existence of wickedness throughout human history, with all mankind dying and sins and transgressions multiplying (Romans 5:12, 15, 16), raises questions about how sin, imperfection, and wickedness originated despite God giving man a perfect start. This challenge against God's sovereignty is a paramount issue involving mankind, with the answers lying in its resolution (Ro 5:12, 15, 16).

Failure to Develop Love and Appreciation

The lack of love and appreciation played a significant role in the challenge against God's sovereignty. The challenger in question was a spirit creature—an angel—who, despite benefiting from God's sovereignty, failed to cultivate a deep knowledge of God and grow in love for Him. Seizing the opportunity presented by the presence of the human couple, Adam and Eve, this rebellious angel sought to undermine God's sovereignty. His plan involved turning Eve, and subsequently Adam, away from their rightful subjection to God's sovereignty, with the aim of establishing a rival sovereignty.

Eve, being the first to be approached, had not fully appreciated her Creator and God, nor had she taken advantage of the opportunity to truly know Him. She listened to the voice of an inferior being—the serpent, who was actually the rebellious angel. The Bible does not indicate any surprise on Eve's part upon hearing the serpent speak. It does mention that the serpent was "the serpent was more [crafty] than any beast of the field which Jehovah God had made" (Genesis 3:1, A.S.V.). Whether the serpent had consumed the forbidden fruit from "the tree of the knowledge of good and bad" and thus gained the ability to speak is not explicitly stated. Nevertheless, the rebellious angel, using the serpent as a mouthpiece, presented Eve with the deceptive promise of independence and becoming like God, knowing good and bad. Tragically, Eve believed the lie and was convinced that she would not die (Genesis 2:17; 3:4-5; 2 Corinthians 11:3).

Adam, who also demonstrated a lack of appreciation and love for his Creator and Provider, succumbed to Eve's persuasion when faced with rebellion within his household. He showed no loyalty to stand up for his God when put to the test, losing faith in God's ability to provide everything good for His faithful servant. This is reminiscent of God's words to David after his sin with Bath-sheba (2 Samuel 12:7-9). Adam's response when questioned about his wrongdoing reflects a sense of offense against God: "The woman whom you gave to be with me, she gave me fruit of the tree, and I ate" (Genesis 3:12). While Adam did not believe the Serpent's lie like Eve did, both he and Eve willfully chose a path of self-determination and rebellion against God (1 Timothy 2:14).

It is important to note that Adam could not claim, "I am being tested by God." Instead, the principle described in James 1:13-15 came into effect: "each person is tempted when he is lured and enticed by his own desire. Then desire when it has conceived gives birth to sin, and sin when it is fully grown brings forth death." Consequently, the angel, Eve, and Adam—all three rebels—exercised the freedom of will bestowed upon them by God, turning away from sinlessness and embarking on a course of deliberate disobedience.

The Central Issue at Stake

What exactly was being challenged? Who was reproached and defamed by this angelic challenger, later identified as Satan the Devil? Did it concern God's supremacy and the existence of His sovereignty? Was God's sovereignty in jeopardy? No, because God possesses ultimate authority and power that cannot be wrested from His hand by anyone in heaven or on earth (Romans 9:19). Therefore, the challenge must have revolved around the rightness, deservingness, and righteousness of God's sovereignty—whether His sovereignty was exercised in a worthy, righteous manner for the best interests of His subjects or not. An indication of this can be seen in the serpent's approach to Eve when it questioned, "Did God actually say, 'You shall not eat of any tree in the garden'?" The serpent subtly insinuated that such a restriction was unbelievable, suggesting that God was unjustly withholding something that rightfully belonged to the human pair (Genesis 3:1).

Failure to Develop Love and Appreciation

The issue of love and appreciation was exemplified in Satan's challenge concerning Job. Satan questioned whether Job's fear of God was genuine, suggesting that Job only served God out of self-interest. Satan accused Job of serving God solely for personal gain and insinuated that if God were to remove His blessings and afflict Job, he would curse God. This accusation not only slandered Job's integrity but also cast doubt on God's sovereignty. Satan claimed that no one could maintain loyalty to God's sovereignty if put to the test.

God Permits the Issue to be Joined

God allowed the issue to be tested, not because He doubted His own righteousness, but out of love for His intelligent creatures. He granted Satan permission to test humanity's loyalty before the entire universe. This gave God's creatures the opportunity to prove Satan wrong, vindicate God's name, and remove the slander against both God's sovereignty and their own integrity. Satan's egotism led him to be given up to a disapproved mental state. He contradicted his own reasoning in his approach to Eve. Although accusing God of unfair exercise of sovereignty, he still relied on God's fairness, thinking that God would let him live if he proved his charge of unfaithfulness among God's creatures.

Settlement of the Issue, a Vital Need

The resolution of this issue was crucial for all living beings in their relationship to God's sovereignty. Once settled, it would never need to be tried again. God desired that every aspect of this issue be fully known and understood. His actions inspire confidence in His unchangeableness, further establishing His sovereignty as desirable and firmly established in the minds of those who choose it.

A Moral Issue

This issue is primarily a moral one, not solely based on raw strength or power. However, due to God's invisibility and Satan's efforts to blind minds, questions about God's power or existence have arisen. Men have misunderstood God's patience and kindness, leading to increased rebellion. Serving God with integrity has required faith and endurance in the face of suffering. Nevertheless, God intends to make His sovereignty and His name known to all. He has allowed time for this world under Satan's rule to develop in wickedness, setting a time for its destruction. The psalmist prayed for God's name to be declared over all the earth, and God Himself has sworn that every knee shall bow and every tongue shall swear allegiance to Him.

The Extent of the Issue

The issue reaches beyond humanity, involving God's heavenly creatures, including His only-begotten Son. Jesus, who always pleased His Father, willingly served to vindicate God's sovereignty. God chose Him for this task and sent Him to earth, born as a male child through the virgin Mary. Jesus maintained perfection and blamelessness throughout His life, even unto a disgraceful death. Satan could not break His integrity, and Jesus declared that the ruler of this world would be cast out. Jesus triumphed over the world and Satan's influence.

The Depth of Human Imperfection: Reflections on Genesis 6:5, 8:21; Jeremiah 17:9; and Paul's Teachings in Romans

Human imperfection has been a recurring theme throughout the scriptures, highlighting the inherent flaws and weaknesses that characterize humanity. Verses such as Genesis 6:5 and 8:21, Jeremiah

17:9, and Paul's teachings in Romans shed light on the depth of human imperfection and its implications. These passages reveal the fallen state of mankind, emphasizing our innate inclination towards evil and the profound challenges it poses. This section aims to explore the level of human imperfection presented in these verses and the implications they have for our existence. Additionally, it will address the question of hope in the face of our deeply flawed nature.

I. Genesis 6:5 and 8:21: The Bent towards Evil: Genesis 6:5 describes the state of humanity before the flood, stating that "the wickedness of man was great in the earth, and that every intention of the thoughts of his heart was only evil continually." This verse portrays the pervasive and all-encompassing nature of human wickedness, emphasizing the deep-seated inclination towards evil that resides within humanity.

Genesis 8:21 provides a post-flood perspective, where God acknowledges that "the intention of man's heart is evil from his youth." This verse indicates that the fallen nature of humanity persists, even after the cataclysmic event of the flood. It reveals that human imperfection and the inclination towards evil are not eradicated through external circumstances but are deeply rooted within our nature.

These passages emphasize the universality and persistence of human sinfulness. They depict humanity's inherent tendency to deviate from righteousness and the struggle to resist the allure of evil. It is a solemn reminder of our frailty and the desperate need for divine intervention.

II. Jeremiah 17:9: The Treacherous and Unknowable Heart: Jeremiah 17:9 states, "The heart is deceitful above all things, and desperately sick; who can understand it?" This verse provides insights into the profound depth of human imperfection by revealing the treacherous and unknowable nature of the human heart.

The "heart" in this context refers to the core of human desires, emotions, and intentions. It is portrayed as deceitful and desperately sick, highlighting the distorted nature of human desires and the capacity for self-deception. This verse suggests that human hearts are prone to corruption, leading to misguided choices and actions.

The unknowability of the human heart poses significant challenges for individuals and communities. It indicates that we are often unaware of our own motivations and inner workings. This lack of self-awareness contributes to our flawed decision-making and adds to the complexities of navigating relationships and society.

III. Paul's Teachings in Romans: The Natural Desire for Evil: Paul's teachings in the book of Romans provide a comprehensive exploration of human imperfection, particularly in Romans 1-3. He presents a compelling argument that all humanity is under sin, highlighting our natural inclination towards evil and our inability to attain righteousness on our own.

Romans 1 describes humanity's suppression of the truth and their descent into idolatry and immorality. It demonstrates the consequence of turning away from God and the subsequent moral decay. Paul emphasizes that human beings, apart from God's intervention, are unable to escape this spiral of sin.

In Romans 2, Paul challenges the self-righteousness of those who claim moral superiority. He asserts that no one is exempt from the effects of sin and highlights the universal need for God's mercy and grace.

Romans 3 concludes this section by declaring that all have sinned and fall short of God's glory. Paul underscores the universality of human imperfection, stating that no one is righteous in themselves.

These teachings by Paul serve to emphasize the gravity of human imperfection and the universal need for salvation. They demonstrate the futility of relying on our own efforts and underscore the necessity of relying on God's grace and redemption.

The Hope in the Midst of Imperfection: Despite the depth of human imperfection portrayed in these verses, the scriptures also offer hope. The recognition of our fallen nature serves as a catalyst for seeking redemption and reconciliation with God.

Throughout the biblical narrative, God's redemptive plan unfolds, culminating in the person of Jesus Christ. Through His life, death, and resurrection, Jesus offers the hope of salvation and transformation for all who believe in Him. He provides a way to overcome our inherent imperfections and be reconciled to God.

The transformative power of the Holy Spirit is also crucial in our journey towards overcoming human imperfection. As believers, we receive the indwelling presence of the Holy Spirit, who guides, convicts, and empowers us to live according to God's will.

The verses explored in this section shed light on the depth of human imperfection and the challenges it poses. From Genesis to Paul's teachings in Romans, the scriptures emphasize humanity's innate bent towards evil, the treacherous nature of the human heart, and our natural inclination to do wrong. However, these passages also point to the hope found in God's redemptive plan. Through Jesus Christ and the empowering presence of the Holy Spirit, we can find deliverance from our fallen state and the transformative power to live in alignment with God's purposes. The recognition of our imperfection serves as a reminder of our need for God's grace, prompting us to seek His redemption and restoration.

Bibliography

Abbot, Nabia. 1938. *STUDIES IN ANCIENT ORIENTAL CIVILIZATIONS*. Chicago: The University of Chicago Press.

Aland, Barbara. 2004. *The Significance of the Chester Beatty in Early Church History, in: THE EARLIEST GOSPEL ed. Charles Horton*. London: Bloomsbury T & T Clark.

Aland, Kurt, and Barbara Aland. 1995. *The Text of the New Testament*. Grand Rapids: Eerdmans.

—. 1987. *The Text of the New Testament*. Grand Rapids: Eerdmans.

Aland, Kurt, Matthew Black, and Carlo M. Martini. 1993; 2006. *The Greek New Testament, Fourth Revised Edition (Interlinear With Morphology)*. Deutsche Bibelgesellschaft: United Bible Society.

Andrews, E. (2020). *FROM SPOKEN WORDS TO SACRED TEXTS: Introduction-Intermediate New Testament Textual Studies*. Cambridge: Christian Publishing House.

Andrews, E. D. (2015). *CRISIS OF FAITH: Saving Those Who Doubt*. Cambridge, OH: Christian Publishing House.

Andrews, E. D. (2023). *ARCHAEOLOGY & THE NEW TESTAMENT*. Cambridge, Ohio: Christian publishing House.

Andrews, E. D. (2023). *ARCHAEOLOGY & THE OLD TESTAMENT*. Cambridge, Ohio: Christian Publishing House.

Andrews, E. D. (2023). *CHRISTIAN APOLOGETICS: Answering the Tough Questions: Evidence and Reason in Defense of the Faith*. Cambridge, Ohio: Christian Publishing House.

Andrews, E. D. (2023). *HOW WE GOT THE BIBLE*. Cambridge, OH: Christian Publishing House.

Andrews, E. D. (2023). *THE BIBLE AS HISTORY: A Historical Journey Through the Bible*. Cambridge, Ohio: Christian Publishing House.

Andrews, E. D. (2023). *THE BIBLE ON TRIAL: Examining the Evidence for Being Inspired, Inerrant, Authentic, and True.* Cambridge, Ohio: Christian Publishing House.

Andrews, E. D. (2023). *THE SCRIBE AND THE TEXT OF THE NEW TESTAMENT: Scribal Activities in the Transmission of the Text of the New Testament.* Cambridge, Ohio: Christian Publishing House.

Arndt, William, Frederick W. Danker, and Walter Bauer. 2000. *A Greek-English Lexicon of the New Testament and Other Early Christian Literature. 3rd ed.* . Chicago: University of Chicago Press.

Baer, Daniel. 2007. *The Unquenchable Fire.* Maitland, FL: Xulon Press.

Bagnall, Roger S. 2009. *The Oxford Handbook of Papyrology (Oxford Handbooks).* Oxford, NY: Oxford University Press.

Balz, Horst, and Gerhard Schneider. 1978. *Exegetical Dictionary of the New Testament.* Edinburgh: T & T Clark Ltd.

Barnett, Paul. 2005. *The Birth of Christianity: The First Twenty Years (After Jesus, Vol. 1)* . Grand Rapids, MI: Wm. B. Eerdmans .

Bauckham, Richard. 1993. *The Theology of the Book of Revelation (NTT).* Cambridge, UK: Cambridge University Press.

Bercot, David W. 1998. *A Dictionary of Early Christian Beliefs.* Peabody: Hendrickson.

Black, David Alan. 1994. *New Testament Textual Criticism: A Concise Guide.* Grand Rapids, MI: Baker Books.

—. 2002. *Rethinking New Testament Textual Criticism.* Grand Rapids: Baker Books.

Bock, Darrell L, and Daniel B Wallace. 2007. *Dethroning Jesus: Exposing Popular Culture's Quest to Unseat the Biblical Christ.* Nashville: Thomas Nelson.

Borgen, Peder. 1997. *Philo of Alexandria: An Exegete for His Time.* Leiden, Boston: Brill.

Brand, Chad, Charles Draper, and England Archie. 2003. *Holman Illustrated Bible Dictionary: Revised, Updated and Expanded.* Nashville, TN: Holman.

Brown, Virginia. 1972. *The Textual Transmission of Caesar's Civil War.* Leiden: Brill.

Capes, David B, Rodney Reeves, and E. Randolph Richards. 2007. *Rediscovering Paul: An Introduction to His World, Letters and Theology* . Downers Grove: IVP Academic.

Carson, D. A, and Douglas J Moo. 2005. *An Introduction to the New Testament.* Grand Rapids, MI: Zondervan.

Carson, D. A. 1994. *New Bible Commentary: 21st Century Edition. 4th ed.* Downers Grove: Inter-Varisity Press.

Clayton, Joseph. 2006. *Luther and His Work.* Whitefish: Kessinger Publishing.

Cmfort, Philip Wesley. 2015. *A Commentary On the Manuscripts and Text of the New Testament.* Grand Rapids: Kregel Publications.

Colwell, E. C. 1969. *Methods in Evaluating Scribal Habits: A Study of P45, P66, P75, in Studies in Methodology in Textual Criticism of the New Testament.* Leiden and Boston: Brill.

Colwell, Ernest C. 1965. *Scribal Habits in Early Papyri: A Study in the Corruption of the Text.* Grand Rapids: Eerdmans.

Comfort, Philip. 2005. *Encountering the Manuscripts: An Introduction to New Testament Paleography and Textual Criticism.* Nashville: Broadman & Holman.

Comfort, Philip W. 2008. *New Testament Text and Translation Commentary.* Carol Stream: Tyndale House Publishers.

Comfort, Philip Wesley. 1992. *The Quest for the Original Text of the New Testament.* Eugene: Wipf and Stock.

Comfort, Philip, and David Barret. 2001. *The Text of the Earliest New Testament Greek Manuscripts.* Wheaton: Tyndale House Publishers.

Cruse, C. F. 1998. *Eusebius' Eccliatical History.* Peabody, MA: Hendrickson.

Deissmann, Adolf. 1910. *LIGHT FROM THE ANCIENT EAST: The New Testament Illustrated by Recently Discovered Texts of the Graeco-Roman World.* New York and London: Hodder and Stoughton.

Dell 'Orto, Luisa Franchi. 1990. *Riscoprire Pompei (Rediscovering Pompeii).* Italy: L'Erma di Bretschneider.

Durant, Will & Ariel. 1950. *The Story of Civilization: Part IV—The Age of Faith.* New York, NY: Simon & Schuster.

Ehrman, Bart D. 2005. *Misquoting Jesus: The Story Behind Who Changed the Bible and Why.* New York: Harper One.

—. 2006. *Peter, Paul and Mary Magdalene: The Followers of Jesus in History and Legend.* Oxford: Oxford University Press.

Ehrman, Bart D, and Michael W. Holmes. 2012. *The Text of the New Testament in Contemporary Research: Essays on the Status Quaestionis. Second Edition.* Leiden and Boston: Brill.

Ehrman, Bart D. Holmes, Michael W. 1995. *The Text of the New Testament in Contemporary Research: Essays on the Status Quaestionis.* Grand Rapids, MI: Eerdmans.

Ehrman, Bart D. 2003. *Lost Christianities: The Battles for Scripture and the Faiths We Never Knew.* New York: Oxford University Press.

Elliott, J. K. 2010. *New Testament Textual Criticism: The Application of Thoroughgoing Principles: Essays on Manuscripts and Textual Variation (Novum Testamentum, Supplements).* Leiden: Brill.

Epp, Eldon J. 1993. *Studies in the Theory and Method of New Testament Textual Criticism.* Grand Rapids: Wm. B. Eerdmans Publishing Co.

—. 1989. *Textual Criticism.* Atlanta: Scholars Press.

Evans, Craig A. 2002. *Fabricating Jesus: How Modern Scholars Distort the Gospels.* Downers Grove, IL: InterVaristy Press.

—. 2012. *Jesus and His World: The Archaeological Evidence.* Louisville: Westminster John Knox Press.

Fahlbusch, Erwin (Editor), Jan Milic (Editor) Lochman, John (Editor) Mbiti, Jaroslav (Editor) Pelikan, and Lukas (Editor) Vischer. German 1986, 1989, 1992, 1996, 1997; English 1999, 2001, 2003, 2005. *The Encyclopedia of Christianity (Vol. 1-3).* Grand Rapids: Eerdmans Publishing Company and Koninklijke Brill NV.

Fee, Gordon D. 1993. *P75, P66, and Origen: The Myth of Early Textual Recension in Alexandria, in: E. J. Epp & G. D. Fee, Studies in the Theory & Method of NT Textual Criticism.* Grand Rapids: Wm. Eerdmans.

Fee, Gordon D. 1974. *P75, P66, and Origen: The Myth of the Early Textual Recension in Alexandria.* Grand Rapids: Zondervan.

—. 1979. *The Textual Criticism of the New Testament.* Grand Rapids: Zondervan.

Ferguson, Everett. 2003. *Backgrounds of Early Christianity.* Grand Rapids, MI: Wm. B. Eerdmans.

Ferguson, Everett. 2005. *Church History , Volume One: From Christ to Pre-Reformation: The Rise and Growth of the Church in Its Cultural, Intellectual, and Political Context.* Grand Rapids, MI: Zondervan.

Freeman, James M. 1998. *THE NEW MANNERS & CUSTOMS OF THE BIBLE.* Gainesville: Bridge-Logos.

Gamble, Henry Y. 1995. *Books and Readers in the Early Church: A History of Early Christian Texts.* New Haven, CT: New Haven University Press.

Geisler, Norman L, and William E Nix. 1996. *A General Introduction to the Bible.* Chicago: Moody Press.

Geisler, Norman, and David Geisler. 2009. *CONVERSATION EVANGELISM: How to Listen and Speak So You Can Be Heard.* Eugene: Harvest House Publishers.

Greenlee, J Harold. 1995. *Introduction to New Testament Textual Criticism.* Peabody: Hendrickson.

—. 2008. *The Text of the New Testament.* Peabody: Henrickson.

Guthrie, Donald. 1990. *Introduction to the New Testament (Revised and Expanded).* Downers Grove, IL: InterVarsity Press.

Hammond, Carolyn. 1996. *Introduction to The Gallic War.* Oxford: Oxford University Press.

Hatch, William Henry Paine. 45. "A Recently Discovered Fragmrnt of the Epistle to the Romans." *Harvard Theological Review* 81-85.

Head, Peter M. 2004. "The Habits of New Testament Copyists Singular Readings in the Early Fragmentary Papyri of John." *Biblica, Vol. 85, No. 3* 399-408.

Hill, Charles E., and Michael J. Kruger. 2012. *The Early Text of the New Testament.* Oxford: Oxford University Press.

Hixon, Elijah, Gurry, Peter J. 2019. *MYTHS AND MISTAKES iN NEW TESTAMENT TEXTUAL CRITICISM.* Downer Groves: InterVarsity Press.

Holmes, Michael W. 1989. *New Testament Textual Criticism.* Grand Rapids: Baker.

—. 2007. *The Apostolic Fathers: Greek Texts and English Translations.* Grand Rapids: Baker Academics.

Hurtado, Larry. 1989. *New International Bible Commentary: Mark. .: .* Peabody, Mass: Hendrickson.

Hurtado, Larry. 1998. "The Origin of the Nominal Sacra." *Journal of Biblical Literature* 655-673.

Johnson, William A. 2012 (Reprint). *Readers and Reading Culture in the High Roman Empire: A Study of Elite Communities (Classical Culture and Society).* Oxford, New York: Oxford University Press.

Johnson, William A, and Holt N Parker. 2011. *Ancient Literacies: The Culture of Reading in Greece and Rome.* Oxford, United Kingdom: Oxford University Press.

Jones, Timothy Paul. 2007. *Misquoting Truth: A Guide to the Fallacies of Bart Ehrman's Misquoting Jesus.* Downer Groves: InterVarsity Press.

Komoszewski, J. Ed, James M. Sawyer, and Daniel Wallace. 2006. *Reinventing Jesus* . Grand Rapids, MI: Kregel Publications.

Lane Fox, Robin. 2006. *Pagans and Christians: In the Mediterranean World from the Second Century AD to the Conversion of Constantine.* City of Westminster, London: Penguin.

Lea, Thomas D., and Hayne P. Griffin. 1992. *The New American Commentary, vol. 34, 1, 2 Timothy, Titus.* Nashville: Broadman & Holman Publishers.

Lightfoot, Joseph Barber, and J. R Harmer. 1891. *The Apostolic Fathers.* London: Macmillan and Co.

Lightfoot, Neil R. 1963, 1988, 2003. *How We Got the Bible.* Grand Rapids, MI: Baker Books.

McCarthy, Dan, and Charles Clayton. 1994. *Let the Reader Understand: A guide to Interpreting and Applying the Bible.* Wheaton, Illinois: BridgePoint.

McKenzie, John L. 1975. *Light on the Epistles: A Reader's Guide.* Chicago, IL: Thomas More Press.

McRay, John. 2003. *Paul: His Life and Teaching.* Grand Rapids, MI: Baker Academics.

Metzger, Bruce M. 1964, 1968, 1992. *The Text of the New Testament: Its Transmission, Corruption, and Transmission.* New York: Oxford University Press.

Metzger, Bruce M. 1994. *A Textual Commentary on the Greek New Testament.* New York: United Bible Society.

Metzger, Bruce M., and Bart D. Ehrman. 2005. *The Text of the New Testament: Its Transmission, Corruption, and Restoration (4th Edition).* New York: Oxford University Press.

Metzger, Bruce. 1981. *Manuscripts of the Greek Bible: An Introduction to Palaeography* . New York, NY: Oxford University Press.

Millard, Alan. 2000. *READING AND WRITING IN THE TIME IF JESUS.* New York, NY: NYU Press.

Mounce, Robert H. 2001. *The New American Commentary.* Nashville, TN: Broadman & Holman Publishers.

Mounce, William D. 2006. *Mounce's Complete Expository Dictionary of Old & New Testament Words.* Grand Rapids, MI: Zondervan.

Myers, Allen C. 1987. *The Eerdmans Bible Dictionary* . Grand Rapids, Mich: Eerdmans.

Nestle, Eberhard, and Erwin Nestle. 2012. *Nestle-Aland: NTG Apparatus Criticus, ed. Barbara Aland et al., 28. revidierte Auflage (Revised Edition).* Stuttgart: Deutsche Bibelgesellschaft.

Orchard, Bernard (Editor), Longstaff, Thomas R. W. (Editor). 2005. "J. J. Griesbach: Synoptic and Text - Critical Studies 1776-1976." *Society for New Testament Studies Monograph Series (Book 34)* xi.

Orchard, Bernard. 1776-1976, 2005. *J. J. Griesbach: Synoptic and Text - Critical Studies* . Cambridge: Cambridge University Press.

Parker, David C. 1992. *Codex Bezae: An Early Christian Manuscript and its Text.* Cambridge: Cambridge University Press.

Parker, David C. 1997. *The living Text of the Gospels.* Cambridge: Cambridge University Press.

Porter, Stanley E. 2013. *How We Got the New Testament (Acadia Studies in Bible and Theology).* Grand Rapids, MI: Baker Publishing Group.

Price, Randall. 2007. *Searching for the Original Bible.* Eugene: Harvest House.

Richards, E. Randolph. 2004. *PAUL AND FIRST-CENTURY LETTER WRITING: Secretaries, Composition and Collection.* Downers Grove: InterVarsity Press.

—. 1991. *The Secretary in the Letters of Paul* . Heidelberg, Germany: Mohr Siebeck.

—. 1990. *The Secretary in the Letters of Paul.* Tübingen: J.C.B. Mohr.

Roberts, C. H. 1970. *Books in the Graeco-Roman World and in the New Testament in the Cambridge History of the Bible, Vol. 1, From the Beginnings to Jerome* . Cambridge: Cambridge University Press.

Roberts, Colin H. 1979. *Manuscript, Society, and Belief in Early Christian Egypt.* London: Oxford University Press.

Roberts, Colin H., and Theodore C. Skeat. 1987. *The Birth of the Codex.* London: Oxford University Press.

Robertson, A. T. 1925. *An Introduction to the Textual Criticism of the New Testament.* London: Hodder & Stoughton.

Royse, James R. 2008. *Scribal Habits in Early Greek New Testament Papyri (New Testament Tools and Studies) (New Testament Tools, Studies and Documents).* Leiden & Boston: Brill Academic Pub.

Schaff, Philip, and David Schley Schaff. 1910. *History of the Christian Church, vol. 2.* New York: Charles Scribner's Sons.

Schurer, Emil. 1890. *A HISTORY OF THE JEWISH PEOPLE IN THE TIME OF JESUS CHRIST (Volume II).* Edinburgh: T. & T. Clark.

Scott, Julius J. Jr. 1995. *Jewish Backgrounds of the New Testament.* Grand Rapids, MI: Baker Academic.

Souter, Alexander. 1913. *The Text and Canon of the New Testament.* New York: Charles Scribner's Sons.

Stark, Rodney. 1996). *The Rise of Christianity: A Socialist Reconsiders History.* Princeton, NJ: Princeton University Press.

Starr, Raymond J. 1987. "The Circulation of Literary Texts in the Roman World." *The Classical Quarterly* 213-223.

Towns, Elmer L. 2006. *Concise Bible Dictrines: Clear, Simple, and Easy-to-Understand Explanations of Bible Doctrines.* Chattanooga: AMG Publishers.

Tregelles, Samuel Prideaux. 1854. *An Account of the Printed Text of the Greek New Testament: With Remarks on Its Revision Upon Critical Principles.* London: S. Bagster and Sons.

Tuckett, Christopher M. 2001. "P52 and Nomina Sacra." *New Testament Study* 544-48.

Wachtel, Klaus, and Michael W Holmes. 2011. *The Textual History of the Greek New Testament: Changing Views in Contemporary Research, Text-Critical Studies.* Atlanta: Society of Biblical Literature.

Wallace, Daniel B. 2011. *Revisiting the Corruption of the New Testament: Manuscript, Patristic, and Apocryphal Evidence.* Grand Rapids, MI: Kregel Publications.

Wallace, Daniel. 2011. *The Reliability of the New Testament: Bart Ehrman and Daniel Wallace in Dialogue.* Minneapolis, MN: Fortress Press.

Warfield, B. B. 1948. *The Inspiration and Authority of the Bible.* Philadelphia, PA: Presbyterian and Reformed Pub. Co.

Wegner, Paul D. 2006. *A Student's Guide to Textual Criticism of the Bible: Its History Methods & Results.* Downers Grove: InterVarsity Press.

—. 1999. *The Journey from Text to Translation.* Grand Rapids: Baker Academic.

Westcott, B. F., and F. J. A. Hort. 1882. *Introduction to the New Testament in the Original Greek.* New York: Harper & Brothers.

—. 1882. *The New Testament in the Original Greek, Vol. 2: Introduction, Appendix.* London: Macmillan and Co.

Whiston, William. 1987. *The Works of Josephus.* Peabody, MA: Hendrickson.

Wright, Brian J. 2017. *COMMUNAL READING IN THE TIME OF JESUS: A Window Into Christian Reading Practices.* Minneapolis, MN: Fortress Press. Accessed March 22, 2017. https://www.academia.edu/18281056/_Ancient_Romes_Daily_News_Publication_With_Some_Likely_Implications_For_Early_Christian_Studies_TynBull_67.1_2016_145-160.

Wright, G. Ernest. 1962. *Biblical Archaeology.* London, United Kingdom: Gerald Duckworth & Co.

Zuntz, Gunther. 1953. *The Text of the Epistles: A Disquisition upon the Corpus Paulinum.* London: Oxford University Press.